Harriet Kettle

For Katy, Jacob, Tara, Jack and Molly

Harriet Kettle

Pauper, Prisoner, Patient and Parent in Victorian Norfolk

Andy Reid

POPPYLAND PUBLISHING

This edition 2021 published by Poppyland Publishing, Lowestoft, NR32 3BB.

www.poppyland.co.uk

ISBN 978 1 909796 84 3

Designed and typeset in 10.5 on 13.5 pt Gilgamesh Pro.

Printed by Ashford Colour Press.

Picture credits:

Author 80, 81, 133, 138, 142, 181
Bethlem Museum of the Mind 148, 150
Brown, Robena 17, 27, 170, 173
Cranworth and Southburgh Parochial Church Council 19
Gurdon family collection 16
Howes, Philip and Herbert 194, 196, 197
Illustrated London News Ltd/Mary Evans cover
Norfolk Museum Service 106, 201
Norfolk Record Office viii, 5
Norwich Heritage Projects 85
Picture Norfolk 84
Poppyland collection 34, 36, 39, 41, 71, 77
Poppyland Ltd. collection 101, 115, 149
public domain 35, 57, 99, 102, 110, 166, 167, 169
The National Archives 37, 48, 49, 62, 89, 98
Wellcome Collection (CC BY 4.0) 117, 122
Wymondham Heritage Museum 139, 140

Contents

Acknowledgements

I am grateful to Helen Bainbridge, Tim Blanche, Robena Brown, Angela Cook, Lord Cranworth, Ian Grosvenor, Adrian Hoare, Philip Howes, Elizabeth Meath Baker, Steve Pope, Andrew Prescott, Rose Sheen and Bridget Yates, for suggesting and/or making available relevant sources. A special thank you to Megan Dennis (Curator, Gressenhall Farm and Workhouse: Museum of Norfolk Life), for connecting me with the Gressenhall workhouse research community and giving me access to relevant documentation. The work done by volunteer researchers at Gressenhall, in helping to make material in Class MH12 at the National Archives available in digitised form, meant that it could be consulted during the worst of the Covid-19 pandemic—an absolute boon. Many thanks to Bridget Yates, Barbara Jackson and Eleanor Reid for reading earlier drafts of this biography and providing helpful comments, and to Sarah Reid for eagle-eyed proof-reading of the near-final text. Any remaining errors and/or infelicities are entirely my responsibility.

The staffs of record repositories visited in person and, in some cases, online—the Norfolk Record Office, the Norfolk Heritage Centre, the National Archives (formerly the Public Record Office), the Bethlem Museum of the Mind and the British Library—were unfailingly helpful. The staff of Norfolk Record Office kindly arranged the photographing of sources to work on when travel across the country was impossible, which was of huge assistance. I am grateful to Gareth Davies and Poppyland Publishing for taking this book on, providing valuable advice and seeing it through to publication. My greatest debt is to my wife, Alison, who has heard about Harriet Kettle over many years, read and commented on every draft of the story of her life and shared our house with her during the Covid-19 pandemic of 2020-21.

Note on sources

This study draws on a range of manuscript sources in the Norfolk Record Office, the National Archives and the Bethlem Museum of the Mind, which have been consulted in the original and also, in some cases, in digitised form. Printed sources, such as the reports of the Poor Law Commission and the national inspectors of prisons, have also been consulted, and reference has been made to the secondary sources and websites listed in the bibliography. Newspapers have been used extensively and were consulted, at different times, in original bound copies, on microfilm and via the British Newspaper Archive website. Footnotes provide references to the documentary and printed sources, using the abbreviations listed below. Secondary works are cited by author and date of publication only, with full details given in the bibliography. In the text, including when quoting from primary sources, I have used capitalisation in the manner recommended by The Economist's Style Book while drawing reassurance from its quotation from Emerson: 'a foolish consistency is the hobgoblin of little minds'.

Abbreviations

BM	Bethlem Museum of the Mind
BNP	Bury and Norwich Post
CLA	County Lunatic Asylum
EDP	Eastern Daily Press
HMI	Her Majesty's Inspector
MC	Morning Chronicle
MLU	Mitford and Launditch Union
MLU Minutes	Minute Books of the Board of Guardians of Mitford and Launditch Union
NC	Norfolk Chronicle
NM	Norwich Mercury
NN	Norfolk News
NRO	Norfolk Record Office
PLB	Poor Law Board
PLC	Poor Law Commission
PP	Parliamentary Papers
TNA	The National Archives

22ᵈ November 1858.

The Clerk reported that he had examined the
Master's Day book and inspected the other books
kept by the Master and that he had examined the
Relieving officers' out door relief Lists abstracts of out
door relief Lists and receipt and expenditure books in
conformity with the Poor Law Commissioners' order in
that behalf.

It appeared by a statement presented by the
Master that during the last week 11. paupers were
admitted into the Workhouse 5 were discharged 1.
died and 249. remain.

Martha Craske a poor person maintained in
the Union Workhouse is brought before the Board
in custody charged with an assault upon Mrs
Butcher the assistant Matron and with gross
misbehaviour and is ordered to be taken before the
Magistrates.

Harriet Kettle a poor person also maintained in
the said Workhouse is likewise again brought before
the Board charged with the like offences and with
having destroyed her bed and bedding and attempted
to set fire to the Workhouse.
Ordered that she also be taken before the
Magistrates and dealt with according to Law.

The Clerk laid before the Board another Letter from
Mr. Tombling dated the 17ᵗʰ instant offering to take
the Boy Pitcher belonging to Shipdham into his
service but refusing to pay him any wages.
The Clerk having called the attention of the
Guardians to the several Provisions of the General
Consolidated order with respect to an apprenticeship
by the Board, it is proposed by the Revd. G. C.
Bailey the Guardian of the parish of Shipdham
and Resolved that with the sanction of the Poor

Extract from the minute book of the guardians of Mitford and Launditch Union, 22 November 1858; NRO, C/GP14/14. Harriet Kettle's entry is the fourth paragraph.

Introduction

MANY years ago, while working through the minute books of the Board of Guardians of Mitford and Launditch Poor Law Union in the Norfolk Record Office, I came across the following entry for 22 November 1858:

'Harriet Kettle a poor person…maintained in [Gressenhall] workhouse is… brought before the board charged with…having destroyed her bed and bedding and attempted to set fire to the workhouse.'[1]

At the time, I was working on secondment from the Norfolk Education Department as liaison officer at what was then called the Norfolk Rural Life Museum, now Gressenhall Farm and Workhouse: Museum of Norfolk Life, which occupies the buildings of the former workhouse at Gressenhall. I was searching for historical source material which would illuminate the experience of life in the workhouse for pupils from primary and secondary schools.

I almost jumped out of my seat in the search room when I found that passage in the minute book. A rebel! Someone who kicked back against the punishing post-1834 regime in the union workhouse. Exactly the kind of case study that might get students interested, that might even lend itself to dramatisation.

The incident actually was dramatised by a teacher and students from one of the Norfolk secondary schools, with the roles of workhouse porter and assistant matron played by the co-ordinator and deputy co-ordinator of the late, much lamented Norwich Teachers' Centre. I subsequently found more evidence about Harriet's life in the guardians' minute books, in the collections of Poor Law records in the Public Record Office (now The National Archives), in the records of the county lunatic asylum and elsewhere.[2] Harriet made a cameo appearance in *Peace and War*, a textbook for National Curriculum history in Year 9, published in 1993,[3] as an example of a workhouse inmate. A transcript of one of the key sources about her life was included, with a commentary, in *The Union Workhouse: A Study Guide for Teachers and Local Historians* in 1994.[4] Harriet subsequently featured in other publications and in displays about the workhouse mounted by the museum.[5]

But who was she? She was not just an example—in fact, she was a far from typical example, because more can be discovered about her than about many others in her situation—and she deserved much more than a cameo. Harriet Kettle was a person with her own, combative voice even though that voice was recorded for posterity by others and not by her. In recovering her story, as far as the evidence allows, it becomes possible to reconstruct her experience of the range of institutions with which she came into contact and her life afterwards, and to create a personalised picture of the grittier side of life in Victorian and Edwardian England. But although more evidence has been gathered over the years and particularly recently, drawing on the wealth of digitised material now available online, there are, inevitably, many gaps. Some may, in time, be filled but others will probably remain unfilled. Harriet's story remains fragmentary.

Workhouse inmate, 'girl on the town', prisoner in Walsingham and Wymondham houses of correction and patient at the county lunatic asylum and Bethlem hospital: the young Harriet earned a degree of notoriety in the restricted circles in which her life was lived. And then, in her late 20s, she married, became a parent and her life became more settled, if not uneventful. She never became famous but, in its way, her career was a triumph. From the most unpromising of beginnings, and against the odds, Harriet survived into grand-motherhood and old age. Born around the time of the accession of Queen Victoria, she died in the year of the Battle of the Somme in World War I. And, in completing the arc of her life, she died at Gressenhall workhouse, where she had grown up.

Notes

1   MLU minutes; NRO, C/GP14/14.
2   Material from these sources that I recorded in the period to 1987 are in NRO, MC1933/27 893x9.
3   Colin Shephard, Andy Reid and Keith Shephard, *Peace and War* (John Murray, London, 1993).
4   A Reid (1994).
5   There is a three-page summary of Harriet's life in S Pope (2006). A briefer account, with several inaccuracies, appears in Simon Fowler, *Workhouse* (The National Archives, Kew, 2008), and R Lee (2005) includes a paragraph about Harriet's trial.

Harriet Kettle's origins and family

HARRIET Kettle's origins are obscure. All that is known of her early life comes from a summary recorded by a medical officer at the Norfolk county lunatic asylum when she was in her mid-twenties: 'Her mother died insane, her father did but little for her, and she was brought up in Gressenhall workhouse'.[1] This was probably what Harriet herself told him, although it may also have been confirmed by her elder sister Matilda during a visit to the asylum.

The first incontrovertible reference to Harriet in historical records occurs in the national census conducted on 30 March 1851, when the enumerator listed her as an inmate of Gressenhall workhouse, aged 12, a scholar (attending the workhouse school), born in the village of Cranworth, Norfolk. 'Harriet Kettle' did not appear in the returns of the census taken 10 years earlier, on 6 June 1841.

However, Harriet had an alias, to which one explicit reference has been found. The Norwich Mercury newspaper's issue of 18 September 1852 carried a brief report on the imprisonment of 'Harriet Kettle alias Harriet Clarke' for 14 days for 'refractory conduct in the union house at Gressenhall'.[2] Harriet Kettle, it appears, was also known as Harriet Clarke.

And there was a Harriet Clarke at Gressenhall workhouse in 1841. The census returns listed 'Harriott Clarke', aged 3, as an inmate. Above her name came Matilda Clarke, aged 5; below it came John Clarke, aged 2. The juxtaposition of the names indicates that the three children were siblings. Their parents are not to be found in the list of workhouse inmates.

More will be said later of Matilda Clarke/Kettle, Harriet's sister. Of John Clarke, Harriet's presumed brother, nothing more can be said at present. So far, he has not been connected definitively with other historical records.

If the ages given for Harriet in 1841 and 1851 were accurate, she was born between 1 April and 6 June 1838. However, exactly when and where she was born is not known. Civil registration had just begun (on 1 July 1837) but Harriet's birth appears not to have been registered. Nor is there any trace of her baptism in the parish registers in Cranworth, her birthplace according to the 1851 census, or other nearby places. There was, however, a Harriet Clarke

Kittle, daughter of John and Elizabeth Kittle, who was baptised at Outwell, in the Norfolk Fens, on 2 January 1838.[3] The name, 'Clarke Kittle' ('Kittle', at the time, being interchangeable with 'Kettle') would strongly suggest that this was Harriet, although there is no other evidence to connect her with the area.

The reference to Cranworth as Harriet's birthplace in the 1851 census returns is consistent with later sources which refer to her 'settlement' being there. The parish where people were 'settled' was their home parish, the place responsible for providing or paying for their relief if they were in need. There were various ways of obtaining a 'settlement'.[4] It is likely that Harriet was settled in Cranworth because (despite the possible baptism in Outwell) she was born there or because her parents were settled in the parish. Later in her life, Harriet could not remember where she was born but, apart from in 1901, her elder sister Matilda consistently gave her birthplace as Cranworth,[5] right up until the 1911 census.

Harriet Kettle's mother is a mystery. If Harriet was the child baptised in Outwell in January 1838, her name was Elizabeth Kittle, but that cannot be confirmed. Harriet took her father's surname and knew who her father was, which suggests that her parents were married, but no convincing record of their marriage has been found.[6] In her mid-twenties Harriet claimed that she inherited a bad temper from her parents; perhaps they had many rows. It is not known when and where Harriet's mother died, except that her death must have been after 7 June 1839, the earliest date on which her son John Clarke could have been born (assuming his age was given accurately in the 1841 census),[7] and before the end of 1848, when Harriet's father John Kettle, now described as a widower, remarried. If Harriet's mother died insane, as stated in the record at the asylum, it was perhaps as a result of post-natal depression exacerbated by extreme poverty, or simply the anguish of being unable to care for her children in the absence (for reasons explained below) of her husband. There is, however, no record of the admission to, or death in, the Norfolk county lunatic asylum of anyone who could plausibly be regarded as Harriet's mother. Perhaps she committed suicide at home and was judged posthumously to have been of unsound mind.

Harriet's father, John Kettle or Clarke, can be identified with more confidence. John Kettle, labourer, was named as Harriet's father on her marriage certificate in 1865. He was also named, with a different occupation—baker— as Matilda Kettle's father when she got married three years earlier.[8] According to the Cranworth parish register of baptisms, he was born, the illegitimate son of Anne (or Ann) Kettle, on 14 December 1813 and baptised as John Kettle in Cranworth three days later.[9] The father was not named. However, John was sometimes referred to as John Kettle alias Clarke or John Clarke alias Kettle,

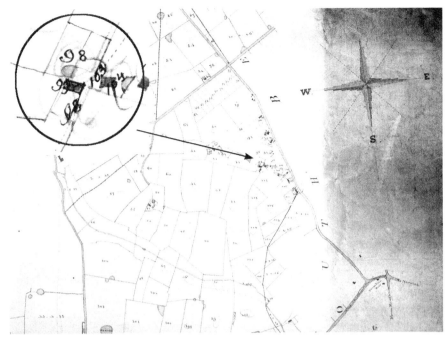

Richard Clarke's house (no. 98) as shown on the tithe map of Cranworth; NRO, DN/TA 106.

which would suggest that his father was called Clarke. Definite confirmation is to be found in the certificate recording John's remarriage in 1848, on which his father was named as Richard Clarke, labourer. So Richard Clarke was Harriet's paternal grandfather.

Anne/Ann Kettle, John's mother and Harriet's paternal grandmother, was probably born in January 1784.[10] She remained single until 1820, but the Cranworth parish register recorded the baptism of no fewer than nine of her children between 1802 and 1818.[11] John Kettle was the sixth. He had two elder brothers called Richard Clark Kettle; the first was born in 1805 and died in infancy, and the second was born in 1809. There was also a younger brother called William Clark Kettle, born in 1816, who died in infancy. The names of these three brothers would indicate that their father, too, was Richard Clarke. He may well have been the father of all nine of the children born to Anne Kettle while she was single.

Richard Clarke was a married man. He had married Mary Houlin in Cranworth on 13 November 1790 but the couple appear to have had no children, or at least none who were baptised in Cranworth or nearby. Mary died in 1819, and when she was buried, in early November, she was referred to in the parish register as 'Mary Clarke wife of Richard'. Her age was given as 70, meaning that she was over 20 years older than her husband. Only two months after her death, on 6 January 1820, Richard Clarke married Anne Kettle.[12] The nature of the relationships among Richard, Mary and Ann while Mary was still alive can only be a matter of speculation. After the marriage, Anne had at least five more children with Richard, a daughter, also called Ann, being born as late as 1829 when she was 45—and Ann may not have been the last.[13]

Richard Clarke, agricultural labourer, was probably born in August 1770 and was therefore 43 when John Kettle was born in 1813.[14] He lived in one half of a double cottage at High Common in Cranworth, situated off the road, behind a Primitive Methodist chapel built in 1835.[15] At the time of the census returns of 1841, he was recorded (accurately) as aged 70, while his new wife Ann [sic] was said to be 50.[16] Living with them were four of the children born to them since their marriage—Robert, William, Thomas and Ann (a fifth, Mary, had died in infancy). Also residing in the house was Charlotte Clarke, whose age was given as 35; she was the first of the nine children born to Anne[17] when she was a single woman. Ten years later, in the 1851 census, Richard was stated to be 82 and Ann's age was given a little more accurately as 70. With them lived their unmarried daughter Ann, now 22, and (as lodgers) their son William, his wife Ann and their four young daughters. Given that the cottage probably had two, or at most three, rooms, it must have been crowded. The occupation recorded for Harriet's grandmother Ann was 'nurse', which probably meant that she was helping to look after her grandchildren during the day, since her daughter-in-law, like her son, was described as an agricultural labourer. Richard Clarke died soon after the census, and was buried at Cranworth on 30 May 1851. Ann appeared in the next set of census returns in 1861, when, aged 81, she was still at High Common, living in her own tenement in a group of three very full houses, and described as a pauper. She died in 1869. Both Harriet's paternal grandparents, therefore, lived into their 80s.[18]

Harriet Kettle had numerous relatives on her father's side—her grandparents, uncles, aunts and cousins—but they were all living in poverty and none was able or willing to take responsibility for her. Her father, John Kettle/Clarke, may have led a wandering life, taking jobs in different places around Norfolk, and, from the age of 19 onwards, he had increasingly serious brushes with the law. He was probably the John Kittle who was charged by William Curson of East Dereham and others in 1832 with stealing a male ass.[19] Four years later, in April 1836, 'John Kettle, alias Clarke', was sentenced to six months imprisonment for stealing potatoes from Thomas Donnell of East Dereham. This, it was noted, was not his first offence.[20]

John's daughter Matilda may have been born while he was serving his sentence and Harriet and his son John would have arrived after his release from prison. However, he might not have seen his son as he was soon in trouble again, and this time the result was that he was sentenced to transportation to Australia. He may have been the John Clarke who, in the week beginning 12 March 1838, appeared at the Norfolk quarter sessions in Norwich and was sentenced to transportation for seven years for receiving stolen hay and barley,[21] although this identification is far from certain.[22] On the Monday after receiving his sentence, this John Clarke was taken from Norwich Castle to the 'Justitia', a hulk at Woolwich.[23] The 'hulks' were decommissioned warships in which convicts were held pending transportation, where conditions were notoriously poor. The 'Justitia' was probably as bad as any; after an outbreak of cholera on board in 1847, it was judged unfit for further use.[24] John Clarke spent almost six months on the hulk before, on 5 October 1839, setting sail for Australia with 265 other convicts on the 'Theresa'. He arrived in New South Wales, which had well established penal colonies, on 31 January 1839.[25]

'Very recently returned from transportation' was how John Clarke/Kettle was described in January 1849, and this time the individual referred to can be identified with confidence as Harriet's father.[26] No doubt he had found a ship on which he could work his passage back to England. John's wife, the mother of Matilda, Harriet and John, probably died while he was serving his sentence, as 'John Clark Kettle' was described as a widower when, on 28 December 1848, he married Mary Ann Dack of Southburgh, the parish adjoining Cranworth.[27] John was resident in Cranworth at the time and his occupation was given as labourer. The marriage took place at Southburgh but John and Mary Ann set up house in Shipdham, a large village three miles north west of Cranworth.[28] Did John take the trouble to visit his children in Gressenhall workhouse during this interlude? There is no way of knowing.

John and Mary Ann had only a brief time together as a married couple. On 19 January 1849, 'John Clarke alias Kittle' aged 36 of Shipdham and Thomas Clarke aged 22 of Cranworth were committed for trial at the spring quarter sessions in Norwich, accused of the theft of five fowls belonging to James Howes of Southburgh, Mary Ann's home village, two days earlier. The Norfolk News reported the theft, the subsequent police investigation and the arrests of John and Thomas Clarke on 27 January. At John's house, the police found 'part of the fowls…concealed under a bed'. According to the newspaper reports, John and Thomas Clarke were 'two notorious characters'. John, of course, had just returned from transportation. Thomas was one of his younger brothers, the fourth of the five children known to have been born to Richard Clarke and Anne Kettle after their marriage and one of those living with them at the time of the 1841 census; he, too, had 'previous'. On 1 January 1845, when aged 18, he had been convicted of the theft of five hare skins, six rabbit skins, one cat skin and a quantity of horse hair from a cart belonging to John Butterfant, an itinerant dealer, in Shipdham, and had been sentenced to four months' imprisonment with hard labour. [29]

The case against 'John Clarke alias Kittle' and Thomas Clarke came before the quarter sessions in Norwich on 14 March 1849. Thomas Clarke, on this occasion, was acquitted but John Clarke was found guilty and, 'having been several times previously convicted, and once transported for 10 years [although it may have been seven, as has been seen], was now sentenced to 15 years' transportation'.[30] The unfortunate Mary Ann, John's new wife, would have seen no more of her husband after March 1849, unless she managed to visit him before his transportation. She had a child, George Kettle, born in Shipdham on 12 January 1850 but the date of his birth suggests that John was not the father.[31]

After his conviction, John Clarke/Kettle was held in the county gaol at Norwich Castle until his transfer in early December 1849 to the convict prison at Millbank in London where he was recorded as being married with three children and, intriguingly, his occupation was given as 'fiddler'.[32] After less than a month there, he was transferred to Pentonville, which was still a fairly new prison, having opened in 1842. Eventually, after a long delay, part of which he may have spent at Gibraltar, John became one of 277 convicts who sailed on the 'Ramillies' to Fremantle, Western Australia, where he arrived on 7 August 1854.[33]

Western Australia was a young colony, settlement having begun only in 1829. Convicts were needed to provide labour and the first shipload had arrived at Fremantle in June 1850.[34] Within a month of his arrival in 1854, John Clarke/ Kettle was granted a 'ticket of leave' allowing him to seek employment rather than remaining in the quarters assigned to the convicts. His details were recorded and it was again noted that he was married, with three children. Now, however, his occupation was given as 'cook', which is interesting, given that Matilda, on her marriage in 1862, recalled him as a baker; perhaps he had worked his passage home after his first transportation as a ship's cook. He was said to be semi-literate, which fits with his signing his marriage certificate in 1848, rather than making a mark as Mary Ann Dack did. He was five feet, six and a half inches tall, was of stout build with a scar on his cheek, and had dark brown hair, hazel eyes and a sallow complexion. John probably found farm work in the area south east of Perth, known by its original inhabitants, the Ballondory people, as the Wergijan and by the colonists as the Wheatbelt. He married Eliza Smith, very likely bigamously, in January 1857[35] and they had five children. John received a conditional pardon in May 1863 and died in the country town of Beverley, Western Australia, in May 1871.[36]

Harriet's father, John, was not the only child of Richard Clarke and Anne

Kettle who got into trouble with the law. Three of his brothers, Richard Clark Kettle, William Clarke and Thomas Clarke, Harriet's uncles, also had criminal records. In 1855, a prison governor noted (perhaps with a little exaggeration) that, 'nearly all [the] family are thieves'.[37] John's elder brother, Richard Clark Kettle (the one who survived infancy), appeared in court in March 1834. It was reported that: 'Richard Clarke [sic], alias Kettle, stood charged with having stolen…one coomb of wheat from Mr James Kiddle, of Cranworth'. Kiddle was one of the principal farmers in the parish. His brother, Robert, who lived and worked in partnership with him, discovered the theft. Together, the two brothers searched Richard Clark Kettle's premises and found wheat, the characteristics of which led them to believe that it was part of that which had been stolen. Richard, 'said that it was corn his wife had gleaned in the harvest'. This cut no ice and the jury found him guilty. He was sentenced to 12 months' imprisonment.[38]

William Clarke (later described as 'labourer and dealer'[39]) and his younger brother Thomas Clarke (he who had been acquitted of the offence for which John Clarke/Kettle was transported in 1849) were charged in November 1851 with having stolen six lambs and two ewes belonging to John Aylmer, one of the largest farmers in Cranworth. They appeared before the quarter sessions in January 1852, when the court heard that William Clarke had tried unsuccessfully to sell the lambs at the Cock public house in Barford and had then found a purchaser at Hingham market. However, the police had been alerted and the lambs were identified by 'marks and peculiarities'. There was insufficient evidence to convict Thomas Clarke, who was again acquitted, but William Clarke was found guilty and sentenced to transportation for seven years.[40] Unlike his elder brother John, however, he did not actually go to Australia. After spending four months in Norwich Castle, he was transferred to Millbank convict prison for nearly eight months and then to the 'public works' prison at Portsmouth, where the comment about the family quoted above was recorded. William behaved well and was discharged on licence on 29 March 1855, returning to his wife and large family at High Common, where he lived for the rest of his life.[41]

Thomas Clarke was undeterred by the experience of his elder brothers. He had married in 1847 and children had been born in 1849 and 1852. The family lived at High Common, near Thomas's parents. Thomas was described variously as a labourer, a fishmonger or fish vendor[42] and a general dealer who 'travels with a dog cart'.[43] On 19 October 1853, he was in court again, charged with stealing a bill-hook and a quantity of beans belonging to Francis Clarke (not a close relation), a small farmer and proprietor of the King's Head, a beer-house at High Common.[44] Francis Clarke had cunningly marked his beans, 'by cutting notches on the sticks which supported them, while standing in sheaves'. When some of the beans disappeared, he went with a police officer to a shed at Thomas

Clarke's house, where they identified the stolen property and found that, 'a pig, belonging to the prisoner, was eating the beans'. This time, there was no escape for Thomas Clarke. After being sentenced to five years' penal servitude,[45] he spent two months in the county gaol at Norwich Castle, where the governor, George Pinson, who had previously been the master of Gressenhall workhouse, described him as being 5 feet six inches tall, with grey eyes, light brown hair, fresh complexion and 'rather shrewd looking'. Thomas was then transferred to Millbank and on to Pentonville. After a year there, he was moved on to the prison at Portland, where he worked in the quarry, and was then placed on a convict ship with 139 others and taken to Bermuda, where he was employed on public works. He fell ill, but recovered and returned to England in March 1858, serving the remainder of his sentence at Portsmouth until his release on 16 October 1858.[46] He returned to Cranworth, but only briefly. His wife had died while he was in prison and on 24 March 1859 he got married again, as a widower, to Frances Ward nee Kittle, a widow.[47] At the time of the 1861 census they were living, with the two children of Thomas's first marriage, in Shipdham. Thomas Clarke, 'dealer', appeared in court again in March 1865, charged with a violent and indecent assault on a female servant in Carbrooke, an adjoining village, and was found guilty of common assault.[48] In November 1867, he was in the county court supporting his daughter's unsuccessful claim for wages from the 'mistress' with whom she had gone into service for a year. According to the press coverage of the case, it was alleged that he was, 'a drunken, dissipated man' and that his wife had therefore agreed with his daughter's employer that the wages would be paid in clothes rather than cash.[49] Thomas Clarke appears not to have been an admirable character.

Harriet's sister Matilda was a more significant figure in her life than either of her parents or any of her other relations. She was a year or two older than Harriet and, on the basis of the ages given for her in census returns, was probably born in 1836 or 1837.[50]

Matilda, like Harriet, grew up in Gressenhall workhouse. In 1849, as Matilda Kettle rather than Matilda Clarke, she was mentioned three times in the guardians' minute book.[51] On 7 May, Matilda and a fellow inmate, Leah Gay, referred to as 'two girls under the care of the schoolmistress', were charged with 'refractory conduct', and two months later, on 9 July, they were both again charged with 'refractory conduct in the workhouse school'. On 23 July, after another incident, Leah, the elder and probably the prime mover, was sent to Walsingham house of correction for 14 days while Matilda was confined in a separate room in the workhouse on bread and water for eight hours on the three following days.[52] And then, less than a week after her punishment, and perhaps recognising that she was 'stir crazy', to use a modern phrase, the guardians at their meeting on 30 July

1849, 'agreed that clothing to the amount of forty shillings be allowed to Matilda Kettle to enable her to go into the service of James Clarke of Great Yarmouth'. Matilda would have been 12 or 13 in 1849, an age at which she could go into service.

The James Clarke for whom Matilda went to work may have been a relative, but as yet that is unproven. What happened to her afterwards is unknown. It is possible that things didn't work out and that she left Great Yarmouth and returned to Gressenhall. A Matilda Kettle, born Cranworth, was listed next after Harriet Kettle in the 1851 census returns for Gressenhall workhouse. Her age, however, was given as five. Matilda was not one of the most common female forenames in Norfolk in this period. Was this another Matilda Kettle from Cranworth, or had the census enumerator (who was the master of the workhouse) made a slip and recorded Matilda's age as five instead of 15?

Later, Matilda Kettle moved to Norwich. She probably visited Harriet when her sister was a patient in the county lunatic asylum in the summer of 1856.[53] In April 1861, aged 24, she was living in Colegate in the household of a unitarian minister, his German wife and their two sons and two daughters, working as a domestic servant; she was the family's cook.[54] The following October, she was still in Norwich but had probably moved out of the minister's house, as Harriet stayed with her. Matilda, whose level of literacy was probably higher, wrote a letter to the Gressenhall guardians on behalf of her sister.[55] Matilda married William Pank, an attendant at the Norwich city asylum, in January 1862 and, when an order was issued for the re-admission of her sister to the Norfolk county lunatic asylum in July 1863, Matilda Pank was named as Harriet's nearest known relative.[56] Matilda was widowed in 1883, after which she made a living as a needlewoman in the parish of St Benedict's, Norwich. She died in January 1926, aged 89.

Although much remains unclear and unproven about Harriet's origins and her family, the sources do agree consistently that both Harriet and Matilda Kettle came from and 'belonged' to the small village of Cranworth. What was the economic and social background from which they emerged?

Notes

1 CLA, case book 1861-1865; NRO, SAH 263.

2 NM, 18 September 1852.

3 Outwell baptism register, accessed via freereg.org.uk. A birth date on or before 2 January 1838 would not quite match the evidence from the census returns.

4 Under legislation of 1662 and 1691, the qualifications for a settlement in a place included birth, parental settlement, marriage, serving an apprenticeship, occupying property of a certain value, paying local rates or living undisturbed in the place for 40 days.

5 Except in 1901, when her birthplace was recorded as Dereham.

6   One possibility is the marriage of John Clarke of Shipdham to Elizabeth Allison of Elmham at Elmham, about which a notice was inserted in the Norwich Mercury on 2 December 1837, but no record of this has been found in freereg.org, and it would have been an ambitious marriage for John Clarke as Elizabeth Allison was the daughter of a farmer—as evident from her baptism on 12 March 1813, accessed via freereg.org.

7   The civil registration records yield no plausible reference to the death of an Elizabeth Kettle between 1839 and 1848. There are several records of the death of an Elizabeth Clarke but, without obtaining original certificates, there is no way of knowing whether any of them was Harriet's mother—whose name, in any case, may not have been Elizabeth, if the person baptised in Outwell in 1838 was not the Harriet who is the subject of this biography.

8   Marriage certificates of Harriet and Matilda Kettle.

9   Cranworth baptism register 1813-80; NRO, PD359/6(S).

10   Ann Kettle, daughter of Robert and Elizabeth Kettle, was baptised in Cranworth on 7 January 1784 and would therefore have been nearly 30 when John was born; Cranworth parish register of baptisms, accessed via freereg.org.

11   At least four, and probably five, died in infancy, and one died aged two.

12   Cranworth marriage register, available via freereg.org. Thanks to Helen Bainbridge for alerting me to this reference.

13   There may have been a sixth, George Clarke, aged 13 in 1845 and therefore born in 1831 or 1832, but there is no record of his baptism in Cranworth or anywhere nearby.

14   Richard Clarke, son of Edward and Mary Clarke, was baptised in Cranworth on 27 August 1770; Cranworth parish register of baptisms, accessed via freereg.org.

15   Tithe apportionment for Cranworth, 1838; NRO, DN/TA 106.

16   The ages of adults were often rounded to the nearest five in the 1841 census.

17   Charlotte was born on 4 March 1802, Anne's name being recorded in the parish register as 'Anne Kiddle'. Information from the Cranworth parish register, accessed via findmypast.com.

18   Information from the census returns of 1841 and 1851, accessed via findmypast.com.

19   TNA: PCOM2 348, page 63, accessed via findmypast.com. John Kittle's age was given as 19.

20   NC, 9 April 1836. Three years later, a John Kettle was acquitted of an unspecified charge at the Norfolk Quarter Sessions; NC, 26 October 1839.

21   NM, 17 March 1838.

22   A petition against the sentence of transportation was supported by Clarke's wife, Hannah Clarke, the person who had brought the prosecution and a number of the inhabitants of Hainford, a village north of Norwich, who stated that John Clarke had resided there 'for some years' (eight years, according to a supporting letter from a barrister). It is this that creates the doubt as to whether this John Clarke was Harriet's father. In a covering letter, the chairman of the Norfolk quarter sessions, John Weyland, said that his understanding was that 'the prisoner has some complaint which makes it doubtful that he outlives his sentence'. Weyland gave his address as Woodrising Hall, very near Cranworth, and wrote that he would have no objection to Clarke not being sent abroad, 'providing he passes seven years away from this neighbourhood'. The petition was unavailing, and a terse 'gaol report' stating, 'character bad—in prison before', which matches the track record of Harriet's father, helps to explain why. Information from TNA: HO17/71/77 and HO19/8, identified via digitalpanopticon.org and accessed via findmypast.com. A search of the records of convicts transported in the

relevant period via onesearch.slq.qld.gov.au has yielded other John Clarkes and a much smaller number of John Kettles and Kittles, but none who could be identified confidently as Harriet's father.

23 NM, 24 March 1839.

24 Information from prisonhistory.org.

25 Information from the convict transportation registers 1787-1867, TNA: HO11/18, p 79(41), accessed via a database compiled by the State Library of Queensland in association with the Australian Joint Copying Project through onesearch.slq.qld.gov. au (subsequent references to this source refer only to onsearch.slq.qld.gov.au). See also convictrecords.com.au. A certificate of freedom issued to a John Clarke (who was said to have arrived on the Theresa in 1839) on 10 December 1844 was for a John Clarke who had been convicted of stealing a goose at Essex quarter sessions on 28 November 1837—clearly not the same person (accessed via records.nsw.gov.au).

26 NN 27 January 1849. See also NC, 27 January.

27 When the banns were read for the third time, there was an objection from the churchwarden who forbade them, 'on the ground of there being no proof of his wife's death' but this objection was presumably overcome, as the marriage went ahead. Southburgh register of banns and marriages, accessed via findmypast.com.

28 Marriage certificate of John Clark Kettle and Mary Ann Dack, 28 December 1848.

29 NC 4 January 1845. Butterfant had bought these items and more from Thomas Clarke in Cranworth, but Thomas and George Clarke (aged 13) had subsequently followed him to Shipdham and removed the articles from the cart when it was parked in a shed at the 'Crown' public house. George Clarke may have been the sixth child born to Richard and Ann Clarke after their marriage. He was acquitted.

30 NC 17 March 1849; NN, 17 March 1849. The figure of 15 years for the length of the sentence of transportation comes from the NN; in the NC, it was incorrectly given as seven. A source in TNA: confirms the figure of 15 years (TNA: PCOM2/348 p. 227, accessed via findmypast.com). Thomas Clarke was also charged with stealing a pig-net from the premises of Mr Howard, tavern-keeper, of Southburgh; he was acquitted of this charge also. John Clarke alias Kittle's age as given in this press report is consistent with the date of John Kettle's birth recorded in the Cranworth baptism register.

31 Birth certificate of George Kettle, 12 January 1850, which named his mother as Mary Ann Kettle formerly Dack while leaving the space under 'name and surname of father' blank. A George Kettle, very likely the same child, died later in the year.

32 TNA: PCOM2/30, p213 accessed via findmypast.com. Here, the length of John Clarke/ Kettle's previous sentence of transportation was stated to be 15 years, which is highly unlikely to have been correct.

33 Information from onesearch.sql.qld.gov.au. The 'Ramillies' left England on 25 April 1854 but 157 of the 277 convicts were picked up at Gibraltar. John Clarke/Kettle may, therefore, have sailed to Gibraltar on an earlier voyage. Further information from convictrecords.com.au and fremantleprison.com.au.

34 R Hughes (1987).

35 Mary Ann Kettle nee Dack was listed in the 1851 census as Mary Kittle, aged 26, living in the house of John Webster, labourer, in Southburgh near the boundary with Cranworth, the same household in which she had been living, as Mary Ann Dack, in 1841. Webster appears to have been her father, as she is listed in 1851 as his daughter. The earliest possible record of her death is in 1858.

36 Information from onesearch.sql.qld.gov.au; further information from convictrecords. com.au, fremantleprison.com.au and beverleywa.com (all accessed 2 December 2020).

37 TNA: PCOM2/105, p 223, accessed via findmypast.com.

38 NM, 8 March 1834. Richard Clarke alias Kettle's age is not given in NM, but the NC, in a much briefer notice, gave it as 24, which is consistent with the date of his birth.

39 TNA: PCOM2/105, p 223, accessed via findmypast.com.

40 NC, 10 January 1852.

41 TNA: PCOM2/105, p 223, accessed via findmypast.com. William Clarke died in 1887, aged 64; information from the Cranworth parish register of burials, accessed via findmypast.com.

42 Thomas Clarke was himself the victim of a theft in 1847: James Goff was convicted of 'stealing six oysters and a pint and a half of nuts, the property of Thomas Clarke, fisherman, of Cranworth'; NM, 3 July 1847.

43 Family and occupational information from the 1851 census returns, accessed via findmypast.com, from the records of civil registration, accessed via freebmd.org, from the Cranworth parish registers, accessed via freereg.org and from TNA: PCOM2/34, accessed via findmypast.com.

44 Later known as the King of the Gipsies and then as the White Hart. It closed in 1919. Thanks to Robena Brown for this information, from the norfolkpubs.co.uk website.

45 NC, 22 October 1853 and NN, 22 October 1853.

46 TNA: HO8/123-138 and PCOM2 34, 49 and 357, identified via digitalpanopticon.org and accessed via findmypast.com.

47 Marriage certificate of Thomas Clarke and Frances Ward, 24 March 1859.

48 NC, 17 December 1864; NM, 14 January 1865 and 25 March 1865.

49 NN, 30 November 1867.

50 The age given for Matilda in 1871 (33) would suggest that she was born in 1838, but the census returns of 1841, 1861, 1881, 1891, 1901 and 1911, and the age given on her death certificate, would all suggest that she was born in 1836 or 1837. The evidence from 1851 is problematic, as explained in the next-but-one paragraph. Census returns accessed via ukcensusonline.com, findmypast.com and ancestry.co.uk.

51 There was another Matilda Kettle, who was older than Harriet's sister and came from Shipdham. She was listed in the 1841 census returns for the Gressenhall workhouse as aged 15 (which, as ages were rounded in 1841, meant that she was aged between 13 and 18), and appeared in the Gressenhall guardians' minutes in 1842 when they agreed to issue her with clothes to wear when going into service; MLU minutes; NRO, C/GP14/5. It seems likely that she was the Matilda Kettle who in January 1844 was convicted at the quarter sessions in Swaffham of stealing a shawl and was transported to Van Diemen's Land (Tasmania). She departed on the 'Angelina' on 25 April 1844, arriving in Van Diemen's Land on 24 August 1844. (Information from digitalpanopticon.org and convictrecords.com.au).

52 MLU minutes; NRO, C/GP14/9. The 1851 census enumerator recorded Leah Gay's age as 20 which would make it most unlikely that she was still at the school in 1849; in the 1841 census returns she was recorded, probably more accurately, as age 8, although that would mean she was 16 in 1849, still too old to be at school.

53 Inferred from the statement in the asylum's case book that Harriet smashed three windows 'because her sister did not come and see her'; CLA, case book 1853-1861; NRO, SAH 262.

54 1861 census returns, accessed via ancestry.co.uk.

55 MLU minutes, 28 October 1861; NRO, C/GP14/16.

56 CLA, Reception Orders 1857-60 and 1860-63; NRO, SAH 168/3. Thanks to Rose Sheen for this reference.

In Cranworth:
the Gurdons and the labourers

CRANWORTH, where Harriet Kettle was said to have been born, was and is a small agricultural village in central Norfolk, 16 miles west of Norwich. In 1836 it was described in White's Directory as 'a pleasant but scattered village and parish'[1], with an area of 1,000 acres (in later directories, revised up to 1,107 acres) and a population of 323. Cranworth's neighbour to the north west, between it and the much larger village of Shipdham, was Letton. Letton was similar in area to Cranworth (1,000 acres of land according to the 1836 directory, later revised to 1,260 acres) but had fewer than half as many people (133). Letton, despite the extensive acreage of the parish, was a 'shrunken' settlement, parts of which had been gradually deserted in the 15th and 16th centuries owing to the enclosure of arable land for sheep-rearing. Letton's church was in ruins by 1560 and only faint traces of the foundations survive. The ecclesiastical parishes of Letton and Cranworth were united in 1546 and became known as 'Cranworth-cum-Letton', although the civil parishes remained distinct. [2]

The dominant figure in both Cranworth and Letton in 1836 was Theophilus Thornhagh Dillingham Gurdon Esq. (1764-1849), whose family had been established in the area since the 15th century and whose name preserved the memory of forbears of his father.[3] TTD Gurdon (as he tended to be known) owned all the land in Letton, which was therefore a 'closed' parish. He owned four fifths of the land in Cranworth, where he was also, 'lord of the manor and patron of the rectory'.[4] His land-holdings extended to several other adjacent parishes as well[5], his property amounting in 1838 to 4,498 acres. The estate, it appears, was 'well run…commanding good rents throughout the 19th century'.[6]

TTD Gurdon resided at Letton Hall, described in White's Directory as, 'a handsome quadrangular mansion of white brick, seated in an extensive and well wooded park,' and in social terms a world away from the labourer's cottage in

Letton Hall, 2020.

15

which Harriet Kettle probably spent her infancy. The hall, which replaced an earlier house nearby, was designed by the noted architect Sir John Soane and was built in 1785-8. It was described by Pevsner as 'not a large house'—that is, by comparison with other country mansions - but the hall and staircase were judged 'very fine'.[7] The park was expanded shortly after the hall was built by moving roads out of the way and enclosing the land. Game was reared there and shooting parties provided recreation for the Gurdon family and their guests. Sheep-rearing continued, alongside arable and dairy farming; in 1840, TTD Gurdon was celebrated as possessing, 'decidedly the best breed of Southdown sheep in the county'.[8] The family was not in residence when the national census was taken in 1841, the only recorded occupants of the hall being four female and two male servants.

TTD Gurdon died in 1849. According to the Bury and Norwich Post, a Whig-supporting newspaper, he would, 'be ever recollected as one of those high-minded country gentlemen of whom Norfolk have [sic] a right to be proud; as an ornament to the society in which he moved, as one who took an honourable lead among those politicians who maintained and supported the Whig principles in this county, as the friend of their great patriot, Mr Coke,[9] and as the enemy of no man'.[10]

Letton Hall passed to TTD Gurdon's eldest son, Brampton Gurdon (1797-1881). At the time of the 1851 census, Brampton and his family were resident at the hall, along with seven female and three male servants. Brampton was a magistrate; he was appointed Sheriff of Norfolk in 1855; and he became the Liberal Member of Parliament for West Norfolk in 1857, serving until 1865.[11] Among the many who enjoyed his hospitality at Letton was Benjamin Armstrong, Vicar of East Dereham from 1850 until 1888, whose diary records several visits there. On 14 August 1855, for example, he wrote: 'Dined at the Gurdons, surrounded by all that wealth & good taste could suggest. The ladies of the family, as usual, most agreeable, diversifying the evening with music and singing.' Four years later, on 28 October 1859, he recorded another visit: 'Dined at Letton Hall, and met an aristocratic party staying in the house. Our dinner plates were silver, & the dessert service Dresden, with 8 powdered footmen to wait'.[12]

In Cranworth, the largest residence was the rectory, occupied by the Revd Philip Gurdon, a younger brother of Brampton Gurdon and someone who, because of the public roles he

The Revd Philip Gurdon as a young man (Joseph Slater), 1825. (Courtesy Gurdon family)

Cranworth Rectory before 1918. (Courtesy Robena Brown)

performed, was to meet his fellow parishioner Harriet Kettle on many occasions. Philip had been born at Letton Hall in 1800, the third son of TTD Gurdon. He graduated from Cambridge University in 1823, was ordained two years later and, as a young man, played county cricket for Norfolk. Having already became rector of Reymerston in 1825, rector of Southburgh in 1828, and rector of Hackford in 1829, he was instituted to the rectory of Cranworth-cum-Letton by his father (who was patron of all these livings) in April 1832, at the same time resigning from Hackford.[13] His total income amounted to the substantial sum of about £1,200 per year.[14] On his death in 1874, Philip Gurdon was described in the London Evening Standard as, 'one of the few remaining pluralists'.[15] Holding multiple incumbencies had been common in the 18th century but became increasingly rare as the Church of England, responding to the challenge presented by Methodism, reformed itself in the 19th century. The Pluralities Act of 1838 stipulated that no clergyman should hold more than two livings and that they should not be more than ten miles apart. Philip Gurdon might have argued that the three ecclesiastical parishes he served were contiguous and contained little more than a thousand people in total. Philip, moreover, complied with the injunction of Edward Stanley, the reforming Bishop of Norwich from 1837 to 1849, who insisted that clergymen of the Church of England should reside in their parishes.[16]

Three months after becoming rector of Cranworth-cum-Letton, Philip married his wife Henrietta. They moved into Cranworth Rectory, enlarged it in 1840, and by the time of the census of 1841 had five daughters, with the needs of the family being catered for by eight servants, six female and two male. In 1851, Philip and Henrietta were again in residence at Cranworth when the census was taken; only two of their daughters now remained at home and the complement of servants had fallen to four females and one male. The following year, Cranworth church was restored and partially rebuilt.

Philip Gurdon served Cranworth-cum-Letton as its rector for 42 years. The Church of England did not have a monopoly of organised religion in the parish, however; the Primitive Methodists had built their small chapel at High Common in Cranworth in 1835, with seating for 35 people, and on 30 March 1851 attracted 20 worshippers in the morning, 45 in the afternoon and 40 in the evening, compared with the 200 who attended the one (afternoon) service in the parish church (plus 50 children who attended Sunday school).[17] Philip's attitude to this competitor appears to have been relaxed and inclusive. The Norfolk News commented approvingly in 1863 on his, 'true Christian charity which respects conscientious differences in matters of religion'. The Primitive Methodists in the parish were not only, 'equal recipients with the rest, of the bounty which is so freely scattered through the parish, but one poor woman amongst their number—noted for the respectability of her character and her regular and tidy habits—has actually the charge of the church, where she attends during the single service that is held there every Sunday, and has been distinctly assured—in answer to her intimation that she could not forsake "the people"— that during the rest of the day she is at perfect liberty to attend the place which her conscience best approves'.[18]

Besides being the rector of Cranworth-cum-Letton, Philip Gurdon farmed the glebe and other lands that he held, amounting to about 50 acres in Cranworth alone,[19] and was a breeder of prize-winning poultry. He was also extremely active in the public life of the County of Norfolk.[20] He was a justice of the peace, sometimes sitting in petty sessions alongside his brother Brampton Gurdon. For several years, he served as honorary secretary of the Norfolk Agricultural Association.[21] He was also an ex-officio member of the Board of Guardians of the Mitford and Launditch Poor Law Union and was elected as its chairman in 1852. In that capacity he often came face to face with Harriet Kettle. He was a member of the committee of visiting justices of the county lunatic asylum at Thorpe from 1860 onwards, and he would have met Harriet there too. As a magistrate, however, Philip Gurdon sometimes got ahead of the ratepayers of his district and was not always popular with them. At a meeting held at the Assembly Rooms in East Dereham on 2 January 1863 to protest against the Highways Act of 1862, which Gurdon supported, the Revd H E Knatchbull of North Elmham, an opponent, said of Gurdon that, 'he was a very clever fellow...He had known him all his life, and that he succeeded in everything he undertook, but his tongue went a great deal too fast'.[22]

Philip Gurdon died at Cranworth Rectory on 1 August 1874 and was buried at the village church six days later. Oddly, there is no memorial to him among the many Gurdon family monuments inside the church (his rather modest grave stands in the churchyard); nor has any obituary been found in the local newspapers. Many of the reports of his death simply referred to him as a 'clerical pluralist' and were limited to noting the livings that he had held and that had become available with his decease. The one exception, improbably, was the London Evening Standard, which noted that Philip was, 'much beloved for his genuine kindness of heart'.[23]

*Grave of Philip Gurdon, 2020.
(Courtesy Cranworth and Southburgh
Parochial Church Council)*

After Philip Gurdon's death, his household effects were offered for sale, and the particulars provide an insight into the nature of his domestic establishment. The items listed included, 'mahogany, birch and painted double and single wardrobes, ditto dressing tables, chests of drawers, wash stands, looking glasses, cane-seated chairs, toilet sets, mahogany, birch and iron four-post and other bedsteads, excellent bordered featherbeds, hair and wool mattresses, blankets, quilts, Kidderminster, Brussels and other carpets, damask and moreen[24] window curtains, mahogany-framed dining room chairs, mahogany, loo[25] and other tables', and other furniture. There was even a refridgerator.[26] The outdoor effects included, 'an easy-running brougham by Elvin [a coachbuilder in East Dereham], a vis-à-vis basket carriage by Elvin, gig [and] luggage cart', along with harness, saddles, bridles and various tools and other equipment.[27] Philip Gurdon and his family enjoyed a comfortable lifestyle.

As well as the Gurdons, White's Directory of 1836 listed the other principal inhabitants of Letton and Cranworth. In Letton, there were four farmers, while in Cranworth the directory mentioned six, along with two shopkeepers, a corn miller, a blacksmith, a wheelwright, a cooper and a schoolmistress.[28] The census returns of 1841 and 1851 recorded the details of the families of the farmers and the few tradespeople and, of course, the people omitted from the directory, who were the most numerous group in the two villages—the families of the agricultural labourers.

In Letton, the four farmhouses were recorded in 1841, three of which contained servants as well as the farmer and his family. The lodges of TTD

Gurdon's gamekeeper and gardener were also noted. In Cranworth, eight inhabitants were described as farmers, five of whom were prosperous enough to employ servants, and there were a grocer, a smith and various other tradespeople. One of the farmers was Amos Potter, father of Robert Potter, with whom Harriet was to clash in court many years later; another was Robert Kiddle, who discovered the theft of grain by Richard Clark Kettle, of whom more below; and a third was John Aylmer, from whom William Clarke stole the ewes and lambs. Not much had altered in 1851. The population of Letton had dropped very slightly from 154 to 150, while that of Cranworth had fallen rather more, from 340 to 310, but the social structure was substantially unchanged.

The tenant farmers in Letton and Cranworth seem to have enjoyed good relations with the Gurdon family, their landlords. The cordiality between them was expressed strikingly in an event less than a month after Philip Gurdon's death. Robert Thornhagh Gurdon (1829-1902), eldest son and heir of Brampton Gurdon, married for the second time in 1874 and the tenants expressed a wish to present the couple with a wedding gift. The bridegroom's parents, Brampton Gurdon and his wife Henrietta, invited, 'all the tenants…with their wives, sons and daughters, to a luncheon and garden party' on 31 August 1874. Henry Stebbings, on behalf of the tenants, presented the newlyweds with a 'magnificent breakfast service' and gave an address in which he referred to, 'the great sympathy and mutual respect which have always existed between the landlord and the tenants of these estates'. He thought that 'the present occasion is one peculiarly fitted for showing our respect to the family, and our great regard for yourselves'.[29] Although it was no doubt in the interests of both landlords and tenants to cultivate good relations, there do appear to have been genuinely warm feelings on both sides. They were to be tested in the great depression in agriculture which began in the late 1870s, when the Gurdons were compelled to lower the rents of the farms, but the relationship of landlord and tenant appears to have remained reasonably amicable.[30]

The lifestyle of the larger farmers of Cranworth and Letton seems to have been not dissimilar to that of the rector, Philip Gurdon, if somewhat less refined. James Kiddle and Robert Kiddle, the brothers from whom Richard Clarke Kettle stole a coomb of wheat in 1834, dissolved their farming partnership in 1837 and the moveable property at their farm near the south-western boundary of Cranworth came on to the market. Offered for sale were '10 capital cart horses and mares, 12 handsome young cows, home-bred steers, 4 bulls, 92 sheep and lambs' along with pigs, '3 good road waggons' and various pieces of farm machinery including 'part of a threshing machine, with carriage'. The farmhouse had 'sleeping-rooms' containing four four-post bedsteads with 'moreen and chintz furniture' and two 'stump bedsteads', together with mahogany chests of drawers and other furniture. Downstairs was a parlour with 'mahogany card and dining tables, 2 Kidderminster carpets, 6 mahogany chairs, 2 elbow chairs' and other items. In the kitchen and pantry were a range of utensils and a 'Capital 8-day clock'. A dairy and cellar, containing equipment for making cream, butter and beer, completed the accommodation.[31] After the sale, Robert Kiddle continued to farm as sole tenant. Aged 56 in 1851, his farm comprised 350 acres and he employed two house servants as well as the agricultural labourers who worked the land. Harriet Kettle would probably have met Robert Kiddle at Gressenhall workhouse, as he served as the representative from Cranworth on the Board of Guardians of Mitford and Launditch Poor Law Union throughout the 1850s.

The agricultural labourers and their families accounted for over two thirds of the households in Letton and Cranworth in 1841 and 1851. In Letton, many of their cottages lay in an area north-east of the hall called Letton Green. In Cranworth, some were to be found around the parish church and rectory on Church Green, while most of the others (including Richard Clarke's) lay about a mile away at High Common, adjoining the parish of Southburgh. The original common land (along with commons in Letton, Southburgh and Reymerston) had been enclosed by Act of Parliament in 1796.

Harriet Kettle, may have spent at least part of her earliest years in one of the labourers' cottages at High Common, where there were other Clarke households in addition to that of her grandparents. There are no descriptions of the homes of agricultural labourers in Cranworth in the 1830s and 1840s, and so the best indication of the conditions in which Harriet spent her infancy is provided by a general report by Edward Twisleton, *On the Dwellings of the Labouring Classes in the Counties of Norfolk and Suffolk*, which was written in 1840 and was one of the local reports accompanying Edwin Chadwick's national *Report on the Sanitary Condition of the Labouring Population* of 1842.

Twisleton stated that a considerable proportion of the labourers lived in cottages with one room on the ground floor and one above it. He commented: 'Although they may be sufficiently commodious for a man, and wife, and very young children, they are manifestly uncomfortable, and the having only one bedroom is even indecent for a man and wife and large growing family; but I have seen many instances where a man, his wife, and six children, of different sexes, have slept together in one room on three and sometimes only two beds'. In some cases, the occupants tried to provide some privacy, by, 'putting curtains to the beds or dividing the room into two parts by pinning old counterpanes together, and sometimes by cutting up and sewing together old gowns and stretching them across the room'. Richard and Ann Clarke's cottage can be imagined to have been like this in the 1840s and 1850s.

The situation in the downstairs room, Twisleton commented, 'is almost equally inconvenient, and where it is necessary to wash linen, to cook, to bake, and to perform all the ordinary household work in the same room with children running and playing about, it is difficult for even the most tidy persons to prevent their house from being, to use a favourite phrase of the district, in a constant "muddle."' The most common type of cottage, however, had, as well as the single bedroom and room on the ground floor, 'an additional room used as a kind of wash-house, scullery, or, as it is frequently termed, a back-house, not to be confounded with bake-house'. In homes of this kind the upstairs room was sometimes divided into two by a wooden partition. Twisleton quoted one of his correspondents, Mr Wallis of the Mitford and Launditch Union, regarding the cases of typhus and other fevers that had occurred in labourers' cottages: 'In many of these cases the dwellings were particularly unhealthy from dirt and want of proper rooms, so that father, mother, sisters, and brothers, and perhaps a lodger, were all crowded into one apartment, perhaps not more than 12 feet square. In most of the cottages there is but one sleeping apartment, one lower room, and perhaps a little back place or shed. In many instances the muck or dirt-hole, which is the receptacle of all the refuse and filth of the cottage, is opposite the door.' Newly built cottages were usually better, with two rooms upstairs and two downstairs. There were not many of these in 1842, although dwellings of this description were built in Cranworth and Letton later.

'The furniture of the cottages in this district', noted Edward Twisleton in his report, 'is generally of a very simple kind. On the brick floor of the principal room there may be five or six strong wooden chairs, two or even three tables, a chest of drawers and sometimes a clock. On the chimney-piece there may be bright brass candlesticks and neat pieces of crockery. On the walls, pictures are not uncommon…The majority of the pictures relate to religious subjects, such as the history of Joseph, of David, or of Christ. Allegorical pictures are not infrequently met with, such as Spring, Summer, Autumn and Winter, represented as persons. Besides those, we may notice portraits very unlike the originals, among which the first place is due to Her Majesty and Prince Albert'. He added that: 'There are in the cottages very few books of any kind, except testaments or prayer-books; and there can be no doubt that the peasantry of Norfolk and Suffolk are on the whole an illiterate race'.

The food consumed by the labourers and their families was simple: 'Bread and butter, together with tea, is the usual food, even for dinner, of the aged and infirm, and of widows with children. The principal meal of the labourers is in the evening, after the day's work is over; when many of them sit down to a comfortable supper of Norfolk dumpling, potatoes, and, now and then, a little bacon or other meat.' The bread, Twisleton noted, was 'best wheaten bread'.

In December 1849, the Morning Chronicle, a national newspaper, gave a not dissimilar, if less sanguine, picture of the labourers' diet: 'The food of the labourer and his family is principally bread, potatoes and frequently, in Norfolk, the Norfolk dumpling, which consists simply of the dough of which bread is made, the difference between bread and dumpling being merely that the one is boiled while the other is baked. In none of the cottages that I have visited...have I ever seen such a thing as a piece of fresh butcher's meat...When meat of any kind is purchased it is mostly bacon or salt pork.'[32]

Harriet Kettle's infancy would have been spent in an environment of this kind. As her mother appears to have had issues and her father was clearly not a family man, the conditions in which she lived were probably worse than those in many of the other cottages in Cranworth. They may even have been like those described by a relieving officer in Roydon, near Diss, quoted by Twisleton: 'I found the poor woman and children without food or firing, and not a sufficiency of clothing to cover their nakedness. Their furniture consists of an old table, one chair, and a form below stairs; a bedstead and three bunches of rags, miscalled beds, but without sheets, blankets, or coverlids, and in a state of filth, and covered with vermin, that cannot be described. The house is without two panes of the girth-lights,[33] their place being supplied with a piece of sacking and rags; the walls and roof is [sic] in a most wretched and dilapidated state, the wind and weather penetrating in every direction; the floor below entirely broken up; one third of the chamber-floor is also broken up; there is no door to the chamber, its place being supplied with a piece of ragged pickling.'[34]

Money would certainly have been short. Labourers' wages, according to Twisleton, varied, 'generally speaking, from 10s [shillings] to 12s [50p to 60p] a week for day labour. There are about 2s or 3s [10p or 15p] more for task-work'. Over the next 20 years, the labourers' income fell, a situation deplored by, among others, FW Keppel, chairman of the board of guardians at Gressenhall, who argued that, to prevent outbreaks of incendiarism in the countryside, the poor should be given employment at 'fair wages'. He also advocated the provision of cottages at affordable rents.[35] James Caird, writing in 1851, reported that in Norfolk wages were only 8s a week but noted that, 'a great proportion of the work on farms is done by task work or contract...Task work will generally bring larger pay to the labourer, but this is more doubtful where the farmer resorts to contract. Hand-hoeing, and other light operations of husbandry, which can be carried on by children, are sometimes paid for by contract, a man engaging to do what is required for so much, and employing all the children he can collect, in gangs, to get through with it.'[36] Over a decade later, the Norfolk News reported in November 1863 that wages in the Cranworth and Letton area were still usually only 9s [45p] a week.[37]

Most of the work for the labourers of the two villages, who included some of the women and boys as well as the men, would have been on the local farms, the seven most substantial of which comprised 100 to 350 acres. Robert Kiddle's, where, according to the census returns, 12 male labourers, three women and two boys were employed in 1851, was the largest. Some of the younger labourers in Cranworth, however, may have worked as a member of a gang of the kind described by James Caird. The gang system was seen as a cause of 'immoral' behaviour as men and women (and, as Caird noted, boys and girls) worked together in the fields and sometimes had to spend the night together in a barn if the farm on which they were working was some distance from their homes. This may have been one of the factors contributing to the high rate of illegitimacy in Norfolk, which, according to the Morning Chronicle, was the third-highest in England.[38] Cranworth was not untypical; Harriet's grandmother Anne Kettle was not the only unmarried woman who had children baptised there.

In 1830, before Harriet Kettle was born, the poverty and distress of the agricultural labourers in Norfolk had resulted in an explosion of protest. There had been similar outbreaks of discontent in 1815 and 1822 but in 1830, during the 'Captain Swing' riots which affected much of the country, a particular focus of the labourers' ire was the threshing machine, which deprived them of an important source of winter employment. In a long report on the 'disturbed state' of the county in that year, the Norfolk Chronicle described a 'spirit of tumultuary combination among the labouring classes, the efforts of whose hostility, directed in the first instance against one obnoxious implement of agriculture [meaning the threshing machine] extend themselves in the natural and speedy course of such proceedings, to the destruction of almost every other piece of machinery, and to the violation by force or by menace, of those laws on which personal security and the rights of property altogether depend'. There was no county police force at that time; the newspaper reported on the swearing-in of 120 special constables in Shipdham, after which, 'having received information that rioting had taken place, and that machinery had been broken in the adjoining parishes,' about 30 or 40 of them rode to the home of the Chief Constable of Mitford Hundred, who was Mr Stebbings, one of the farmers in Letton.[39] There, 'they were met by the tenantry of TT[D] Gurdon Esq and with that gentleman, B Gurdon Esq and the Revd P Gurdon, proceeded in pursuit of the rioters'. They were joined by a small detachment of Royal Dragoon Guards and caught up with the 'mob' of 350 to 400 labourers at East Tuddenham, 'where they had just completed the demolition of two threshing machines'. This was class war in the Norfolk countryside but, given the balance of forces, there could only be one outcome: the rioters were dispersed and 11 arrests made.[40] Notably, in Cranworth and Letton, the landowner, parson and farmers were all lined up against the labourers, unlike in other parts of Norfolk where farmers sometimes colluded with the labourers to secure a reduction in the tithes to which their land was subject and which, as occupiers, they had to pay.[41] That the parson in this instance was the son of the landlord probably helped to spare him any unwelcome attention from the tenants.

As a result of the riots, some of the farmers temporarily dismantled or dispensed with their threshing machines, which may have been why the Kiddles' farm in Cranworth had only 'part of a threshing machine' when its contents were sold in 1837. The machines soon reappeared afterwards but the disturbances did have the effect of making the propertied classes more aware of the desperation of the labourers and the potential for violent protest, and, in some areas at least, steps began to be taken to improve both their material lot and their attitudes.

Philip Gurdon took a leading role in the establishment, in March 1833, of the Hundred of Mitford Society[42], 'for promoting good conduct and encouraging industrious habits amongst servants, cottagers and labourers,' and served as its secretary until 1846. On 25 October 1833, with Philip's father TTD Gurdon in the chair, the society met at the Kings Arms Inn in East Dereham to distribute rewards to those judged deserving of them. They included two sovereigns to Aaron Able of Letton, 'who has served as team-man [in charge of the heavy horses] with TT[D] Gurdon Esq for 36 years without intermission, and was never intoxicated when with his team', and one sovereign to be divided between two Cranworth labourers, Garner and Walker, 'for the growth of oats on their allotments'. After drinking toasts, the officers of the Society congratulated themselves on, 'the advantage of bringing the several classes of society more into communication with each other, and the practically showing to the poor, that those in superior situations do really take an interest in their well-being'.[43] The presentation of rewards and premiums became an annual event.

The aims of the society were restated in 1848, and included: 'to stimulate to good conduct the servants of farmers and tradespeople, by rewarding them for length of servitude; to check intemperate and careless habits…; to encourage the cottagers who devoted their leisure hours to the culture of gardens and allotments; to urge to greater watchfulness and recompense liberally, the shepherd who reared the greatest number of lambs, with the smallest loss of ewes; to increase the stores of the economical, by adding a large percentage to their deposits at the Savings Bank; to foster the love of, and desire to excel in, agricultural pursuits by rewarding the skilful ploughman; and to incite to diligence females who were incapable of going out to service, and who could only knit'.[44]

Such philanthropic initiatives by the propertied were complemented by constructive actions by the labourers themselves. FW Keppel, the chairman of the board of guardians at Gressenhall, wrote in a letter of April 1841 to Edward

Twisleton: 'The people have begun to take care of themselves by forming benefit and medical clubs; though some existed previous to the passing of the Poor Law, they have increased of late years'.[45] William Watling, an agricultural labourer from High Common in Cranworth, was a member of such a benefit club in 1852, reporting that, 'we have money out when we are ill'.[46]

Emigration offered a means of providing unemployed labourers with new opportunities while, at the same time, reducing the numbers dependent on poor relief. In 1837, Philip Gurdon had made all the arrangements to enable a Cranworth family to emigrate to the United States, under the terms of a scheme managed by the Poor Law Commission. James Hubbard, a labourer, his wife Ann, two sons, aged 13 and seven or eight daughters ranging in age from 14 to under one, sailed for New York (where James had a brother) on the 'Ontario' on 17 May 1837, with the parish taking out a loan of £50 (repayable over five years) to cover the cost of their passages and provisions for the journey. The family was not receiving poor relief but were perhaps considered likely to require it in due course; the outlay for their emigration, the equivalent of providing them with poor relief for a year, would spare the ratepayers of Cranworth expense in the future.[47] The Hubbards were among 3,354 emigrants whom the Poor Law Commission assisted to leave Norfolk in 1835-7.[48]

Another initiative taken by Philip Gurdon was to create allotments for the labourers in Cranworth to cultivate in what spare time they had. He was quoted on the evils of the gang system in the Morning Chronicle, which published a series of articles about 'labour and the poor' in 1849 and 1850. Gurdon, 'stated that the mischief which these gangs caused to society was extensive and very much to be deplored'. Because he wanted to discourage the labourers from, 'perambulating the several parishes in search of employment', Gurdon successfully secured the allotments by arranging the division of land at High Common (north of the Primitive Methodist chapel) that had been allocated for the maintenance of the poor at the time when Cranworth High Common was enclosed in 1796. The allotments were of half an acre each and were let to the labourers so that they could grow crops and keep pigs on them. There was opposition from the farmers, who had a 'strong prejudice' against the plan, perhaps because they feared that their crops would be stolen to feed the labourers' pigs. However, no doubt helped by the fact that most of the farmers were his father's tenants, Philip Gurdon was able to carry his plan forward and it seems to have had some success.[49]

It appears that the Gurdons were well regarded and commanded the respect of many if not all of the poorer inhabitants of Cranworth and Letton. When TTD Gurdon died in March 1849, the people of the two villages expressed their feelings about his qualities as a landlord and benefactor by turning out in numbers for his funeral. As the cortege travelled the mile or so from Letton Hall to Cranworth

The former 'Milk's Yard' in Cranworth—where 20 people, in five households, lived in 1851, c1930.
(Courtesy Robena Brown)

Church, 'every yard of the road was lined by mourners, who felt the loss they had sustained in the death of their neighbour and friend, and who, chiefly poor, and many of them aged, exhibited the very touchstone of heartfelt grief…' The path up to the church was 'lined by the children of the village schools, the girls clad in deep mourning,' and there was standing room only inside.[50]

Over a decade later, when the Norfolk News investigated the 'cottage homes of England' in the autumn of 1863, its reporter found much to praise in Cranworth and Letton, finding conditions there much better than in most of the other places he visited. 'As the sun shone brilliantly on the well thatched roofs, the unbroken walls, the brightly cleaned windows of the cottages and upon gardens kept with more than ordinary neatness,' waxed the lyrical account, 'we were not long in…divining that the "squire" discharged his duties to the poor somewhat better than many "squires" are wont to do'. The report continued, 'the cottagers…informed us that both the squire [Brampton Gurdon] and the clergyman [Philip Gurdon] were heartily seconded in the kind consideration for the people by their wives and daughters'. Every cottage on the Gurdon estate was found to have at least two bedrooms and an outdoor privy. The rents were lower than usual and repairs were done promptly.[51]

However, not all was perfect. Even allowing for the fall in the population of the villages (Cranworth's had declined to 264 and Letton's to 111 in 1861, while the number of houses remained about the same as ten years earlier) there were still insufficient cottages on the farms to house all the workers. Moreover, only half the cottages in Cranworth were on the Gurdon estate;[52] the other half were probably more overcrowded and let for higher rents. In 1860, the three houses at High Common, Cranworth, which included the elderly Ann Clarke's residence, were offered for sale by auction; they were 'let in 6 tenements…at annual rents amounting to £25', a high figure for such property in the period.[53] According to the 1861 census returns, no fewer than 31 people (including Ann) lived in these three houses.

And living on 9s [45p] per week was far from easy. As one poor woman who had a husband and four children put it to the reporter from the Norfolk News: '"Sir, it's a penny a meal each for six days and nothing for the Sunday—leaving out all thought of how we are to pay for the boots and shoes, clothing, firing, candles, soap, soda and lots of other things that must be put down as necessaries." "Then how do you live," we asked. "Well Sir,"—was the reply—"My heart is often broken for the children's sake because we have not food enough for them, and if it were not for the kindness of the 'ladies' we should not live at all."' This was a reference to Brampton Gurdon's wife Henrietta and unmarried daughter Amy Louisa, who ran a Sunday school at the hall, supported clothing clubs for the poor and distributed soup and blankets. Philip Gurdon's wife Henrietta and four eldest daughters, now in their early 20s, were also reported to be, 'constantly engaged in deeds of benevolence', providing clothing for poor widows and large families.[54]

The paternalism and philanthropy of the Gurdons helped to ensure that Cranworth and Letton remained largely if not entirely peaceful places in the mid-19th century. Many of the poorer parishioners, no doubt, were grateful for what was done for them. However, not all necessarily benefited, and there may have been an element of selectivity in what was provided. As one writer has noted of East Anglia in this period, 'the worthy poor were rewarded whilst the unworthy went hungry'.[55] Villagers with less deferential attitudes found other means to satisfy their needs, demonstrating scant respect for property and the propertied. After the riots of 1830, a low-level insurgency continued in the Norfolk countryside, characterised by episodes of stack-burning, theft, animal-maiming and poaching. Poachers took game from the reserves maintained by landowners like the Gurdons, both to feed their families and for profit, their bags being sold to intermediaries who conveyed them to the towns, where they found a ready market.[56]

Although no records have been found of stack-burning or animal-maiming in Cranworth and Letton, the two communities were not immune from theft and poaching. Harriet Kettle's father John Kettle/Clarke and her uncles Richard

Clark Kettle, William Clarke and Thomas Clarke may have been among the main offenders, but were not alone in turning to illegal means of enhancing their incomes. In 1853, for example, Edward Pooley of Letton, aged 24, was tried for the theft of two coombs of wheat from James Goddard, one of the Letton farmers, and was found to have three 'picklock keys' on his person when arrested.[57]

Two years earlier, in 1851, a series of cases of poaching had occurred in the Letton area, culminating in a direct attack on the house of George Whitear, Brampton Gurdon's head gamekeeper, which was besieged by a gang of poachers who had become notorious in the area. A week later, on the night of 6 December 1851, there was a 'serious affray' at Letton between the gang, whose members had blackened their faces with wet gunpowder, and Gurdon's gamekeepers, supported by members of the recently-formed county police force.[58]

Two of the policemen who confronted the poachers at Letton, including the most senior officer, Superintendent Parker, were hit by shots fired by the gang. There were fears that wounds sustained in the face by Parker would prove fatal but he recovered—and, seven years later, was the person who escorted Harriet Kettle to appear before the magistrates after her attempt to set fire to Gressenhall workhouse. Three of the gang of poachers were arrested, two more being picked up at their houses later. They all appeared before the Revd Philip Gurdon, again acting as the local magistrate, who remanded them to appear at the next Norwich Assizes. A further two were arrested at a later date and were remanded by the Revd Thomas Paddon, another magistrate and one of Philip Gurdon's predecessors as chairman of the board of guardians at Gressenhall workhouse. The alleged ringleader, however, appears to have escaped. Two of the accused lived in Letton Green and one of them, Robert Buckle, occupied a house which, according to the 1851 census returns, contained nine other family members spanning three generations. Three of the poachers (those who had been armed) were sentenced to ten years' transportation, three (including Robert Buckle) to two years' imprisonment with hard labour, and one was acquitted. The deployment of the police to apprehend the poachers was questioned by the judge: 'If gentlemen will preserve their game…they are to preserve that game at their own expense… The police force is paid for by the ratepayers of the county, and is intended for the preservation of the public peace,' although he did acknowledge later that the police had been deployed, not to protect game but because the gamekeeper and his wife had been threatened.[59]

Less than 18 months later, on a bright moonlit night in March 1853, there was another incident of poaching and assault, this time in Cranworth but again involving Brampton Gurdon's gamekeeper, George Whitear. He attempted to apprehend three poachers on land owned by Gurdon but was knocked down. His gun was taken but was later recovered from a ditch. Two men were arrested, one from Cranworth and one from Shipdham, but again the ringleader escaped and in his absence the two prisoners were acquitted. It was a feature of the continuing low-level conflict in the countryside that efforts to investigate cases of arson and poaching tended to meet a wall of silence, as the labourers and their families closed ranks around the perpetrators.[60]

This was the society into which Harriet Kettle was born and in which she spent her earliest years, and her perceptions may have been coloured by it, however dim her memories of her life before she arrived at Gressenhall. She and other workhouse inmates may have been influenced by the culture of resistance which existed, alongside the habits of deference, among the labouring poor.

Harriet Kettle and the Revd Philip Gurdon came from opposite ends of the social spectrum in Cranworth, but they faced each other on numerous occasions. Gurdon, as mentioned above, was a member of the Board of Guardians of Mitford and Launditch Union, the body responsible for Gressenhall workhouse, where Harriet Kettle was brought up. He was elected chairman in 1852 (replacing FW Keppel) and, having been re-elected each year, was still performing that role in 1863. He was the person before whom Harriet Kettle appeared when summoned to the board at regular intervals, charged with various misdemeanors.

Exactly when Harriet left Cranworth for Gressenhall is not known, but it was at a very early age. It was at Gressenhall that she spent most of her childhood.

Notes

1   William White, *History, Gazeteer and Directory of Norfolk*, 1836.
2   Alan Davison et al, *East Anglian Archaeology 44: Six Deserted Villages in Norfolk* (1988); P Carroll (2011).
3   P Carroll (2011).
4   Cranworth tithe apportionment, 1838; NRO, DN/TA 106; William White, ibid.
5   Southburgh, Reymerstone, Garveston and Thuxton - see S Wade Martins (1991).
6   S Wade Martins (1991).
7   N Pevsner, *The Buildings of England: North-West and South Norfolk* (1962).
8   NN, 5 December 1840.
9   T W Coke, Earl of Leicester, of Holkham Hall.
10 BNP, 21 March 1849.
11 NN 14 March 1857. Brampton Gurdon's election for West Norfolk was uncontested because the Liberals and Conservatives had made a deal: each party provided one member for the two-member constituency. The NN, a radical newspaper, sometimes expressed scepticism about the depth of Brampton Gurdon's Liberal convictions, referring to him on 19 May 1860 as, 'the once liberal Mr Brampton Gurdon'.
12 C Armstrong (2012).
13 Information from theclergydatabase.org.uk.
14 NM, 11 August 1874.
15 Evening Standard, 10 August 1874.

16 S Wade Martins (2018).

17 Norfolk Record Society, *Religious Worship in Norfolk: the 1851 Census of Accommodation and Attendance at Worship*, 1998.

18 NN, 14 November 1863. The name of the 'poor woman' was Mary Ann Rose, wife of an agricultural labourer, 'who cleans Cranworth Church', according to a report in NN, 5 November 1859.

19 Cranworth tithe apportionment, 1838; NRO, DN/TA 106.

20 As were many Anglican clergymen in Norfolk at the time; see R Lee, *Rural Society and the Anglican Clergy* (Boydell and Brewer, Woodbridge, 2006).

21 NM, 18 May 1861, for example.

22 NN, 10 January 1863. The Highway Act of 1862 gave the county magistrates the power to transfer the maintenance of local roads from parishes to districts under the supervision of the County Surveyor. The opponents of the measure claimed that this would result in a higher county rate and unemployment in the parishes.

23 Evening Standard, 10 August 1874.

24 Damask was a patterned fabric made from a range of textiles. Moreen was a strong ribbed cotton fabric used mostly, as here, for curtains.

25 Loo was a card game.

26 Perhaps an ice-making machine (invented 1854) rather than what is understood by the term today.

27 NN, 3 October 1874.

28 The Cranworth tithe apportionment of 1838 mentions a schoolroom rented by Mrs Gurdon, and the accompanying map shows its location near the church; NRO, DN/TA 106. A new school was built by T T D Gurdon in 1844.

29 NC, 5 September 1874. Robert Thornhagh Gurdon was created the first Baron Cranworth in 1899 and became the first chairman of Norfolk County Council. His first wife had died in 1864, aged 28, after only two years of marriage, after giving birth to a daughter. His second wife was 21 years his junior.

30 P Carroll (2011).

31 NM, 7 October 1837.

32 MC, 26 December 1849.

33 Dormer windows—D Yaxley (2003).

34 Very coarse linen—Ibid.

35 BNP, 17 October 1849.

36 James Caird, *English Agriculture in 1851* (1852).

37 NN, 14 November 1863. £1 in 1840 would equate to £102.54 in 2020, according to the Office for National Statistics composite price index, accessed 16/06/2020.

38 MC, 29 December 1849.

39 Stebbings may have been the father of Henry Stebbings, who presented the wedding gift to Robert Thornhagh Gurdon and his wife in 1874.

40 NC, 4 December 1830.

41 E J Hobsbawm and G Rude (1973); R Lee (2005).

42 The first such society in Norfolk, in Launditch Hundred, was established two years earlier, in 1831; Digby (1978).

43 NC, 9 February and 2 November 1833.

44 NC, 28 October 1848.

45 Appendix to the Seventh Annual Report of the PLC, PP XI, 1841.

46 NN, 20 March 1852. Watling was called as a witness during the trial of the poachers referred to below.

47 TNA: MH12 8475/10-12, 33-34, 50, 59-62.

48 Digby (1978).

49 MC, 26 December 1849.

50 NM, 24 March 1849. The building of the village schools had been paid for by T T D Gurdon in 1844.

51 NN, 14 November 1863.

52 Cranworth tithe apportionment, 1838; NRO, DN/TA 106.

53 NN, 8 September 1860. Digby (1978) states (p.21) that a labourer's rent was typically £4 a year, but could range from £2 to £6.

54 NN, 14 November 1863.

55 J E Archer (1990).

56 M J Carter (1980).

57 NN, 2 July 1853.

58 M J Carter (1980). The Norfolk County Police Force had been established in 1839, under the provisions of the Rural Constabulary Act; by 1841, the county was served by 143 police officers, and the numbers grew steadily over subsequent years.

59 NN, 13 December 1851, 20 December 1851, 20 March 1852. See also Carter (1980).

60 NN, 19 March 1853.

Growing up in Gressenhall Workhouse

G RESSENHALL workhouse, the large institution in which Harriet Kettle was brought up, provided accommodation for the poor of the Mitford and Launditch Poor Law Union in central Norfolk.[1]

The union comprised 60 parishes, 50 in the 'hundreds' (historical districts) of Mitford and Launditch together with ten from Eynesford Hundred. Cranworth was in Mitford Hundred. The union was created following the passage of the Poor Law Amendment Act of 1834, which established new, stricter and more systematic arrangements for the relief of people in need, and could be seen as part of the drive to reform the morals of the labouring poor after the disturbances of 1830. The management of the union was in the hands of a board of guardians. The guardians had to occupy property rated at £35 per year,[2] and were elected by open ballot of the property owners and ratepayers of the parishes, although there was often only one candidate. Most parishes elected one guardian, but the market town of East Dereham had four representatives and Shipdham had two, and at a later stage North Elmham and Mattishall also elected two guardians. The local magistrates were ex-officio members of the board, increasing its membership to around 70, but only a small fraction of the guardians attended meetings regularly.

The costs of poor relief were met from rates levied on the occupiers of land and buildings, with each parish having to cover the costs of its own poor. As a result, the level of the poor rate varied greatly from parish to parish. The most significant ratepayers were the farmers, and farmers constituted the great majority of the elected members of the board of guardians. For them, keeping the poor rates as low as possible was a matter of self-interest.

The guardians of Mitford and Launditch Union held their first meeting at Gressenhall workhouse on 19 May 1836 and met weekly thereafter, their proceedings being recorded in a minute book by their clerk.[3] As their first chairman, they elected Frederick Walpole Keppel (1797-1858), of Lexham Hall, who was a magistrate and ex-officio guardian.[4] Keppel, praised at a celebration of his birthday a few days after his election as, 'a gentleman whose life is devoted to the service of his fellow men,'[5] was a strong supporter of the Poor Law Amendment Act. In May 1841, he said of himself: 'I am an advocate for reform;

Map showing the parishes served by the workhouse at Gressenhall.

I do not call myself a Whig of the old school, but of the new; I am not afraid of reform' - although not, he added, to the extent of supporting the Chartists.[6] On his death in December 1858, the following tribute appeared in one of the local newspapers: 'Although possessing a somewhat rough manner, no man could possess a kinder heart or a more open hand to the poor…In politics Mr Keppel was a consistent and unflinching supporter of Liberal opinions, and was a not less strenuous advocate for economy in public expenditure…'[7] Keppel served as chairman of the board of guardians until 1842, upon which his fellow ex-officio guardian, the Revd Philip Gurdon of Cranworth (whom Dr Kay had called, 'one of the most active members of the visiting committee' at Gressenhall in 1838[8]), proposed an address which was endorsed by the board and subsequently printed in the Norwich Mercury newspaper. In fulsome prose, the guardians praised Keppel's, 'unsullied integrity and active zeal for the public welfare, together with a kindly feeling to your fellow creatures', adding that, 'the great reduction of the rates demonstrate [sic] your faithful guardianship of the public purse'.[9] The new chairman was the Revd Thomas Paddon, vicar of Mattishall[10] and a magistrate, who served until 1849. FW Keppel then returned for a further three-year stint as chairman before handing over to Philip Gurdon in 1852. It was perhaps largely thanks to Keppel and Gurdon that the poor of Mitford and Launditch were spared some of the excesses of brutality which were reported elsewhere.

The work of the board of guardians was supervised by assistant poor law commissioners, from 1847 known as poor law inspectors, appointed by the Poor Law Commission (replaced in 1847 by the Poor Law Board), whose offices were at Somerset House in London. The Mitford and Launditch guardians' first meeting was attended by the assistant poor law commissioner, Dr James Kay, who continued to visit regularly until he was moved to another part of the country in 1838. Later, as Dr James Kay-Shuttleworth (after his marriage to Janet Shuttleworth in 1842), he became a noted educational reformer. Kay and Keppel established a good working relationship, and together were able to subdue the initial opposition to the new Poor Law of some of the guardians.

James Kay, c1871.

Most large workhouses in England were built in the years after the passage of the Poor Law Amendment Act. Gressenhall workhouse had a longer history. Its main buildings had been opened in 1777 as a 'house of industry' under the provisions of an Act of Parliament of May 1775, which united the parishes of Mitford and Launditch hundreds in an 'incorporation'. Similar initatives were taken in several other parts of East Anglia in the final third of the 18th century, inspired by a desire to provide humane treatment for the poor at a lower cost to ratepayers. The intention was that the helpless would be well looked after while the able-bodied would work and thereby help to defray the running costs of the whole establishment. The house of industry was built on a lavish scale, and the regime in it was relatively relaxed. [11]

After the passage of the Poor Law Amendment Act, the incorporation was dissolved and replaced by the Mitford and Launditch Poor Law Union. Gressenhall workhouse became a harsher place with a more parsimonious and rigorous regime. This was deliberate: the theory was that conditions in the workhouse would act as a 'test', deterring all but the destitute from applying for help. The inmates were 'classified'—that is, divided into separate categories by sex and age. Families were split up. In 1835, work began on alterations and additions to the workhouse buildings to meet the requirements of the new system, the completion of which was supervised by Dr Kay. A wall was constructed to enclose the front of the building, with a gateway guarded by a porter's lodge. The

The House of Industry at Gressenhall depicted in an oil painting by Robert Kerrison, 1810.

space behind it was divided into separate yards by partition walls.

In the autumn of 1836 the works were sufficiently complete for the inmates to be 'classified'. The process took place in October, in the presence of a sergeant and three constables from the Metropolitan Police. As noted in the previous chapter, there was no county police force in Norfolk before 1839, and some of the inmates of the former house of industry would certainly have resisted the changes, as Dr Kay realised.[12] According to reports in the local newspapers, on 7 April 1834, shortly before the passage of the Poor Law Amendment Act: 'A revolt took place at the workhouse at Gressenhall…Twelve of the most refractory inmates were committed to Walsingham Bridewell, and order has been restored.'[13] Disturbances took place in several other parts of Norfolk when workhouses were built or modified: for example, there were riots at Bircham in Docking Union[14] and at Kenninghall in Guiltcross Union[15]; and an arsonist struck the Heckingham Workhouse in Loddon and Clavering Union.[16] The anxiety of the authorities was well founded but, in the event, the police presence helped to ensure that there was no trouble, and the classification of the inmates was completed without incident.

Harriet Kettle was admitted to the Mitford and Launditch Union Workhouse as a child. Exactly when, and in what circumstances, is not known[17] but, assuming that the identification of Harriet Kettle with the Harriott Clarke listed in the 1841 census returns is correct, it would have been before 1841 and Harriet

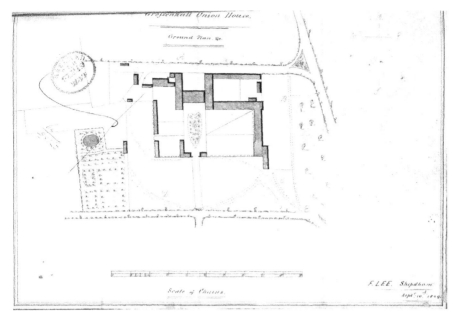

Plan of Gressenhall workhouse dated 1849 showing the alterations made to the workhouse buildings after 1834 Act, (TNA: MH/12/8478/325).

would have been no more than three years old when admitted. A few years later, in 1845 and 1846, there was a surge of admissions to Gressenhall; these were years of hunger (and, in Ireland, famine) that precipitated the repeal of the Corn Laws in 1846. The number of tramps admitted rose from 29 in 1841 to 376 in 1847,[18] while the total number of inmates reached a peak of 503 in January 1846. In reporting to the Poor Law Commission in January 1845 that the workhouse was full and that its official capacity of 477 had been exceeded, the guardians noted that a great number of those admitted were children and infants. No doubt many, like Harriet, had been abandoned by parents no longer able or willing to support them.

The usual process for admission to the workhouse was by application to one of the union's three[19] relieving officers, who were the eyes and ears of the guardians in the parishes. Harriet Kettle and her siblings could have been delivered to the parish overseer of the poor, who would have passed them on to the relieving officer, or to the relieving officer directly. John Kettle was not at home from March 1838 onwards; perhaps Harriet's mother found that she could no longer support the children, or perhaps she 'died insane' and Harriet's grandparents took responsibility for delivering the children to the overseer. We don't know.

What is surely beyond doubt is that arriving at the workhouse would have been a disturbing and frightening experience for Harriet. She might never have left Cranworth before, and she almost certainly would never have seen such a large building, far bigger than the Revd Philip Gurdon's rectory, the largest house in Cranworth; bigger, even, than Letton Hall, where TTD Gurdon lived. To a child, the walls surrounding the workhouse must have seemed intimidatingly high. Harriet, Matilda and John probably arrived at Gressenhall together; perhaps Matilda was carrying John and Harriet was clinging to her sister as they approached the gate.

At the gate, there was a bell that could be rung to attract the attention of the porter. After being let in, Harriet's first stop would have been a receiving ward. In accordance with the regulations, she would have been bathed and 'thoroughly cleansed'[20] in a tub. At an early stage, she would have been examined by the workhouse's medical officer, William M Warcup, a surgeon with a practice in East Dereham. Harriet's admission would have been recorded and reported to the next meeting of the board of guardians. She would have been issued with workhouse clothes, her own being taken away, sterilised and stored. The workhouse clothing was largely of serge, flannel, calico (cotton) and Haverhill drabbet (a coarse linen fabric)[21], with linsey-woolsey and duffield (types of woollen cloth) also being mentioned occasionally in the guardians' minute books. The girls' clothing was probably a smaller version of that issued to women, which included shifts of calico (white, blue or olive), flannel or serge petticoats, and probably an over-gown of blue calico or cotton checks. The men were clothed in grey 'stout twist calico' shirts, trousers (perhaps of serge or drabbet), 'highlows' (lace-up ankle boots), stockings and probably drabbet smocks or perhaps jackets of fearnought (a thick woollen cloth). There were hats for the men and caps for the boys. Clothes were made up and shoes manufactured in the workhouse from the materials supplied by contractors, which also included thread, tapes, buttons, leather, nails and shoe oil.[22]

After the process of admission had been completed, Harriet would have been allocated to the girls' ward. According to the national regulations, children under seven and girls aged seven to 15 were different 'classes', but at Gressenhall, although they may have used different rooms during the day, girls aged five to 16 were accommodated in the same dormitory. The girls' accommodation was probably in one of the L-shaped eastern wings, built as part of the original house of industry in 1777, and before 1834 divided into separate partitioned areas or 'cottages' for married couples behind an open arcade, an arrangement described later by Dr Kay, disparagingly, as 'not unlike the streets of Bologna'.[23] By the time Harriet entered the workhouse, the eastern wings had been 'gutted', the cottages swept away and the arcades walled in as part of the modifications of 1835-6. The girls' dormitory would have been on the first floor and the day room or rooms, which served as school rooms, on the ground floor, opening on to a yard enclosed by high walls, including one running diagonally from the angle of the 'L'. The yards were gravelled and each had a privy, often in a less than salubrious state, with an open drain running from it: the smell must have been offensive at the best of times.[24]

The dormitories contained iron bedsteads, supplied by Messrs Ostler and Gidney of East Dereham. The mattresses were of straw, less comfortable than the flocks with which they were filled before 1834. The walls were whitewashed. The dormitories, and the whole building, were supposed to be locked at night but this did not prevent occasional escapes, as in June 1845, when the master and schoolmaster were, 'reprimanded severely…for not having the doors of the workhouse properly closed and secured according to the orders of the poor law commissioners', following the escape of two boys 'between the hours of four and five in the morning'.[25]

Iron bedstead, introduced following the 1834 Act.

The sleeping accommodation was very crowded, the girls' dormitory in which Harriet slept particularly so. According to a return of August 1842, the girls aged five to 16, numbering 58, occupied a dormitory measuring 56 by 20 feet (17 by 6 metres) and a day room of 28 by 14 feet (8.5 by 4.25 metres). The boys' accommodation was larger but it, too, was overcrowded.[26]

Eleven years later, in January 1853, the poor law inspector, Sir John Walsham, raised concerns about the impact of the overcrowding on the children's health, after measles and ophthalmia had spread rapidly through the dormitories. The guardians' clerk reported that the girls' dormitory contained 34 beds, nine with two occupants and the remainder with three, 12 of which were occupied by three girls over seven. There was a total of 90 girls sleeping in the dormitory. Sir John pointed out that it was against the regulations for three children over seven to sleep in the same bed, and that the total number of occupants of the girls' dormitory exceeded the permitted maximum. The following month, the guardians obtained some additional beds and, in April 1853, they increased the sleeping accommodation for the girls by opening a new dormitory. This may not have benefited Harriet Kettle, however, as she probably left the workhouse shortly after January 1853, having spent the preceding years sleeping two or three to a bed in very cramped conditions. The boys' dormitory, as reported by the clerk in January 1853, contained 38 beds, with all boys over the age of seven sleeping two to a bed; previously, however, before the outbreaks of ophthalmia and measles, there had been 30 beds, ten with two occupants and 20 with three, most occupied by two boys over seven and one under seven, or two under seven and one over seven.[27]

It needs to be borne in mind that the cottages in Norfolk villages occupied by agricultural labourers and their families were also crowded, as has been seen. Nevertheless, sharing space with other family members would have been a different and no doubt better experience than the institutional impersonality of the workhouse environment.

It is not known whether Harriet suffered illness as a result of spending her nights in an overcrowded dormitory and her days in a day-room and yard in close proximity to other children and to a noisome privy and open drain, but it is very likely that she did. By later standards, the death rate among the children was high and, although it was sometimes claimed that the health of the inmates was good, epidemics of various diseases occurred from time to time. No specific figures for the deaths of infants and children are available for the 1830s and 1840s, but a list indicating the causes of death of all inmates who died at Gressenhall between 15 November 1836 and 25 May 1841 showed that deaths from consumption (tuberculosis), measles and influenza occurred from time to time.[28] For the 1850s and 1860s (to 1869) details of burials were recorded in the chaplain's books, and these show that from 1850 to 1857 there was an average of 6.25 burials per year of children aged two and under in the workhouse, with the high total of 11 deaths (half the total of all deaths in the workhouse) in 1852. At least one child aged between three and 16 also died in each of these years; 1857, when there were six deaths in this age-group, was a particularly bad year. After 1857, the numbers of both infant and child deaths were lower.[29]

In 1834, before Harriet's time and before the creation of the poor law union, there had been an outbreak of cholera in the house of industry.[30] It was claimed later by one of the guardians that, 'not less than half the inmates' had been afflicted and 23 had died. In 1839, the guardians viewed 'with anxiety the alarming increase of sickness within the house, the cases of influenza alone amounting to 100'. There were also at this time 200 cases of 'itch' (scabies); it 'made its appearance' again in January 1850. In September 1842, 26 out of the 66 boys and 17 of the 58 girls in the workhouse were showing symptoms of scrofula (a complaint causing swelling of the glands around the neck and inflammation of the skin), and there was a suggestion that the close confinement of the children was aiding its spread.[31] In the summer of 1844 there was an epidemic of both typhus and measles, affecting 80 children. In January 1853, as noted above, the poor law inspector, Sir John Walsham, expressed concern about the prevalence of ophthalmia (inflammation of the eyes, a severe form of conjunctivitis) among the boys and thought that it might have been spread because too many individuals were sleeping in each bed. In the same month, measles had again swept through the girls' ward and at the time of Sir John's visit, 31 girls were in bed with it.[32] Perhaps Harriet was one of them, if she had not already left the workhouse. Scarlatina broke out among the children in the schools in 1857, no doubt accounting for the high number of deaths of school-age children that year.[33]

The guardians were not indifferent to the health of the inmates, particularly when the children were affected. They were required to ensure that the young inmates were washed in tubs once a week[34] and later, in 1861, Sir John Walsham was to order that this should be done, 'in a bath with warm water and soap every Saturday afternoon under the superintendence of the schoolmaster and schoolmistress'.[35] In 1838 and 1839, the guardians arranged for the children to be vaccinated against smallpox, and the exercise was repeated in subsequent years, including for 50 unvaccinated children—perhaps

A bath thought to be from the workhouse found on a farm being used as a water-trough.

including Harriet Kettle—in April 1845. In March 1850, the guardians received a complaint about, 'the dirty state of the children's heads in the workhouse female school'—which Harriet, aged 11, would have been attending at the time - and as the complaint proved well founded, the schoolmistress was, 'severely reprimanded for allowing the children to be so neglected and the matron was 'admonished to be more attentive to her duty in this respect'.

Harriet grew up in these overcrowded and unhealthy conditions in the company of many other children and adults although, because of the system of classification, it would have been only with the girls that she had direct contact. A return of March 1847 listed the numbers of boys and girls at Gressenhall by age and reason for their confinement. There were 98 boys and 105 girls in the workhouse at that time; 17 girls, including ten over the age of seven, were listed as 'children deserted by father'. Harriet, then aged eight, may have been one of them as the guardians appear to have been unaware that her father had been transported. Other categories included orphans; illegitimate children; the children of widows, widowers, imprisoned fathers or able-bodied parents who were themselves workhouse inmates. All these groups were represented at Gressenhall.[36]

Apart from the children, the other inmates of the workhouse were largely the old, the sick, adults with physical or mental disabilities, and able-bodied women who were unmarried or had been deserted by their husbands, together with their infant children. Until a separate ward for those deemed 'respectable' was erected in 1853, elderly married couples were split up and the men and women sent to separate wards, but in other respects their treatment, in the context of the parsimonious workhouse regime, was merciful. As FW Keppel put it in 1841: 'The board of guardians have always made it a rule to relieve the aged liberally, certainly higher than under the old law…and also in cases of accident or illness… The orders of medical men for meat or porter have been rarely refused, though I consider there exists much abuse on that head; but the guardians have always decided on the necessity of not attempting to interfere with the surgeon's orders, for fear any accident should happen to the pauper, and the charge be laid on their shoulders.'[37] Unmarried able-bodied women with infant children, however, received harsh treatment, which included having to wear a distinctive 'overdress or jacket', a practice which, despite being against the rules, continued until 1866 and earned them the name, 'jacket women'.[38]

Able-bodied men were also admitted, many of whom were vagrants who stayed for one night or for a short period. However, in contravention of the original intention of the 1834 Act there were also many able-bodied men, both the unemployed and the sick, to whom relief continued to be given outside the workhouse, in money or in the form of tickets exchangeable for flour. Contractors for the provision of the flour were required to deliver it to 'stations' in some of the parishes (including Cranworth) for distribution, 'in such small quantities to the poor there as may be directed by the board,' the recipients handing over their tickets for redemption by the contractors.[39] It was actually cheaper to maintain an able-bodied person outside the workhouse than inside it and payments ostensibly for the relief of sickness enabled farmers (who, as noted above, comprised most of the members of the board of guardians) to maintain a pool of labour to draw upon at haysel and harvest time.[40] In February 1850, there were five times as many people receiving 'outdoor relief' in Mitford and Launditch Union as were being accommodated in the workhouse.

Harriet would not have seen much of the inmates in the other 'classes' since, apart from at mealtimes, they would have been hidden behind high walls. She would, however, have seen the workhouse officers. Her most significant contact would have been with the schoolmistress, of which more later, but she would also have been aware of the master and matron (a husband and wife), the porter and assistant matron (also a husband and wife), the medical officer, the chaplain, the schoolmaster, the infant schoolmistress (from 1850), the messenger and (from 1852) the nurse. She would probably have been able to observe most of them at mealtimes, since in 1838 the guardians had stipulated that, 'the subordinate officers of the workhouse do take all their meals together and not be allowed to take any part of their provisions to their separate apartments'.

The first master and matron with whom Harriet had contact were George and Rhoda Pinson, who were appointed in February 1837 and remained in post for nearly seven years, until December 1843, when Harriet would have been four or five.[41] George had previously been a turnkey in the county gaol at Norwich Castle, which the guardians may have regarded as highly relevant experience.[42] Initially, the remuneration was £100 per year for the master and £20 for the matron, but their joint income was raised to £125 in 1840, and £100 for the master and £25 for the matron remained the standard rate thereafter. Edward Twisleton, the assistant poor law commissioner, said of the Pinsons that they were among the best masters and matrons in the district, while the number of inmates in the workhouse was greater than in any other. On their departure, George having been appointed as Governor of the County Gaol, Twisleton's successor, Sir John Walsham, commented: 'This is a most serious loss. I never saw any workhouse which could compare with the Gressenhall workhouse under the management of Mr and Mrs Pinson.'[43]

The Pinsons were replaced by George and Emma Whelan who moved from the county lunatic asylum at Hanwell, Middlesex, where George had been steward. He had a difficult start at Gressenhall, arriving in Norfolk later than expected and then being admonished for taking unauthorised leave and making incorrect entries about it in the master's report book. He expressed regret and reaffirmed his commitment to performing his duty, 'firmly, kindly, honestly and obediently'.[44] The Whelans served only until June 1846, when they resigned owing to George's illness, during which Emma had done as much of his work as she could. George subsequently became master of the Haydock Lodge Lunatic Asylum in Lancashire. The Whelans were succeeded by Stephen and Sophia Wade, who moved to Gressenhall from Wicklewood Workhouse near Wymondham. Stephen Wade, on his appointment, was regarded by Sir John Walsham as a 'promising officer' but he and his wife found their duties 'arduous' and had to resign in September 1850 owing to the illness of Mrs Wade.[45] The new master and matron were Henry and Margaret Harrison, who moved from Oulton Workhouse in Suffolk because Gressenhall was a 'better appointment'.[46] They were initially characterised by Sir John Walsham as 'tolerably effective'[47] but after Henry had died in service in July 1858 Sir John praised him posthumously as 'an excellent officer'. Robert and Mary Ann Scraggs, the last master and matron of whom Harriet had experience, then took over. The Scraggs served for ten years until 1868 when, after Mary Ann's death, Robert resigned.

During the period when Harriet Kettle was an inmate, Gressenhall's masters and matrons seem to have been generally competent officials. The effectiveness of the porters and assistant matrons was much more variable and their turnover more rapid. The first three porters appointed after Gressenhall became a union workhouse were all found to be unsatisfactory; two were dismissed and one resigned. One of the dismissals resulted from the porter's use of 'indecent language with several married women' and the action taken provides an indication of the high standards the guardians expected of their officers. The usual salary for the porter was £20 per year plus £5 for his wife as assistant matron, together with board and lodging in the workhouse. This was not a princely income but, as will be recalled, it was more than agricultural labourers earned during this period. Over time, moreover, the role of porter became a stepping stone to higher office. John Cary[48], who served as porter for almost eight years to 1849, during part of which period he also took on the role of workhouse barber, moved on to the position of relieving officer within the union at £105 per year (lowered to £95 as provisions became cheaper under the impact of the repeal of the Corn Laws but then raised back to £105 in 1855). There were initial doubts about his ability to perform the role: Sir John Walsham commented that he was 'a respectable and well disposed person and not a bad porter' but expressed concern about his ability to keep accounts and write legibly. However, he seems to have succeeded in learning the necessary skills.[49] Cary would have been the first porter known to Harriet Kettle and, in 1864, over a decade after his appointment as relieving officer, one of his duties was to meet Harriet on her discharge from the county lunatic asylum, whereupon they had a noisy argument. Perhaps Harriet remembered him from her time in the workhouse.

Cary's successor as porter, William Roberts, whose wife Elizabeth became assistant matron, had been a grocer in Hingham, and at 46 was above the normal age limit for the appointment but no candidate meeting the normal criteria had applied. Sir John Walsham was sceptical—'a grocer who has not prospered in his business does not provide a promise of efficiency'—and Roberts and his wife were to resign, owing to Elizabeth's illness, less than two years later. The next three porters, who served in the 1850s, all moved on, with their wives, to become masters and matrons of workhouses.[50] For a porter to become a master (or a relieving officer, as John Cary had done), and for an assistant matron to become a matron, was a big step up, entailing a significant advance in status and a corresponding increase in salary. The next porter and assistant matron at Gressenhall, Thomas Butcher and his wife Mary Ann, who served from November 1857 to March 1863, were less effective and more problematic, both for Harriet Kettle and for the guardians, as will appear later.

The workhouse medical officer was not resident but was a regular visitor. From 1846, when he took over from William M Warcup of East Dereham, until 1874, the role was performed by Dr James Vincent, who had been Warcup's partner. The salary was £35 per year, with extra for attending women after childbirth, and until December 1862 Dr Vincent supplemented this with the salary for serving also as medical officer for one of the eight districts into which the Mitford and Launditch Union was divided for the provision of medical services to the poor. The salary for a district medical officer was £50 and, according to an advertisement of 1840, this was meant to include remuneration for, 'attendance on the poor at their own cottages, for medicine, for assistance in such cases of midwifery as may be required by the board of guardians, the performance of surgical operations, the provision of surgical instruments (trusses excepted) and of every other matter requisite for the treatment of disease or accident, and vaccination for all poor persons permanently or casually resident in any of the parishes of the district, whether belonging to those parishes or not'.[51] Quite a comprehensive job description, indicating that, on paper at least, medical care at the time was more extensive than might have been thought.

In 1852, a professional nurse, at the salary of £15 per year, was appointed to the workhouse establishment, nursing duties having previously been performed by female inmates. The appointee, Anne Webster, subsequently left owing to 'ill-health induced by fatigue', according to Dr Vincent. Vincent mentioned these circumstances when he lobbied the Poor Law Board successfully for an increase in his own salary in 1853, citing the expansion of the provision in the workhouse for the sick. A replacement nurse was appointed in 1853, but finding and retaining suitable candidates for the role was challenging and there was a rapid turnover of postholders over the following years.[52]

The chaplain, like the medical officer, was not resident but, also like him, was a regular visitor. The first chaplain, appointed by the board of guardians in June 1836 at £40 per year, was Levi Walton, who subsequently also became curate in the church at Longham but resigned from his post at Gressenhall in January 1841, owing to ill-health. He was followed by Joseph Thompson, initially at the same salary, who served until November 1863. In 1848, Thompson accepted the board's requirement that he should visit on Sunday and two other days of the week, upon which his salary was raised to £60 a year. The records that he kept show that he generally maintained the required frequency of his visits, with substitutes deputising for him as necessary. The chaplain or his substitute visited the sick, read prayers and preached on Sundays, administered communion, conducted baptisms, burials and the 'churching' of women after childbirth, and prepared young inmates for confirmation as members of the Church of England. Joseph Thompson appears to have been well regarded, 'beloved by both officers and inmates for his general kindness to all', as stated in the Norwich Mercury in 1858.[53]

The services held on Sundays, Christmas Day and Good Friday in the dining hall of the workhouse prompted little comment but on 5 September 1854 the chaplain noted that: 'The girls in the tramps room [were] very ill behaved during divine service. It was a great cause of annoyance and disturbance both to the minister & congregation.' He may have been referring to female vagrants although it seems more likely that the miscreants were the single women with children. By contrast, one of Joseph Thompson's substitutes, Henry Tacy, a noted preacher who, like Thompson himself, was of low-church persuasion[54], invariably commented that the congregation was 'attentive' (and, on one occasion, 'remarkably attentive'). Inmates who were adherents of one of the nonconformist churches were not required to attend but were generally happy to do so.[55] As well as prayers and preaching on Sunday, there were special services on Good Friday and at other times to mark significant moments in the life of the nation, such as the outbreak and conclusion of the Crimean War. On 7 October 1857, there was a special prayer 'for restoration of tranquility in India' at the time of the 'Indian mutiny'.[56] Harriet Kettle may have been an inmate of the workhouse at this time and, if she was, it is interesting to speculate on how much or little this prayer might have meant to her.

The chaplain also visited the workhouse schools, usually once or twice, and occasionally three times a month, although the frequency of these visits declined over time to no more than once a month. Thompson and his successor, the Revd William Ray Eaton, generally limited their comment on these visits to 'satisfactory', which in Thompson's case is disappointing, as he ran a school himself throughout the 23 years he served as chaplain and might have been expected to have more to say.[57] Thompson's school was the East Dereham Select Classical and Mathematical School, later known as the Guildhall School, a school for 'young gentlemen'.[58] Despite holding high church views, the Revd Benjamin Armstrong, Vicar of East Dereham, sent his two sons there for three years before they went on to Bury St Edmunds Grammar School, commenting on Thompson in his diary: 'He has not always been the best friend to me, but his school is a good one.'[59] Joseph Thompson would undoubtedly have come into contact with Harriet Kettle when visiting the girls' school at Gressenhall but whether he had cause to take particular notice of her is not known.

The humblest member of the workhouse establishment was the messenger, a role performed by William Baxter until his death on 9 February 1855. Joseph Thompson buried him, presumably in an unmarked grave in the workhouse burial ground, commenting that, 'he had been the messenger to the workhouse for more than 40 years'.[60] Baxter must have been a well known figure at Gressenhall and was, it seems, quite a character. It was not only the chaplain who took unusual pains to honour him. In the Norwich Mercury, the following notice of his death appeared: 'at the Gressenhall union workhouse, William Baxter, aged 72[61], messenger ever since the formation of the union, an old seaman, who formerly sailed under Captain Dundas (the late admiral of our Black Sea fleet). He was a thorough seaman in his speech and habits, but of strict integrity, one that will be long remembered by the tradesmen of the neighbourhood for his blunt speech and facetious manners. All the officers of the union paid the last respect to his memory by following him to his final resting place.'[62]

If William Baxter had been the messenger for more than 40 years, then he must have started performing that role in the old house of industry of the Mitford and Launditch Incorporation, no later than 1815, the year of the battle of Waterloo.[63] He called the guardians to meetings and would have travelled regularly the three miles to and from East Dereham, taking letters to the post, receiving incoming mail and carrying messages to and from the tradesmen of the town. A married man until widowed in 1850, Baxter was almost dismissed by the guardians for 'improper conduct' in 1838 but was saved by the intervention of the master, George Pinson, and seems to have led a blameless life thereafter. If his terms and conditions were the same as those offered to his successor, he earned £6 per year and occupied accommodation in 'the cottage or gate house belonging to the union workhouse', which was no doubt a useful vantage point for receiving and sending messages. Perhaps he was at his post there when Harriet Kettle arrived at the workhouse in the 1840s.

According to a later source[64], it was the 'irksome monotony and confinement' of the workhouse that Harriet Kettle resented. After getting up in the morning, she would have answered to her name when the schoolmistress conducted a roll-call, as required by the regulations. School would have been an important part of Harriet's daily routine, and was supposed to occupy her for at least three hours, but no details of the actual hours of instruction at Gressenhall appear to have survived. In 1846, the guardians agreed that 'the boys in the schoolroom be allowed one day's half holiday during each week to enable them to be washed and attended to by the matron as heretofore' and later in the year they ordered that the boys should be, 'employed in the open air for two hours in each morning' and, 'allowed to play two hours in each evening in the summer and from two till four o'clock in the afternoon during the winter'. Presumably, time in school was fitted in between those two periods. Nothing, however, was said about open-air activities for the girls, although they probably, like the boys, had time to play.

Harriet Kettle would have heard the bell above the central block of the workhouse which was rung to summon the adult inmates to their work and meals, according to a routine which was modified slightly in 1851. In the summer, they rose at 5.45 am, had breakfast from 6.00 to 7.00, worked from 7.00 until 6.00 pm with a break for lunch from 12.00 to 1.00 pm; had supper from 6.00 to 7.00 pm and went to bed at 8.00 pm; while in the winter they rose, breakfasted and started work an hour later but finished at the same time. [65]

With the exception of gardening for the old men and, later, farming for the boys, the work was done within the walls of the workhouse. Textile and sack manufacturing which, along with farming, had been the main forms of employment for the able-bodied poor in the house of industry before 1834, had come to an end and all the machinery had been sold. Now, the few able-bodied men were required to break stones, pump water and cart gravel, although when the number of inmates in this group dropped, the provision of work seems to have lapsed, which earned the guardians a rebuke from Sir John Walsham in 1847.[66] In January 1854, oakum-picking was introduced as the task for able-bodied men over 16 at Gressenhall. 'Casuals', admitted for one night, were required to pick a pound of oakum before being discharged from the workhouse.[67] The task was to disentangle the strands of twisted, tarry rope, so that the fibres could be used for caulking boats. In October 1854, oakum-picking was extended to able-bodied single women at Gressenhall. With that exception, the women laboured in the kitchens, the sick wards, the laundry and at cleaning and other domestic tasks around the buildings. Old men worked in the garden in front of the main block.

Meal-times, announced by the ringing of the bell, were the only times in the day when Harriet Kettle would have seen the inmates of 'classes' other than her own. The food and drink were served in the dining hall in the main, central block of the workhouse, in the presence of the workhouse officers. Girls and boys

Women oakum-picking in a workhouse, c1910 (TNA: 30/69/1663).

would have had no opportunity to talk to each other at these times, however, as 'silence, order and decorum' had to be maintained. Breakfast, according to the dietary of 1836, comprised bread and gruel. Dinner on most days was bread and cheese (or, for women on Tuesday and Friday, butter), with suet pudding and vegetables on Thursday, broth on Monday and meat pudding with vegetables on Sunday. Supper was bread and cheese. The quantities of each item were precisely specified and meagre, with the men always receiving a little more than the women. In December 1849, the ingredients, too, were specified: gruel to be made with seven ounces of groats (grains including bran) and three of flour; suet pudding with nine ounces of flour and three quarters of an ounce of suet; meat pudding with 10 ounces of flour and 6 of meat. Children over nine were allowed the same portions as adult women and those under nine were 'dieted at discretion'.[68]

The diet in the workhouse was minimal but so was that of the labouring

MITFORD AND LAUNDITCH UNION.

TO THE GUARDIANS OF THE POOR
OF THE
MITFORD AND LAUNDITCH UNION, IN THE COUNTY OF NORFOLK;

To the Clerk or Clerks to the Justices of Petty Sessions, held for the Division or Divisions of the said County in which the Parishes and Places comprised in the said Union are situate:—and to all others whom it may concern.

We, THE POOR LAW COMMISSIONERS FOR ENGLAND AND WALES, in pursuance of the Provisions of an Act passed in the fourth and fifth Years of the Reign of His present Majesty King WILLIAM the FOURTH, intituled " *An Act for the Amendment and better Administration* " *of the Laws relating to the Poor in England and Wales,*" do hereby order and direct that the Paupers of the respective Classes and Sexes described in the Schedule hereunto annexed, who may now or hereafter be received and maintained in the Workhouse or Workhouses of the Mitford and Launditch Union, shall, during the period of their residence therein, be fed, dieted, and maintained with the Food, and in the manner described and set forth in the said Schedule.

AND WE DO HEREBY FURTHER ORDER AND DIRECT, that every Master of the Workhouse or Workhouses of the said Union, shall cause two or more Copies of this our Order and of the said Schedule, printed in a legible manner, and in a large type, to be hung up in the most Public Places of such Workhouse or Workhouses, and to renew the same from time to time, so that it be always kept fair and legible, on pain of incurring, in case of disobedience, the Penalties provided by the aforesaid Act.

Given under our Hands and Seal, this first day of November, in the year One Thousand Eight Hundred and Thirty-six.

(Signed,)

T. FRANKLAND LEWIS.
J. G. S. LEFEVRE.
GEO. NICHOLS.

DIETARY FOR ABLE BODIED PAUPERS OF BOTH SEXES.

		BREAKFAST		DINNER							SUPPER	
		Bread.	Gruel.	Suet Pudding with Vegetables.	Bread.	Cheese.	Butter.	Meat Pudding with Vegetables.	Broth.		Bread.	Cheese.
		oz.	Pints.	oz.	oz.	oz.	oz.	oz.	Pints.		oz.	oz.
SUNDAY.	Men	7	1½	-	-	-	-	14	-		7	1
	Women	6	1½	-	-	-	-	12	-		6	¾
MONDAY.	Men	7	1½	-	7	-	-	-	1½		7	1
	Women	6	1½	-	6	-	-	-	1		6	¾
TUESDAY.	Men	7	1½	-	7	1	-	-	-		7	1
	Women	6	1½	-	6	-	¾	-	-		6	¾
WEDNESDAY.	Men	7	1½	-	7	1	-	-	-		7	1
	Women	6	1½	-	6	¾	-	-	-		6	¾
THURSDAY.	Men	7	1½	14	-	-	-	-	-		7	1
	Women	6	1½	12	-	-	-	-	-		6	¾
FRIDAY.	Men	7	1½	-	7	1	-	-	-		7	1
	Women	6	1½	-	6	-	¾	-	-		6	¾
SATURDAY.	Men	7	1½	-	7	1	-	-	-		7	1
	Women	6	1½	-	6	¾	-	-	-		6	¾

OLD PEOPLE of 60 years of age and upwards, may be allowed 1 oz. of Tea, 4 oz. of Butter, and 4oz. of Sugar per Week, for those whose age and infirmities it may be deemed requisite.

CHILDREN under 9 years of age, to be dieted at discretion ; above 9 to be allowed the same quantities as Women.

SICK to be dieted as directed by the Medical Officer.

BARKER, PRINTER, DEREHAM.

Gressenhall dietary 1846 (TNA: MH/12/8477/440).

poor outside the workhouse, as has been described in the previous chapter. The difference was that the inmates of the workhouse were subject to an institutional regime and could exercise no choice.

The board of guardians invited tenders for the supply of foodstuffs and, given their commitment to saving the ratepayers' money, were no doubt inclined in practice to accept the lowest bid. Unsurprisingly, the quality of the food sometimes left much to be desired and occasionally the guardians refused to accept that which had been supplied. They changed the contractor responsible for delivering bread to the workhouse, for example, in March 1845 after inferior bread had been sent. In May 1851 they instructed the clerk to write to the bread supplier, 'complaining of the condition of the bread recently supplied by him as being heavy, sour and generally of a bad quality'. There was little improvement and so in August the guardians again changed their supplier. The workhouse inmates themselves occasionally made complaints about the quality of the food, as in April 1860, when their protest about the bread supplied was endorsed by the guardians' visiting committee.

An improvement in the diet for the boys aged 10 to 16 was made in 1846. The guardians were concerned about their health and felt that they were not sufficiently prepared for the lives of physical labour which, they anticipated, awaited them. They proposed that the boys should have meat broth instead of bread and cheese on Wednesdays and Fridays, and bread and cheese instead of suet pudding and vegetables on Thursdays. When the poor law commissioners asked why the girls were not to have an improved diet as well, the guardians directed their clerk to reply that they did not consider this necessary. The commissioners did not pursue the matter and sanctioned the proposed changes for the boys.[69] There was no benefit, therefore, for Harriet Kettle.

On rare occasions, the rigour of the dietary regime was relaxed, as on 28 June 1838, the day of Queen Victoria's coronation, when the inmates were 'allowed a pint of ale each and beef and plumb pudding' and on 10 February 1840, when ale and buns were provided in celebration of Queen Victoria's marriage to Prince Albert. The only regular exception to the normal dietary occurred on Christmas Day. In 1852, for example, the inmates, 'were bountifully supplied with roast beef, plum pudding, potatoes, ale and tobacco…The women, in addition, had tea, sugar, butter and snuff; and the juvenile branches [which would still, just, have included Harriet Kettle] had afterwards nuts and oranges given them'. The advertisement in a local paper expressing their appreciation concluded: 'The day was altogether to them one of great joy and cheerfulness. They desire to express their thanks to the guardians for this liberal feast.'[70]

Later, some of the guardians objected to spending any money at all on the

Christmas dinner. In 1854, and again in 1855, an 'economical' faction on the board proposed that no Christmas dinner be provided but was outvoted. Someone clearly decided that the appreciation of the inmates for their treat needed to be recorded in the Norwich Mercury. On 30 December 1854, it was noted that, when the 'substantial and plentiful dinner of roast beef and plum pudding' had been consumed, three cheers were raised for the guardians, and, 'afterwards tobacco, tea, &c, was distributed, from a subscription raised among some guardians and friends'.[71] After the 1855 Christmas dinner, on 5 January 1856, the Norwich Mercury reported that the inmates, 'evinced their gratitude heartily and merrily (after grace) to their kind benefactors in three such hearty cheers, and one cheer more, as would have made a convert of the most rigid economist. At an early hour they all retired to their respective rooms, highly satisfied.'[72] The following week, there was a riposte from 'A Guardian of Mitford and Launditch Union,' who had clearly taken the reference to the 'rigid economist' personally and argued that the cost of the Christmas dinner should be raised only from voluntary subscriptions and not from the poor rates. In 1856, despite the opposition of FW Keppel, the members of the economical faction got their way and no Christmas dinner was provided from the union's funds. On Mr Keppel's proposition, it was, however, restored by a unanimous vote in 1858 'at the cost of the union as in former years' and continued to be provided thereafter.

In January 1858, the chaplain, the Revd Joseph Thompson, on the 17th anniversary of his appointment, had taken an initiative of his own by giving 'a treat' to the 150 children in the workhouse, inviting 120 to his residence in East Dereham, 'where they were regaled with buns, wine [watered, perhaps], oranges, nuts, &c, and money [was] given to each on leaving'. Some of the fare was sent to 'the younger ones, who remained at home'. The children must have been impressed by Thompson's home, which (admittedly, ten years later, when he was about to leave East Dereham) contained walnut furniture, three pianos, a harmonium and 800 books.[73] Ostensibly, the event was to commemorate the marriage of the Princess Royal, Queen Victoria's eldest daughter, but it may have helped to shame the guardians into providing Christmas dinner in 1858 and subsequently.

For the most part, Harriet Kettle cannot have had much fun in the workhouse. However, from time to time, there was some small act which implied a recognition that the girls and boys in the schools were children, and not to blame for their poverty. The Bishop of Norwich, Edward Stanley, took an interest in workhouse education and sent, 'a few presents for the school children' after a visit to Gressenhall in January 1840. In January 1843, the guardians ordered that a tree be taken down, 'for the purpose of erecting a swing for the children', specifying that the cost should not exceed 40 shillings. If this swing was in the girls' yard,

Harriet would, no doubt, have used it; or perhaps, more likely, the boys and girls shared it, using it at different times of the day. Three years later, the assistant poor law commissioner, Sir John Walsham, was thanked, 'for his recent present of bats and balls to the boys in the Workhouse School' but there is no reference to an equivalent gift for the girls. However, one highlight, which Harriet, at the age of 11 or 12 would undoubtedly have enjoyed, was the occasion at the end of February 1851 when, 'Mr George Wombwell…gratuitously admitted all the children of the workhouse schools to his exhibition of wild beasts at East Dereham'. Harriet can be imagined staring wide-eyed at Mr Wombwell's exotic animals.

Such excitements were very few and far between. Day by day, Harriet's life would have been dominated by the routines of the girls' school in Gressenhall workhouse.

Notes

1   The main sources for this chapter are the MLU minutes; NRO, C/GP14/2-12; and the Correspondence of the PLC and PLB with Assistant Commissioners and the MLU, TNA: MH12 8474-8482.
2   NM, 10 March 1838.
3   The first clerk, Samuel King, whom Dr Kay praised in March 1837 as carrying out his duties with 'considerable ability', disappeared in 1844 and, shortly after his departure, was accused of embezzlement. His successor, Charles Wright, served the union faithfully for many years. TNA: MH12 8476/160-172, 303.
4   Keppel was the great-grandson of the second Earl of Albemarle, whose father had come to England from the Netherlands with William III in 1688. His great-grandmother was the daughter of an illegitimate son of Charles II (thepeerage.com, geni.com, accessed July 2020). Keppel owned nearly all the land in East Lexham, and had cousins who held land in several parts of East Anglia, including the then current Earl of Albemarle, whose seat was Quiddenham Hall in Norfolk (White's Directory of Norfolk, 1845).
5   BNP, 8 June 1836.
6   BNP, 11 May 1841. The Chartist movement for parliamentary reform was then at the height of its influence. The occasion was a celebration of the birthday of the Earl of Leicester, the doyen and rallying point of those of liberal opinions in Norfolk.
7   NM, 1 January 1859.
8   TNA: MH12 8479/191.
9   NM, 2 April 1842.
10 Revd Thomas Paddon was Vicar of Mattishall for 40 years, from 1821 to 1861.
11 A Reid, *Gressenhall Workhouse*, Norfolk Museums Service Information Sheet (1988); S Pope (2006). The nature of the regime in the house of industry has been explored recently with the aid of a digital reconstruction of the building by S Ottaway and A Mason, *Reconsidering poor law institutions by virtually reconstructing and reviewing an eighteenth-century workhouse*, published online by Cambridge Univesity Press, 2020.
12 TNA: MH12 8474/127.
13 BNP, 16 April 1834; NC 12 April 1834.
14 D Adams (2013).

15 J Crowley and A Reid (1983).

16 A Reid, *Fire at the Workhouse* (Bridge Publications, Great Yarmouth, 1988).

17 The workhouse admission register no longer survives and from 10 October 1836 onwards the guardians' minute books recorded only the numbers, not the names, of those admitted.

18 Note from F W Keppel to the PLB, 20 June 1848; TNA: MH12 8478/180.

19 Until 1839, four.

20 PLB, General Order (Consolidated) (1847).

21 There is a pub in Haverhill in 2021 called 'The Drabbet Smock'.

22 See NC, 10 March 1838; NM 23 May 1840, NM, 26 August 1843, NM 25 May 1844 and many similar advertisements.

23 PLC, Second Annual Report (1836).

24 TNA: MH12 8478/325.

25 There was a similar incident in May 1863 when two boys were charged with, 'leaving their bed rooms at an improper hour in the night and making their escape from the house'.

26 TNA: MH12 8476/269. The boys' dormitory, then accommodating 66 aged five to 16, was 90 feet long and 27 feet wide (27.5 by 8.25 metres), and their day room measured 46 by 18 feet (14 by 5.5 metres).

27 TNA: MH12 8479/429-30. The adult male inmates normally slept in single beds, although sometimes they had to share, which prompted a critical comment from the commissioners in lunacy after an inspection visit in May 1852, and rapid rectification of the situation by the guardians. The women slept two to a bed and this continued to be the case for many years.

28 TNA: MH12 8476/176-7.

29 MLU, Chaplain's Books, 1850-58, 1858-69; NRO, C/GP14/102 and 103.

30 NC, 22 November 1834.

31 TNA: MH12 8476/269.

32 TNA: MH12 8479/415, 429.

33 TNA: MH12 8480/335.

34 An experience recalled by one former inmate, who spent his childhood in the workhouse, as 'like dipping sheep' (Mr Johnson, Ovington, recorded 1987).

35 TNA: MH32 84.

36 TNA: MH12 8478/35.

37 F W Keppel to Edward Twisleton, 20 April 1841, annexed to Edward Twisleton's report in PLC, Seventh Annual Report (1841).

38 A Reid (1994) includes a transcript of a letter from Sir John Walsham about the practice.

39 NM 15 December 1838.

40 A Digby (1978).

41 They replaced Edward and Martha Tice, who had been the master and matron of the house of industry since 1826 and continued in these roles for a short time after Gressenhall had been converted into a union workhouse.

42 S McConville (1995).

43 TNA: MH12 8477/75.

44 TNA: MH12 8477/131.

45 TNA: MH12 8477/435, MH12 8479/100.

46 TNA: MH12 8479/100.

47 TNA: MH12 8479/98.

48 Sometimes spelt 'Carey'.

49 He served as a relieving officer for many years, as well as farming 12 acres of land (according to the 1861 census returns) and his daughter Agnes was appointed as the infant schoolmistress in the workhouse in 1865.

50 Two of them, William Owen (who had become master of the Wayland Union Workhouse at Rockland All Saints) and William Lock (who had become master of the Guiltcross Union Workhouse at Kenninghall) subsequently expressed interest in the post of master at Gressenhall when it fell vacant after the resignation of Robert Scraggs in April 1868, but, at the ages of 46 and 47 respectively, they were deemed too old to apply.

51 NM, 13 June 1840.

52 One of those appointed (in 1857) was a workhouse inmate, Mary Howard, a woman with two children who had been deserted by her husband. Her salary was £20 per year but she was required to take her children out of the workhouse.

53 MLU, Chaplain's Books, 1850-58, 1858-69; NRO, C/GP14/102 and 103; NM, 30 January 1858.

54 S Wade Martins (2018).

55 Although Sir John Walsham noted in April 1860 that the small number of Wesleyan Methodists were visited by their own minister.

56 MLU, Chaplain's Books, 1850-58, 1858-69; NRO, C/GP14/102 and 103.

57 MLU, Chaplain's Books, 1850-58, 1858-69; NRO, C/GP14/102 and 103.

58 As mentioned, for example, in announcements in NM on 16 January 1841, 15 January 1843 and subsequently; and in NC on 24 July 1854.

59 C Armstrong (2012).

60 MLU, Chaplain's Book, 1850-58; NRO, C/GP14/102.

61 Joseph Thompson had given his age as 70.

62 NM, 17 February 1855.

63 His service with Admiral Dundas must have been during the Napoleonic Wars, in which, at different times, Dundas captained ships in the Baltic and Mediterranean.

64 CLA, case book 1861-65; NRO, SAH263.

65 TNA: MH12 8479/253.

66 TNA: MH12 8478/65, 73.

67 Return relating to Casual Poor in Workhouses, PP LII, 1864.

68 TNA: MH12 8474/181.

69 TNA: MH12 8477/440-1, 444-8.

70 NM, 3 January 1852. In the early years of the new Poor Law, able-bodied men and unmarried mothers were excluded from the Christmas treat, presumably because they were considered unworthy of enjoying it.

71 NM, 30 December 1854.

72 NM, 5 January 1856.

73 NM, 2 January 1869.

At school in Gressenhall Workhouse

UNDER the new Poor Law, boards of guardians were obliged to provide schooling for the boys and girls in the workhouse.[1] The regulations stated that: 'The boys and girls who are inmates of the workhouse shall, for three of the working hours at least, every day, be instructed in reading, writing, arithmetic, and the principles of the Christian religion, and such other instruction shall be imparted to them as may fit them for service, and train them to habits of usefulness, industry and virtue.'[2] Both the poor law commissioners and the board of guardians hoped that by educating the children in the workhouse schools, they would enable them to gain employment, which would both benefit those leaving the workhouse as individuals and, equally (if not more) important for them, help to reduce the burden on the ratepayers in the future. Although it did not enable her to gain the kind of employment envisaged by the authorities, Harriet Kettle undoubtedly gained some benefit from the education she received in the workhouse.

From 1812, there had been a school in the Gressenhall house of industry, established by the National Society for Promoting the Education of the Poor in the Principles of the Established Church in England and Wales, an organisation founded the previous year which, along with the non-denominational British and Foreign School Society, became one of the major providers of elementary education until (and after) the passage of the Education Act of 1870. In 1817, the school had 58 pupils aged from 4 to 14, organised in five classes. As well as those resident in the house of industry, it took some pupils from neighbouring villages.[3]

After Gressenhall became a union workhouse in 1836, the board of guardians, under the oversight of the Poor Law Commission, became responsible for the provision of education for the young inmates and the National Society was no longer involved. Schools for the boys and girls were nurtured by the assistant poor law commissioner, Dr James Kay, who believed strongly in the potential of education to lift workhouse children out of poverty, and his arguments won the support of many of the guardians. According to Kay, 'education is to be regarded as one of the most important means of eradicating the germs of pauperism from the rising generation, and of securing in the minds and in the morals of the people the best protection for the institutions of society'.[4]

As Dr Kay later recalled: 'Having succeeded the late Sir Edward Parry in the administration of the Poor Law Amendment Act in Norfolk, the organisation of the workhouse schools for pauper children occupied my attention. I procured teachers from Mr Wood's Edinburgh Sessional School, and from Mr David Stow's schools in Glasgow…An organising master from Mr Wood's school (Mr Horne, afterwards a master in Battersea Training College), successively resided in several workhouses of the Eastern Counties for a month or two. He reconstructed the school in each workhouse. Wherever the schoolmaster was capable, he placed him—with improved knowledge of method, a better organised and disciplined school, new desks, books, and apparatus—in charge of the training of the children, in humble learning, religion and industry…' Dr Kay had already recommended books to be purchased for the schools at Gressenhall and sanctioned an increase in the schoolmaster's salary from £20 to £25 per year. In September 1837, Mr Horne was temporarily employed at Gressenhall to provide training for Robert Rudd, the schoolmaster of the boys' school and his wife Mary Rudd, the schoolmistress of the girls' school. The guardians agreed that the boys and girls should be taught reading and writing in the same room 'during Mr Horn's [sic] stay at the workhouse'. At Gressenhall, according to Dr Kay, 'Mr Horne found an intelligent, active schoolmaster, who entered eagerly into all our plans. The garden, the school and the workshops…flourished under his care.' Subsequently, when Mr Rudd was temporarily taken ill, a 13-year-old pupil called William Rush spontaneously took over the teaching in the boys' school, ensuring that, 'the whole discipline and routine of the garden, workshop and class instruction went on unbroken,' and greatly impressing the chairman of the board of guardians, FW Keppel, and Dr Kay. Rush earned himself an appointment as assistant schoolmaster and the episode inspired Dr Kay to introduce what became known as the pupil teacher system.[5]

Dr Kay's initiatives were opposed by some Church of England clergymen, who wanted the church to control the education of the young and were alleged, by opponents, to be Tories motivated by their opposition in principle to the Poor Law Amendment Act. The Revd Kirby Trimmer, curate of Stanhoe in Docking Union, wrote to the Norfolk Chronicle to denounce the books used in Mr Wood's school in Edinburgh, because they were not aligned with the doctrine of the Church of England and also, 'because it is absurd to teach pauper children in an agricultural district, and whose occupations are for the most part those of crow [sic] keeping, pig minding, and turnip pulling, that minerals are, as the case may be, 'brilliant', 'opaque', 'malleable', 'ductile', or 'fusible'; and because such a system is not suited to that station in which it has pleased providence to place the agricultural poor'. He added, 'Why, when we have so excellent a system of education as that which our National School Society affords... why must we go as far as Scotland and Ireland for experimental plans to instruct the children of the poor?', noting that, 'the new Irish system' had been introduced at Gressenhall and in the Lynn Union workhouse.[6] Trimmer had family as well as religious reasons for objecting to the direction in which the education of children in workhouses was developing. His uncle, James Rustat Trimmer, served on the committee of the National Society[7] and his grandmother, Sarah Trimmer, had written abridgements of the Old and New Testaments, three copies of each were recommended for each group of 12 children at the National Society's schools. Her other book entitled, 'Teacher's Assistant', was in use at the school in Gressenhall house of industry before 1836; when the National Society inspected the school in 1824, the inspector commented that the children in the fourth class 'read well from Mrs Trimmer's Teacher's Assistant'.[8] Kirby Trimmer's arguments were also set out in a pamphlet, to which Mr Wood of

CONTENTS.

The contents pages of Sarah Trimmer's The Teacher's Assistant, pub. 1836.

Edinburgh, who was a prominent member of the Scottish Episcopalian Church, responded in 1838 in a pamphlet of his own.[9]

Trimmer's letter to the Norfolk Chronicle brought a response a week later from a member of the board of guardians of Docking Union, who argued that the Bible and Catechism were used to teach the workhouse children and that books containing, 'selections from the Old and New Testaments, [and] some interesting lessons on natural history, and on arts and industry, adapted to the understanding of children' were unobjectionable. He also maintained that as there was high unemployment among agricultural labourers, a broader education would equip the workhouse children to obtain employment in other fields. The same issue of the Norfolk Chronicle also contained a letter from the chaplain to the Lynn Union, confirming that Dr Kay had sent a teacher from Edinburgh to 'organise the schools' in the workhouse and praising the 'method of instruction' used. He stated that the books used were printed in Dublin and entitled, 'Lessons for Schools of Industry', but agreed with Trimmer that they, 'are not suited to the instruction of pauper children', and continued, 'it surely is not necessary to require of such children the rules of grammar, nor the Greek and Latin roots of the words they meet with in the course of their reading'.[10] However, the chaplain of Docking Union, the Revd Edmund Senkler, had seen the books in use at Gressenhall workhouse and was full of praise for them, as was the Bishop of London.[11]

Two weeks after the publication of Trimmer's letter, Edward John Howman wrote: 'As a guardian… of the Mitford and Launditch Union, to which Mr Trimmer alludes, I think it proper to state, that in the school of the union house at Gressenhall, the three first books published in Dublin, for the use of parochial schools, are only used, and in which I can discover nothing objectionable—that the children read the Bible and Testament every day according to their classes— that they are instructed in the Church Catechism every day—that a chaplain, a clergyman of the Church of England, is part of the establishment, whose duty it is to attend to the religious instruction of the children, and to which I believe he scrupulously attends…What Mr Trimmer means by the 'Irish System', as used at Gressenhall, I know not…The system which, I am happy to say, is there adopted, is the system used with such admirable effect in the Sessional School at Edinburgh, of the superiority of which, in the results produced on the minds and manners of the children, even over our English National System, I have been firmly convinced, ever since I had an opportunity of seeing it in full operation in Edinburgh, under the personal direction of its amiable, talented and indefatigable inventor and promoter, Mr Wood…'[12] So Dr Kay had apparently gone so far as to arrange for a guardian from the Mitford and Launditch Union to visit Edinburgh to see at first hand the methods and materials that he proposed to introduce in Norfolk workhouses.

A year after the schoolmaster and schoolmistress at Gressenhall had been trained by Mr Horne, in July 1838, the board of guardians found reason to give notice to Robert and Elizabeth Rudd that their services would be dispensed with at the end of the quarter, owing to their 'general misconduct'. Mrs Rudd's conduct was judged so bad that she was suspended from her duties, Dr Kay commenting that the relationship between the master of the workhouse (George Pinson) and her and her husband had broken down, in the context of what appears to have been a general tightening up of the expectations of the workhouse officers at the time.[13]

The board appointed as their successors John Gibson and Harriet Pinson, the latter being the daughter of the newly appointed master and matron of the workhouse, who was aged only 14 on her appointment.[14] Their remuneration was low: £20 per year for the schoolmaster and £15 for the schoolmistress, with board, lodging and washing provided. The poor law commissioners commented that they would be prepared, 'to sanction a moderate increase in their salaries, which are at present lower than those usually given'.[15] In the Fourth Report of the Poor Law Commission, published the same year, Dr Kay had stated that £35 or £40 per year would be the salary required to secure a schoolmaster from Scotland, while the salary for a good schoolmistress would be £20 per year, in both cases with board and lodging provided. In their communication to the board of guardians, the commissioners also referred to, 'the propriety of making arrangements for [the] comfort' of the schoolmaster and schoolmistress, and 'for placing them in a situation in the household in which they shall be exempt from all menial duties, and be enabled to devote their whole time to the religious and industrial training of the children, whose well being they are require to promote by constant vigilance and care'. John Gibson's salary was raised to £25 in December 1839 as, according to the guardians, he had fulfilled his duties in an efficient manner. Edward Twisleton, now the assistant poor law commissioner responsible for Gressenhall, agreed; Gibson, he commented (in a curiously ambivalent assessment), was, 'a very good second rate schoolmaster and he deserves the increase in salary'.[16]

Only three months later, in March 1840, John Gibson resigned as schoolmaster following a disagreement with the master, the details of which were undisclosed. Twisleton noted that his salary was too low, despite the recent increase, especially as, 'Gressenhall workhouse contains more children than any other school in the district'. Gibson moved on to become schoolmaster at the workhouse school in Docking Union in north west Norfolk. The chairman of the guardians at Gressenhall, F W Keppel, after visiting Docking, commented: 'Gibson is improving the children fast.'[17]

As Gibson's successor, the guardians appointed Robert Bradfield, aged 24 and with no teaching experience. His remuneration was the same as that received by Gibson during his final three months at Gressenhall: £25 per year. Twistleton was scathing: 'From stinginess, the board has lost a good opportunity of obtaining a first rate school master.' He noted that there were 54 boys in the school and suggested that the appointment be sanctioned provisionally for three months. Bradfield, he commented, 'seems willing to learn and the chaplain [Levi Walton], himself a schoolmaster was giving him a lesson in teaching today when I visited Gressenhall workhouse'. The appointment was confirmed in September 1840.[18] Bradfield went on to serve as schoolmaster for 34 years, becoming a highly effective teacher, as the reports following inspection visits testified.[19]

The girls' school, meanwhile, was thriving under the management of Harriet Pinson. A small 'Arnott stove' had been ordered to heat the schoolroom in November 1839 and a year later £3 was spent on books specifically for the girls. In 1842, a further £6 was invested in books for both schools. Later that year, alterations were made to the girls' schoolroom. In December 1841 or January 1842, both the boys' and the girls' school were visited by a deputation from the Norwich Court of Guardians.[20] The members of the deputation were impressed: 'at Gressenhall, the boys…received as good an education as many tradesmens' sons in this city; they were taught reading, writing, arithmetic and geography, by an experienced master [which flattered Robert Bradfield, still in only his second year of teaching]; and the girls were taught reading, writing and needle work. They saw some of the embroidery work executed by the girls, and could aver it was such as would not disgrace any house in the county; it was really beautiful.'[21]

When Harriet Pinson's parents, George and Rhoda Pinson, resigned as master and matron at Gressenhall at the end of 1843, following George Pinson's appointment as governor of the county gaol at Norwich Castle, Harriet Pinson resigned as well. On her departure, the guardians recorded, 'their best thanks to Miss Pinson for the exemplary manner in which she has discharged the duties of schoolmistress to the Gressenhall workhouse'. Their sentiments were echoed by the assistant poor law commissioner, Sir John Walsham who, after praising the departing master and matron, continued: 'The girls' school too under Miss Pinson's care was equally conspicuous for excellence and was the only workhouse school in my district in which singing on Wilhems plan was taught.'[22]

Harriet Kettle may have been taught by Harriet Pinson in her last year in the post. Initially, as an infant, she would have been supervised by a workhouse inmate, Lydia Thompson, who was given ten shillings (50p) in October 1843, 'for her good conduct in and industry in the infant school'. Similar gratuities were paid to other female workhouse inmates in subsequent years, but later reports made clear that, even if the women who received the gratuities were conscientious in caring for them, the children learned little. While they were infants, they were supervised rather than taught.

After Miss Pinson's departure, the girls' school went through a period of instability. The next schoolmistress, who took up her post on 5 January 1844, was Mrs Anna Youngs. Aged 27, she was the widow of a ship owner and captain of King's Lynn who, with his ship and crew, had been lost at sea the previous November. Anna's father was a schoolmaster in Grimston, West Norfolk, and she claimed she had worked in his school for 19 years. She was also the niece of Mary Rudd, the first schoolmistress of the union workhouse.[23] Sir John Walsham did not consider her application strong and the Poor Law Commission sanctioned the appointment for only three months. In the event, the guardians decided to dismiss Mrs Youngs summarily after less than two months, a 'measure rendered indispensible by her want of authority and management in the school'.[24]

The guardians' action resulted in a complaint to the Poor Law Commission from Anna Youngs' schoolmaster father, Francis Beets. According to him, on 26 February, when the guardians were meeting, Anna 'went into the committee room to report some of the girls for being very impertinent and disobeying her commands', but those guardians who remained (some, he claimed, had left, and were surprised when they learned later what had happened), 'disregarded her report and told her they heard she was <u>enceinte</u> [pregnant], and…she must immediately leave her situation that night or the next morning'. Anna, said Beets, had denied the report but left in the morning and, 'had to take refuge in the village' (no doubt with her aunt) until her mother could come from Grimston to fetch her. Mrs Beets confronted the master, who denied any knowledge of the reasons for Anna's dismissal and, 'knew no fault that she should be sent so hastily away'.[25] According to Mr Beets, the person responsible for Anna Youngs' dismissal was the porter's wife, who had expected Anna to 'assist in cutting cheese' for the inmates, which required her to, 'leave her children 20 [minutes] before the proper time', and about which she had complained. Sir John Walsham, to whom Beets' letter was referred, had no doubt that Mrs Youngs was 'inefficient' but was of the view that the guardians were out of order in dismissing her, as that was something only the Poor Law Commission could do: if they considered her incompetent, they should have invited her to resign or suspended her.[26] The guardians denied Francis Beets' allegations but acknowledged their error in dismissing Anna Youngs. They took the action suggested by Sir John and, after receiving Mrs Youngs' resignation, they paid her the salary due for the full quarter. Meanwhile, the pupils in the girls' school, Harriet Kettle among them, were receiving very little, if any, education.

Although the advertisement for a successor to Mrs Youngs again offered a salary of only £15 per year (with board, washing and lodging), the guardians were able to appoint an experienced teacher, Eliza Underwood, who was aged 25 and had been an assistant teacher at the National School in Gorleston.[27] Her arrival at Gressenhall was delayed until 25 March 1844, after Anna Youngs' resignation had been received, but she proved satisfactory and was 'highly commended' by the guardians. Her resignation in August 1845 was occasioned by the illness of her father and her consequent desire to return to Gorleston to take up a teaching post there.[28] This was understandable, but Miss Underwood's departure did Harriet Kettle no favours.

Eliza Underwood was succeeded by Emily Ward, who arrived on 18 September 1845 and remained for a year and a quarter. Miss Ward was aged 25 and appears to have had no teaching experience, but at first the guardians were

Mitford and Launditch UNION.

TABLE, shewing the number, &c., of Children in the Workhouse of the *Mitford and Launditch* — Union, on Thursday the Eighteenth day of March, 1847.

CHILDREN IN THE WORKHOUSE	BOYS				GIRLS			
	Under 3 years Old	3 years Old and under 7	7 years Old and upwards	TOTALS	Under 3 years Old	3 years Old and under 7	7 years Old and upwards	TOTALS
Illegimate,—their Mothers in the Workhouse	6	8	4	18	7	4	6	17
Illegimate,—their Mothers not in the Workhouse	1	1	3	5	1	–	2	3
Children of Widows who are in the Workhouse	1	4	4	9	1	–	3	4
Children of Widows who are not in the Workhouse	–	2	4	6	–	–	5	5
Children of Widowers who are in the Workhouse	–	1	1	2	–	1	2	3
Children of Widowers who are not in the Workhouse	–	–	–	–	–	–	–	–
Children whose Father and Mother are dead	2	4	23	29	–	5	23	28
Children deserted by Father	–	–	7	7	3	4	10	17
Children deserted by Mother	–	1	2	3	–	–	3	3
Children deserted by both Parents	–	–	1	1	–	–	1	1
Children whose Father is transported, or suffering imprisonment for crime	2	–	–	2	1	–	–	1
Children whose residence in the Workhouse is caused by the bodily or mental infirmity of their Father or Mother	–	–	1	1	2	2	2	6
Children of able-bodied Parents who are in the Workhouse	4	1	6	11	3	5	7	15
Children of able-bodied Parents who are not in the Workhouse	–	–	1	1	–	–	–	–
Children not falling within any of the foregoing Classes	–	2	1	3	–	–	2	2
TOTALS....	16	24	58	98	18	21	66	105

NOTE.—No Child is to be enumerated more than once, though such Child might fall within more than one Class.

Summary of Children in the Workhouse.

Boys.......... 98
Girls.......... 105
TOTAL.. 203

Signed this 31st day of March 1847.

_____ Clerk to the Guardians.

Gressenhall, table showing numbers of children, 1847 (TNA: MH12 8478/35).

satisfied with her. In March 1846, they agreed to the erection of a new lean-to playroom for the girls' school, which must have helped to relieve the pressure of the large numbers of young female inmates in the workhouse at that time on the very limited space in the schoolroom. Harriet Kettle, now aged seven, no doubt appreciated this new facility.

However, the guardians changed their minds about Emily Ward and, on 4 January 1847, received her 'voluntary resignation…due to the progress of the children under her care being unsatisfactory to the union'.[29] The following week, with encouragement from the poor law commissioners, they decided to raise the salary for the vacant post from £15 to £25 per year. On 1 February, they appointed Miss Mary Wardlow to the position, ignoring the application of Emily Ward who, no doubt attracted by the increased salary, had applied for her former position. Mary Wardlow was 42 and had been 'mistress of a National School for upwards of three years', this being the National School for girls in Gressenhall Village, which she had left because a master and mistress, possibly a married couple, were appointed to the school, which was now to admit boys as well as girls. Miss Wardlow had also 'kept a school on her own account in Norwich for four or five years', and had been 'educated for a schoolmistress' by the wonderfully named Misses Beady and Matchett in Norwich.[30] Mary Wardlow's arrival at Gressenhall was delayed, causing a hiatus in the girls' education, and when she did arrive, she was a disaster. The guardians decided very rapidly not to retain her services as she was 'incapable of carrying out her duties', and again advertised the position.[31] More disruption for Harriet Kettle's education.

The chairman of the board of guardians, FW Keppel, wrote to Sir John Walsham on 16 March: 'Out of the frying pan is an old adage, & I think likely to prove true at Gressenhall, we aimed high at your recommendation for a schoolmistress & now are worse than we were, the last [Emily Ward] was Queen Log, this [Mary Wardlow] is a crazy woman without the least power over her scholars, but there was no other candidate & what was to be done. Her month is up next Monday & the board have decided upon that day to dispense with her services. We have advertized [sic] again in four county newspapers and in the London Times. I fear our success is doubtful, the supply of the article is not equal to the demand…Our late schoolmistress [Emily Ward] is I understand elected to the Erpingham Union where no doubt she will be a treasure, if she has nothing to do.'[32] Which helps to explain why the guardians did not re-appoint Emily Ward to the post at Gressenhall.

When they advertised for Mary Wardlow's successor, the guardians, disregarding Dr Kay's advice about exempting the schoolmaster and schoolmistress from menial duties, decided that the appointee should also help the matron and 'make herself generally useful', which Emily Ward (and before her, Anna Youngs) may have conspicuously failed to do. The person they appointed to the vacancy had to withdraw owing to ill-health and they decided not to re-advertise; instead, on 26 April 1847, they 'secured the services' of Miss Charlotte Sparrow. There had been a gap of six weeks or so between the departure of Mary Wardlow and the arrival of Charlotte Sparrow during which it must be assumed that, yet again, Harriet and the other girls were supervised by adult female inmates and received no proper teaching.

Charlotte Sparrow, aged 23, had over seven years' experience as a teacher, having worked in the schools in Guiltcross (Norfolk) and Stow (Suffolk) union workhouses and in a National School in Suffolk, and spent a short period in the Model Training School in Norwich. Sir John Walsham had doubts about the appointment: 'My impression is that Miss Sparrow was not thought an efficient schoolmistress at Stow Workhouse—and as she is a near relation of the present master and matron of the Gressenhall house [Stephen and Sophia Wade] one is somewhat induced to suspect what is commonly called "a job".' Miss Sparrow's appointment was sanctioned on trial for three months, at the end of which the guardians professed themselves 'perfectly satisfied' with her.[33]

It was during Charlotte Sparrow's tenure, on 4 November 1847, that the boys' and girls' schools were inspected for the first time by HG Bowyer, HMI. An inspectorate for workhouse schools had been established by the Committee of (the Privy) Council on Education in 1846. At the same time, a system of certificates at four levels ('permission', 'probation', 'competence' and 'efficiency', with three sub-divisions at each level) was established for the teachers, upon which the level of their salaries depended. Grants were provided to cover the cost of the salaries, providing that the guardians supplied the books and equipment required for the school. Bowyer served as HMI for workhouse schools for over a quarter of a century and made regular visits to Gressenhall, forming a close working relationship with Sir John Walsham, the poor law inspector.

Harriet Kettle would have been about eight at the time of Bowyer's first inspection of the workhouse schools. He wrote a report in the visitors' book (which does not survive) and it was reproduced in full in the guardians' minute book. It began: 'I may say that I was not only satisfied but surprised at the quickness and intelligence evinced by the boys in their answers upon scripture and their general proficiency which far surpasses that I have hitherto witnessed in the county. The girls are more backward but I have no doubt that their present mistress will soon raise them to the level of the boys.' Despite this vote of confidence, and Sir John Walsham's judgement after his visit in January 1848 that both workhouse schools were 'very well managed indeed', Charlotte Sparrow did not stay much longer, resigning her position in March 1848 after less than a year in post. She intended to leave teaching, no doubt because she was about to get married.[34] Her successor was Miss Anna Cooper, aged 22, of East Dereham, who had had no training for or experience of teaching since leaving school five years previously, and whose work experience was confined to needlework and 'occasionally assisting as barmaid in an inn kept by her father'. She was the only candidate.[35]

A few months after Miss Cooper's appointment, in June 1848, HMI Bowyer conducted another inspection of the schools. Apart from the perfunctory statement, 'I find the girls improved in their scripture knowledge', his report focused entirely on the boys. HMI Bowyer found that they, 'answered admirably in the scriptures and geography, and they also exhibited a tolerable acquaintaince with English history…In reading, however, the first class [the oldest boys] are far from what they ought to be, and there ought also to be a greater number of good writers.' However, he continued, 'notwithstanding this deficiency the condition of the school is highly creditable to the teacher; and the graduation of attainments from the lowest to the highest class, affords evidence that he has not confined his attention to the highest classes'. He added, 'If the schoolmaster makes himself acquainted with grammar he will next year probably be entitled to a certificate of competency'.[36]

Bradfield was examined in March 1849 and received his 'certificate of competency' in October, entitling him to the significantly higher salary of £40 per year. His results in religious knowledge, arithmetic and geography were 'good', while in spelling, 'penmanship' and grammar they were 'fair'. 'Fair' was the third point on the generally used scale of: excellent, good, fair, moderate, imperfect and failure, and meant, in effect, a pass.[37] The result in history was 'moderate'. HMI Bowyer assessed Bradfield's reading as good and the state of the school was reported to be 'very good, but reading and writing require attention'. The following year, following his examination in May, Bradfield's results in all subjects apart from grammar ('imperfect') and history ('fair') were 'good', while his skill as a teacher and the state of the school were judged 'very good', this time with no qualification.[38] In 1851, the boys' schoolroom was enlarged, to extend across the whole of the east wing of the workhouse.

HMI Bowyer's report of 1848 had said nothing about the competence of the schoolmistress, Anna Cooper, but the guardians evidently had concerns about her. The chaplain, Joseph Thompson, was asked to monitor Miss Cooper's progress and, in November 1848, reported: 'I consider her to be so evidently improving in the discharge of her duties that the period of her trial may judiciously be extended to March next when the government inspector will again visit the house to test her qualifications by an examination.'[39] Sir John Walsham was less enthusiastic, reporting that: 'The girls …seem to be still backward—and far inferior to the boys', adding that there were 'one or two objectionable points in connection with the training of girls' to which he had drawn the chaplain's attention. Of Miss Cooper, he observed, 'I fear she is not equal to the task of efficiently teaching and managing the 60 or 70 girls who are always in this large workhouse.'[40]

The guardians received Anna Cooper's resignation on 5 March 1849, their clerk reporting to the Poor Law Board, 'I have to observe that Miss Cooper tended [her] resignation just before the intended visit of the inspector of schools... and that she was considered by the guardians as incompetent...'[41] Miss Cooper could see the writing on the wall: she jumped before she was pushed. The 1851 census returns recorded Anna back at the Cherry Tree Inn in Theatre Road, East Dereham, no doubt helping behind the bar as before. It is hard not to feel some sympathy with young women like her who were pitched with no preparation into what was clearly a thankless task—which included teaching Harriet Kettle, now aged ten.

Following his visit, HMI Bowyer's only recorded observation on the girls' school came in a postscript and was damning: 'I found the girls inferior to the boys in every respect.' Of the boys, he reported that they, 'answered remarkably well in the scriptures. Indeed their religious knowledge would do credit to any school'. He continued: 'Their arithmetic is very fair, and they possess greater knowledge of geography than is usually the case in schools of [this] description. I however think that more attention has perhaps been bestowed on the higher and more showy branches of knowledge than in the humbler but essential one, of reading and writing. Their reading, though certainly better than it was at my last visit is still much below their other attainments, and inferior to that in many schools of humbler pretensions. Their writing, though certainly fair, might be improved; and they are imperfect in writing from dictation which is a great defect in a school. I hope, however that, by devoting more time to these things the defects I have mentioned will be speedily corrected.'[42]

Harriet Kettle had been taught by no fewer than seven teachers in rapid succession by the time of Anna Cooper's resignation in 1849. In the boys' school, by contrast, Robert Bradfield provided stability, continuity and growing expertise. The level of his certification as a teacher rose, reaching the highest level, (certificate of efficiency, first division) in 1856, when the state of the school was judged 'excellent' by HMI.[43] His salary was now £60 per year, with an additional £10 per year for his supervision of the 'industrial farm', of which more below.

For the girls' school, in 1849, the guardians yet again needed to appoint a new schoolmistress. The person selected was Miss Charlotte Wigg, whose appointment was confirmed on 19 March 1849. She was aged 22, had been living in East Dereham, working as a dressmaker, and had 'visited the National & British Schools, and had been engaged in Sunday school teaching', probably for the Independents, with whom she was reported to have been associated. Sir John Walsham viewed the appointment of Miss Wigg as, 'on the face of it, unpromising', and when the Poor Law Board sanctioned it for a trial period of three months, this was, 'on the understanding that she will undertake to teach the church catechism to those children belonging to the Church of England'. The guardians stated of Miss Wigg that they had 'every reason to [believe] that although she has hitherto been unaccustomed to the duties of any similar office she will be found able to perform those required'. [44] This time, they were right.

Charlotte Wigg brought much-needed stability to the school, staying in her post for almost a decade, during which (in 1855) the girls' schoolroom was enlarged and the school's performance became consistently satisfactory, if no more. On her resignation, reported to the board on 14 February 1859, long after Harriet Kettle had ceased to be a pupil, the guardians were to record their regret 'in the loss of such a servant'. The clerk to the guardians reported to the Poor Law Board that Charlotte had resigned, 'to take a situation in a private family, assigning no other reason than that she desired this change as a relief from the arduous duties devolved upon her as mistress of this school'.[45] However, she subsequently obtained the post of schoolmistress in the workhouse at Saffron Walden in Essex. She returned to her home town, East Dereham, the following year and married Richard Watson, a solicitor's clerk, on 5 December 1860.[46]

It was hard going for Miss Wigg at first. When HMI Bowyer visited Gressenhall in November 1849, after expressing himself, 'quite satisfied with the condition of the boys' school—The defects which I adverted to in my last report have been completely corrected', he continued: 'The girls' school is somewhat improved but its progress has been much retarded by the laxity of the discipline, which the present schoolmistress has had great difficulty in overcoming. It is however too large a school to be efficiently managed without some assistance in the shape of permanent monitors or pupil teachers for which it is however at present in far too backward a state.'[47]

Charlotte Wigg persevered. At the end of February 1850, following an examination the previous November, she was awarded a 'certificate of probation'. The results of her examination papers in religious knowledge, spelling, arithmetic and reading were 'good', and in penmanship and industrial skill they were 'fair'. Her skill as a teacher, however, was judged only 'moderate'.[48] Nevertheless, when he inspected both schools on 16 May, HMI Bowyer was, according to Sir John Walsham, 'much pleased with the progress exhibited'.[49] His report, placed before the guardians on 20 May 1850, was considered 'highly satisfactory'. In December 1850, Charlotte was examined again by HMI Bowyer. Although the overall result, reported to her in February 1851, was the same (certificate of probation, first division), this time she sat examination papers in grammar and geography as well as in the subjects she had taken the previous year; the assessment of her skill as a teacher had gone up from 'moderate' to 'fair' and the state of the school was described as 'improved'.[50] Perhaps in recognition of her efforts, Charlotte was permitted to take a holiday of two weeks in June 1850, and a year later the guardians paid for her bedchamber to be papered. In September 1854, she was even allowed to go to East Dereham, 'once in each week to take lessons in music for her improvement'. At last, in November 1855, Charlotte Wigg received a certificate of competency, third division. The state of the school, with 63 pupils, was again judged 'improved', With this, Miss Wigg's salary rose to £28. The following two years, she received a certificate of competency, second division, and a salary of £32, and in 1857 her skill as a teacher of her 60 pupils was judged 'good'.[51] A great story of successful professional development in challenging circumstances.

The appointment of pupil teachers in the boys' school had been advocated by HMI Bowyer in his report of March 1849. He commented on the impossibility of one man attending properly to a school of 80 boys, adding: 'Most of the deficiencies in the lower classes evidently proceed from this cause.' Bowyer recommended appointing two or three of the 'more promising' boys as pupil teachers. The guardians responded promptly; in the autumn of 1849, two of the monitors in the boys' school, William Parke and William Seaman, were given official status, granted £3 each for extra clothing and started on the process of training and qualifying as pupil teachers during which they were given gratuities of ten shillings per half year. In 1850, HMI Bowyer recommended books on history, geography and English grammar for use by the pupil teachers and the guardians agreed to buy them. Both pupil teachers eventually became schoolmasters in the schools of other workhouses but after their departure from Gressenhall Robert Bradfield had to make do with monitors, as the guardians would not support the expense of pupil teachers from the common fund of the union. No pupil teachers were appointed in the girls' school; there, Miss Wigg soldiered on alone. Relief for her was to come, not from the appointment of pupil teachers but from the creation of an infant school superintended by an infant schoolmistress.

HMI Bowyer had recommended the appointment of an infant schoolmistress in his report of March 1849, in which he observed that: 'There are about 30 infants who receive, at present, no other instruction than that which can be afforded by the pauper women of the house; and they consequently come into the other schools knowing hardly anything. So large a number of infants would form a good infant school, and I would recommend that an infant schoolmistress should be procured for them.' There was no immediate response from the guardians, and so in November 1849 Bowyer had to remind the board that the establishment of a proper infant school, 'would relieve both the other schools of a number of little children who cannot be well instructed by the methods which are suited to the elder ones'.

It proved difficult, however, to find an infant schoolmistress. In May 1850, HMI Bowyer noted the guardians' failure to fill the vacancy and commented that the services of an infant schoolmistress were 'greatly needed—for the schoolmistress has to teach single handed between 70 and 80 girls', which suggests that Charlotte Wigg had more responsibility for supervising the women who cared for the infants than Bowyer's earlier comments would imply.[52] The guardians were reluctant to advertise the post, fearing, 'the election of an untrained or incompetent person'. In May 1850, after unsuccessful approaches to various training institutions they took HMI Bowyer's advice and appointed Miss Harriet Perfect to fill the vacancy.

Miss Perfect was 21 and had six years' experience as an assistant teacher in the Bedford Infant School. She took up her duties at Gressenhall, at the salary of £20 per year, on 15 July 1850.[53] Within weeks of her arrival, a transformation took place. The guardians' clerk was instructed to obtain 40 scripture prints, 40 natural history prints, a full-sized numerical frame, a form and colour box, six lesson posts, 40 daily lessons on boards and 40 spelling and reading books on cards, all, 'stated by Miss Perfect…to be necessary for the use of her infant school'. The guardians also converted a room in the women's ward (the 'upper bastardy ward') for use as an infant schoolroom. Clearly, Miss Perfect possessed considerable powers of persuasion; perhaps both she and the guardians were aware that the Committee of Council on Education might not reimburse the union for her salary if she was not provided with the equipment she needed. When Sir John Walsham visited Gressenhall in November 1850, he commented that, 'the establishment of an infant school in accordance with Mr Bowyer's and my own recommendations has added considerably to the efficiency of the girls' school,' the number of pupils in which had fallen to 55 in December.[54] Although Harriet Kettle was too old to have benefited directly from Miss Perfect's work in the infant school, she benefited indirectly by being taught in a more manageable girls' school.

Sir John Walsham considered Harriet Perfect's fitness for her post to be 'unquestionable'.[55] After being examined by HMI Bowyer in December 1850, she received a certificate of probation, first division, the same qualification as that held by Charlotte Wigg. Her religious knowledge was 'fair', spelling and penmanship were 'good', and her skill as an infant teacher was judged, 'very fair'. In 1856, a year after Miss Wigg, she received a certificate of competency, third division, and her salary rose to £28 per year. Her certificate remained at the same level in 1857, when her skill as a teacher of her 45 pupils was again judged 'very fair'.[56] Miss Perfect was well regarded; the chaplain often recorded his pleasure with the infant school, and in 1858 the guardians described her conduct as 'exemplary'. She was to remain infant schoolmistress at Gressenhall until November 1859, when she resigned in order to take up another position; in the 1861 census returns she was recorded as the schoolmistress in the Wayland workhouse, where the master and matron were William and Ada Owen, formerly porter and assistant matron at Gressenhall. Harriet Perfect's strength of character served her well but may have led to a clash with Harriet Kettle in 1852, resulting in the latter's first experience of prison.

All three schools at Gressenhall benefited from the stability of their staffing in the 1850s. In May 1851, Sir John Walsham reported that HMI Bowyer's most recent report on the schools had been 'as favourable as usual, more particularly in reference to the boys and infant schools'.[57] When HMI Bowyer assessed the teachers in July 1851, there were 76 pupils in the boys' school, 54 in the girls' school and 36 in the infants' school.[58] These numbers, and the general tenor of the reports by HMI, remained broadly similar over the next few years, while the level of the teachers' certification rose. In September 1856, HMI Bowyer, according to Sir John Walsham, 'made as usual a very favourable report of all the three schools'.[59] The chairman of the board of guardians, now the Revd Philip Gurdon of Cranworth, in a letter to Sir John Walsham in 1861, stated his belief that: 'the education our orphans are receiving is far superior to that in our village schools'.[60] That this was true of workhouse schools in general had been suggested by a report in the Morning Chronicle in 1849: 'The education afforded in these schools is in many respects superior to that which is given in many of the other schools; and it is not at all an uncommon complaint to hear among the farmers that the pauper children are receiving too much education',[61] making them better educated than the children of agricultural labourers.

What was the content of the education that Harriet Kettle and her peers received? The pattern may have been that the morning was devoted to religious instruction followed by academic lessons and the afternoon to vocational activities. As indicated by the examinations taken by the teachers and the books ordered for the pupils, the curriculum covered reading and writing, including spelling and handwriting, along with arithmetic and religious knowledge. In 1854, a return published in a parliamentary paper indicated that in the schools at Gressenhall there was a, 'scripture lesson every morning, and religious instruction three times a week in [the] boys', girls' and infant schools'.[62] For the older pupils, the curriculum also included grammar, history and geography. Singing may have featured, reflecting an enthusiasm of Dr Kay[63], and building on the legacy at Gressenhall of Harriet Pinson, and there may have been gymnastic exercises of some kind in the yard.

After a morning spent studying academic subjects, the vocational element in the curriculum probably occupied the afternoon. For the boys, from 1850 onwards, this received increased emphasis. In March 1849, HMI Bowyer asked the board of guardians to consider, 'the expediency of providing some industrial training for the boys, besides shoemaking, and tailoring [which were taught by inmates of the workhouse]; as these trades are neither calculated to enable them to earn a subsistence, nor to render them sufficiently vigourous [sic] to perform

Gressenhall Museum, 2006.

the duties of an agricultural labourer. The appearance of the boys clearly shows that they have been too delicately brought up. They have not the vigourous and healthy countenances of rustic lads, but the white and delicate faces of girls; and it is evident they are not calculated to support the labourious [sic] life to which they are destined.' He suggested that the board develop an 'industrial farm' on which the land would be cultivated 'on the most approved principles of spadehusbandry', yielding profit to the union as well as benefits for the boys. The guardians duly took back some of the land around the workhouse from the tenant farmer to whom it was leased, and an 'industrial farm' of 8 acres was established, on which around 25 boys were employed. Large quantities of potatoes and cabbages, along with wheat straw and faggots, were sent to the workhouse, and pigs, oats, wheat, barley and peas were sold. The guardians had set up a committee of five of their number to run the farm, which reported in November 1852 that: 'The improved appearance of the boys since they have been employed upon the land speaks for itself, and has been the subject of comment by many guardians and other gentlemen'. The following year, they added that the employment of an average of 30 boys had not caused the school to suffer.

The girls received training in domestic work and in needlework and knitting but in 1849, HMI Bowyer had suggested an outdoor vocational element in their education as well: 'By keeping a few cows, the girls might also be instructed in the business of the dairy, which would greatly increase their chance of finding employment.' As well as making them more employable, in their case as dairy maids, these measures would also mean that the 'children would also turn out much better'.[64] The guardians were reluctant to adopt the idea, although it was supported by their industrial farm committee in 1852, whose report stated: 'Your committee are therefore emboldened to extend their experiment to the purchase of two cows with a view to the instruction of the girls in dairy work.' But the initiative came to nothing: in 1856, the 'industrial training' for girls at Gressenhall still amounted only to 'needlework, knitting, washing, ironing and kitchen work'. [65] It was, in any case, too late for Harriet Kettle.

A decade earlier, in 4 November 1847, HMI Bowyer had also made a recommendation about the teaching method to be adopted in the workhouse schools, advocating, 'an alteration in the arrangement of the desks, at present they are ranged along the walls a disposition now abandoned in the best National Schools as affording no facilities for simultaneous instruction. Parallel desks are now being generally adopted and have been everywhere strongly recommended by Her Majesty's Inspectors of National Schools.'[66] In effect, Bowyer was recommending that the monitorial system, according to which the teacher taught the older pupils, or monitors, who then taught the other children in groups, should be replaced by direct teaching of the whole class by the teacher. Robert Bradfield, it appears, was slow to adopt this approach in the boys' school, while the girls' school was in an unstable state at the time and the mistresses were hardly in a position to make radical changes of this kind.

In the reports written after his visits, HMI Bowyer provided advice on the books he felt that the guardians should order for the schools. In November 1847, he suggested that the purchase of, 'a sufficient number of secular books conveying useful and entertaining information', recommending (Like Dr Kay before him) those published by the Irish Commission for National Education. He continued, 'I also recommend Dr Davies's History of England, a set of penny magazines and Saturday magazines would also form an useful little library to occupy the leisure hours of the boys....A copy of Tales' Arithmetic and Sullivan's Geography Generalised would also be a great help to the master.' In response, the clerk was directed to obtain two volumes of the books by Davies, Tales and Sullivan. The former chairman of the board of guardians, FW Keppel, had already been asked to purchase 'a map of the world and other maps for the schools'. Later, he obtained nine volumes of penny magazines for the boys and girls, for which he was reimbursed by the board.

In June 1848, HMI Bowyer reported that more resources were still needed, noting that the oldest pupils had read their reading books 'several times through'. In January 1849, the guardians submitted a large order for books and the Poor Law Board despatched them, 'by goods train by Eastern Counties Railway to Dereham and then by carrier to Gressenhall workhouse'. The items were ordered from a printed list supplied by the Poor Law Board and provide clues to the content of the education of both pupils and teachers. The list included, for pupils: four dozen copies of 'Rudiments of English Grammar' by A. Reid A.M.; two dozen copies of 'A Treatise on Arithmetic', half a dozen copies of 'A Treatise on Mensuration' and half a dozen copies of 'Elements of Book-keeping', all published by the Commissioners of National Education in Ireland; two dozen copies of 'An Introduction to Geography'; and two dozen copies of 'The Young Child's Geography', the latter published by the Scottish School Book Association. For the teachers, the guardians ordered: two copies of 'English Grammar' and the 'Agricultural Class Book'; one copy of each of a 'Key to the Elements of Book-keeping' and various titles by J.W.Parker ('Useful Hints for Labourers', first and second series; 'The Useful Arts Employed in… the Production of Food/the Construction of Dwelling Houses/the Production of Clothing'); and, finally, 'Instructions in Household Matters' by 'A Lady'. The first four of these were described as 'useful to schoolmasters and pupil teachers in the preparation of lessons on household economy and domestic arts', while the last was said to be be 'useful to schoolmistresses for oral lessons', and was no doubt used by Charlotte Wigg to prepare the lessons that Harriet Kettle received in the girls' school.[67]

In October 1850, perhaps at the instigation of Charlotte Wigg, the guardians agreed to obtain supplies of the secular reading books published by the Irish Commission for National Education specifically for the use of the girls' school, three dozen of the third and fourth classes being ordered. Acquisitions of books (including Bibles and prayer books) and maps continued in subsequent years. 'Daily Lessons, numbers 1, 2 and 3' were procured in May 1851 and more reading books in September 1852, when there was also a request for the 'latest' map of Australia and New Zealand. Perhaps it showed the colony in Western Australia where John Kettle was to arrive two years later.

By the time of the 1851 census, when Harriet Kettle was listed as a scholar, aged 12, she was being taught in a school which in July 1851 numbered 54 girls. Up to that point, Harriet's experience of education in the workhouse would have been mixed. After spending time with the infants, supervised by workhouse inmates, she may have benefited briefly from the teaching of Harriet Pinson before experiencing the rapid turnover of schoolmistresses of variable effectiveness. As a ten-year-old, she would have witnessed, and may well have contributed to, the indiscipline that greeted Charlotte Wigg on her arrival in 1849, and she certainly clashed with Miss Wigg on two occasions in 1851. However, she would also have benefited from the improvement in the school from 1849 onwards and the reduction in its size when the infant school was created in 1850.

There are references in later sources to Harriet's intelligence and she certainly learned to read, as she was reported to be able to read (but not write) when admitted to the county lunatic asylum in July 1856.[68] She may have had some limited ability to write as she was able to sign her name when she married in 1865. Harriet would also, in all probability, have learned some arithmetic, history and geography and she would undoubtedly have acquired some religious knowledge, both from the school and from the Sunday services held in the dining hall. In all likelihood, she learned to knit and do needlework, as training in these skills was provided for the older girls and Harriet was recorded later, in the county lunatic asylum, as knitting. A later source refers to her 'moderate' level of education[69] and, such as it was, this is testimony to the efforts of her teachers in the girls' school at Gressenhall workhouse.

However, at the age of 12, Harriet was becoming a rebel.

Notes

1   The main sources for this chapter are the MLU minutes; NRO, C/GP14/2-15; and the Correspondence of the PLC and PLU with Assistant Commissioners and the MLU; TNA: MH12 8474-8482.
2   PLB, General Order (Consolidated) (1847).
3   B Yates (2020). I am grateful to Bridget Yates for sharing relevant content from her study of education in the parish of Gressenhall in advance of its publication.
4   PLC, Fourth Annual Report, 1838.
5   Sir James Kay-Shuttleworth, *Four Periods of Public Education* (1862).
6   NC, 17 February 1838.
7   H J Burgess, *Enterprise in Education: The story of the work of the Established Church in the education of the people prior to 1870*, (1958).
8   NRO, DN/NDS 278. Thanks to Bridget Yates for this and the preceding reference.
9   D Adams (2013).
10 NC, 24 February 1838.
11 D Adams (2013).
12 NC, 10 March 1838.
13 TNA: MH12 8475/191. On 18 June 1838, the guardians had seen fit to stipulate that, 'the subordinate officers of the workhouse do take all their meals together and not be allowed to take any part of their provisions to their separate apartments. Also that no washing be done except in the laundry...'
14 Harriet Pinson was born on 17 January 1824 and baptised at St Michael at Plea in Norwich on 2 February 1824. Her father George's occupation was recorded as 'weaver'; baptism register accessed via freereg.org.uk.
15 TNA: MH12 8475/195.
16 TNA: MH12 8476/73.
17 TNA: MH12 8476/93, 109.

18 TNA: MH12 8476/98, 118.

19 He did, however, clash with the master (Stephen Wade) in 1848 about keeping a dog in the workhouse, and had to dispense with the animal. Sir John Walsham characterised the incident as 'something like a personal collision' but decided not to intervene as, 'the dog is gone, and the guardians have contrived 'componere lites' [to settle the issues], and as both combatants are very good officers, and now very good friends'. (TNA: MH12 8478/215) In 1863 Bradfield was reprimanded for his 'frequent absences from the House' and told that his duties included 'seeing the boys under his care properly to bed'. He also denied, in 1868, an allegation that he had caused the pregnancy of a female inmate, Elizabeth Rudd. After an investigation, the charge was found 'not proven'. The episode was included as a case study, with transcripts of the key sources, in A Reid (1994), and a dramatised version features in R Lee (2005).

20 Poor relief in Norwich remained the responsibility of an incorporation which was not to be reorganised as a poor law union until 1863, and a pre-1834 workhouse remained in use until 1859. See A Digby (1978).

21 NM, 22 January 1842.

22 TNA: MH12 8477/75.

23 Her mother, Sarah, born Fox, was the sister of Mary Rudd, born Fox. Thanks to Bridget Yates for this information.

24 TNA: MH12 8477/107-8.

25 Although, in a letter of 20 March 1844 to the PLC, he stated that he had known Mrs Youngs for only 21 days and considered that 'no duration of acquaintance would have improved her'.

26 TNA: MH12 8477/109-11.

27 TNA: MH12 8477/136.

28 TNA: MH12 8477/320. The 1851 census returns show Eliza Underwood, aged 30, schoolmistress, along with Eliza Dunham, schoolmistress (and former inmate of Gressenhall workhouse), aged 27 and a male painter, lodging in the house of a slightly older schoolmistress, Phoebe Cooper, aged 43. On 3 June 1853, Eliza Underwood married George Watling, cordwainer, in Longham, where she was now resident; Longham marriage register, accessed via freereg.org.uk.

29 TNA: MH12 8478/17.

30 Ibid.

31 TNA: MH12 8478/31.

32 TNA: MH12 8478/34.

33 TNA: MH12 8478/40-2, 82-3.

34 The marriage of Charlotte Sparrow was registered in Depwade, Norfolk, in the second quarter of 1848: freebmd.org.uk.

35 TNA: MH12 8478/163.

36 TNA: MH12 8478/181.

37 See Instructions to HMI upon the Administration of the Revised Code (1862), available on educationengland.org website.

38 TNA: MH12 8478/326.

39 TNA: MH12 8478/210.

40 TNA: MH12 8478/215.

41 TNA: MH12 8478/254.

42 TNA: MH12 8478/270.

43 TNA: MH12 8480/305.

44 TNA: MH12 8478/254-6. The independents were a nonconformist church, who had a chapel in Dereham, now known as the 'Cowper church' as it was built on the site previously occupied by the poet's house.

45 TNA: MH12 8481/452-3.

46 Richard and Charlotte had one child, Alice Mary, baptised on 11 December 1861. Charlotte may have returned to teaching as she was listed as 'schoolmistress' on the census returns of 1871 and 1881. The family continued to live in East Dereham and were prosperous enough to employ a servant. Charlotte died in 1886, her age being given as 57 (information from East Dereham parish registers and census records, accessed via findmypast.com).

47 TNA: MH12 8478/349.

48 TNA: MH12 8479/24.

49 TNA: MH12 8479/55.

50 TNA: MH12 8479/183.

51 TNA: MH12 8480/126, 306, 399.

52 TNA: MH12 8479/55.

53 TNA: MH12 8479/70,76.

54 TNA: MH12 8479/98.

55 Ibid.

56 TNA: MH12 8479/183; MH12 8480/307, 400.

57 TNA: MH12 8479/193.

58 TNA: MH12 8479/242.

59 TNA: MH12 8480/335.

60 TNA: MH 32 84.

61 MC, 29 December 1849.

62 PP LV, 1854.

63 Dr Kay suggested that, 'the children march into the school from the garden, the workshop, and the playground, singing such moral songs as have been introduced into infant schools with success; the intervals of any change of lesson or occupation are filled up with singing…' PLC, Fourth Annual Report (1838).

64 TNA: MH12 8478/270.

65 Committee of Council on Education, Reports of HMI of Schools on Workhouse Schools, PP XXXIII, 1857, session 2.

66 MLU minutes, 8 November 1847; NRO, C/GP14/8.

67 TNA: MH12 8478/237-8.

68 CLA, admission register 1845-61; NRO, SAH 175.

69 Criminal patients' admission register, BM ARD02.

Rebel in Gressenhall, 'girl on the town' in Norwich

T HERE was a strict disciplinary regime in the workhouse.[1] The rules were prominently displayed, or at least that was the requirement. In June 1847, Sir John Walsham pointed out that details of the punishments for various misdemeanors were not displayed in Gressenhall workhouse when they should have been, but no doubt his intervention resulted in the situation being rectified.[2]

There were consequences when the rules were broken. The normal punishment for minor offences was confinement in a 'separate room' or 'solitary room' for periods of up to 12 hours—up to 24 hours was permissible—on a diet of bread and water. One such separate room at Gressenhall, initially referred to as the 'dungeon' or 'black hole' was the refractory cell, the location of which was identified in 1986, whereupon it was opened to visitors to the museum. It was created on the instructions of Dr Kay in 1836 by blocking up a window on the ground floor of the east wing and was equipped with a heavy iron door with gratings. More serious infractions of the rules resulted in an appearance before a magistrate, which usually led to confinement for short periods in Walsingham house of correction or, later, for females, Wymondham house of correction.

Among the inmates, including the boys and girls in the workhouse schools, there were many who complied with the rules—and some who did not. As Harriet Kettle's frustration with the constraints of the institutional environment increased and her rage against the workhouse authorities grew, there were other rebellious inmates whose example she could follow, and who provided role models for her to emulate. One, perhaps, was her elder sister Matilda who, with her accomplice Leah Gay, had rebelled briefly before going into service with James Clarke in 1849. Another was Martha Craske of East Dereham.

Martha Craske, aged 24 in 1851 and therefore 12 years older than Harriet, had a long record of misdemeanors in the workhouse, dating back to 25 August 1845, when she was found to have

The refractory cell, Gressenhall, 2006.

been guilty, 'of refractory conduct to the mistress and inmates of the workhouse'. The guardians ordered that she, 'be punished by confinement in the solitary room for six hours during tomorrow and the three following days and during such time kept on a diet of bread and water'. The following March, Martha and two other women were charged with misbehaviour and taken before a magistrate. This happened again in January 1847. On 2 July 1849, Martha and her younger sister Elizabeth Craske, 'having been brought before the board charged with misbehaviour towards the master and with refractory conduct in the house, Ordered that the said Martha Craske be taken before the magistrates and that Elizabeth Craske be punished by solitary confinement and kept on bread and water diet for six hours on Tuesday, Wednesday, Thursday and Friday next'. The following week, it was reported that Martha Craske had been sentenced to 20 days in Walsingham house of correction.

The incidents continued. On 14 January 1850, Martha was charged, 'with an assault upon Mrs Tilney a servant in the workhouse'. Mrs Tilney, an inmate, was in charge of the workhouse laundry. Martha was taken before the magistrates again and this time sentenced to two months in Wymondham house of correction. On 18 October 1852, Martha and Elizabeth Craske were again brought before the board, 'the said Elizabeth Craske being charged with assaulting George Mason the porter and using threatening language towards Ann Mason his wife, and the said Martha Craske charged with breaking windows in the young women's day room…' They were taken before a magistrate but the punishment on this occasion is not recorded.

The next time Martha and Elizabeth were in trouble, Harriet Kettle had joined them. Perhaps she had witnessed and been influenced by the incidents recorded above and others of a similar nature.

Harriet's first misdemeanor, however, did not involve Martha Craske. On 7 April 1851, immediately after she had been recorded in the census return of 30 March, Harriet's name occurred for the first time in the guardians' minute book following a clash with the schoolmistress, Charlotte Wigg. It was stated that: 'Harriet Kettle of Cranworth and Elizabeth Butters of Hoe…having been brought before the board charged with insubordinate and other improper conduct towards the schoolmistress, Ordered that the said Harriet Kettle and Elizabeth Butters be punished by solitary confinement and bread and water diet on Tuesday and Wednesday next.'

Being brought before the board must have been an intimidating experience for Harriet Kettle, at least on the first occasion. The boardroom, with its turkey carpet, was a place that she would never normally have visited. The average age of the guardians elected in April 1851, all men of course, was 48. Seven-eighths were farmers, with farms ranging in size from under 100 to over 1,000 acres, but most commonly of between 100 and 300 acres. Three of those elected were rectors of parishes, and others included a corn merchant, builder, coachbuilder and lawyer.[3] And then there were the magistrates who acted as ex-officio guardians, including FW Keppel, the Revd Thomas Paddon, Brampton Gurdon and the Revd Philip Gurdon. In total, there were about 70 guardians, although on average only around 20 attended the meetings.[4] They can be imagined sitting at a long table, the chairman, flanked by the vice-chairman and the clerk, at the centre, with the cupboards and shelves where minute books and other records were stored behind them. For a 12 year-old to stand on the carpet, the matron and schoolmistress at her side reciting her misdeeds, facing a room-full of farmers, clergymen and magistrates, cannot have been much fun. Nor can the punishment have been an enjoyable experience.

However, on 21 April, only two weeks after her first appearance, Harriet was again brought before the board, whose membership had now changed slightly as most of the guardians had just been 'elected' by their parishes. This time, Harriet was charged with, 'refractory conduct in repeated disobedience of the orders of the schoolmistress' and was ordered to be kept in a separate apartment for six hours on the 23rd, 24th, 25th and 26th instants'. Charlotte Wigg, having won the battle to establish her authority in the school, was obviously determined to maintain it.

The following year, on 5 July 1852, there was another case of refractory conduct by Harriet Kettle, which resulted in her being confined in a separate room for 24 hours on bread and water. And then, on 13 September of the same year, Harriet's clash with the infant schoolmistress was reported. The guardians' minutes recorded that, 'on the complaint of Miss Harriet Perfect the mistress of the infant school Harriet Kettle is ordered to be taken before a magistrate for disorderly and insubordinate conduct'.

Harriet was sentenced to 14 days' imprisonment with hard labour: the first of several periods she was to spend in prison.[5] She was aged 13, or possibly 14. How did she respond to this new experience, which must have been unpleasant, even though the time she had spent at Gressenhall would have familiarised her with life in an institution? Possibly like this: '…a little shawled figure is brought in by a policeman, a little, dark, wistful face…It is evidently her first experience, and as the matron asks her name and questions her she begins to cry—such a pathetic, frightened sound of the trapped animal.'[6] Or perhaps the view taken of Harriet in Walsingham was more like that of the governor of Coldbath Fields prison in London who, reporting on the arrival of inmates from various workhouses in the capital, wrote: '…we witnessed in the demeanour of the young girls… such revolting specimens of workhouse education, that the exhibition was at

Walsingham House of Correction, 2020.

once frightful and disgusting. The inconceivable wickedness of those girls was absolutely appalling. Their language, their violence and their indecency shocked every beholder.'[7]

After serving her time at Walsingham, Harriet returned to Gressenhall. A little over a month later, on 3 November 1852, she was imprisoned again, for the longer period of 21 days.[8] And then, on 10 January 1853, the guardians received a report from their visiting committee that: 'Martha Craske and Elizabeth Craske…of East Dereham and Harriet Kettle of…Cranworth…had on the fifth instant been guilty of great misbehaviour by destroying the food and other property of the guardians and by wilfully disobeying the orders of the master and by making a great noise and disturbance and by using obscene and violent language. Ordered that they be forthwith taken before a magistrate and dealt with as the law directs.' It sounds as though there had been a major fracas in the dining hall which the master, Henry Harrison, had had some difficulty in quelling.

For Harriet, the result was that she was sentenced to 42 days in prison. She may or may not have returned to Gressenhall workhouse afterwards, or she may have returned and then been discharged or absconded. There was now, in any case, a gap of three years, until 7 January 1856, in the references to Harriet in the guardians' minute book. During this period, on 21 September 1855, she was reported later to have been convicted and sentenced to 42 days' imprisonment but there is no reference in the guardians' minute book to any incident in the workhouse at that time.

For at least part, if not for all, of the time between 1853 and 1856, Harriet Kettle was leading a very different life from that which had been her fate previously. She was making a living as a 'girl on the town', or sex worker, in Norwich.

There are no statements attributed to Harriet Kettle that relate directly to her sex work, but one reference that is very likely to her as a 'girl on the town', using her alias Harriet Clark, has been found. The source is a newspaper report on proceedings in the Norwich police court in October 1853, when William

A cell in Walsingham House of Correction, 2020.

Humphrey charged William Cannell with stealing £10 from him. The former stated, 'that at about 12 o'clock the preceding evening he was in company with [Cannell], whom he had known before. They went to a house in St Lawrence, taking two young women with them. He was not sober at the time. When they arrived at the house he sent one of the girls for some ale and in the meantime fell asleep. When he entered the house he believed he had £20[9] about him, a £5 note of Gurney's bank and the remainder in gold. He put it in his watch pocket in his waistcoat, the coin being wrapped up in the note, and a receipt for property tax that day paid over it. When he awoke, he missed some money, and he asked the girls where it was. They said his friend had taken it. He found the note and £5 10s in gold in his pocket. Harriet Clark and Mary Ann Hubbard confirmed the foregoing statement. As the prosecutor could not declare positively what sum he had in his possession, the case was dismissed, the girls being warned to abandon their present course of life.'[10] The reference to 'their present course of life' was of course to sex work. Harriet Kettle would have been 14 or 15 at the time.

Apart from this probable reference, such evidence as there is for this phase of Harriet's life comes from later sources. Edward Casson, medical officer at the county lunatic asylum, where Harriet was to spend five periods as a patient, referred in 1856 to 'her irregular life she having been a girl on the town in Norwich for some time previous to her committal to prison...'.[11] Charles

White, a later medical officer, writing in 1863, cast Harriet as the victim of her circumstances: 'She left [the workhouse] to seek her own living when quite a girl, being tired of the irksome monotony and confinement of the union. From this point her evil courses date. Inheriting a bad disposition and violent passions, having been deprived of a mother's care, or the gentler influences which might have guided so uncertain a nature, and being surrounded by the moral effluvia of a workhouse, a place always and necessarily unfavourable to any advance in rectitude, it is not wonderful that when set free in the world young and ignorant she yielded to her inclinations and got into trouble.'[12]

It was not inevitable, however, that Harriet would become a sex worker on leaving Gressenhall workhouse; nor was it the case that, 'being surrounded by the moral effluvia of a workhouse' was 'necessarily unfavourable to any advance in rectitude'. There were many examples to suggest the contrary: children who, benefiting from the education provided in the workhouse schools, went on to regular and, in some instances, notably successful employment.[13]

Placing young people who had been educated in the workhouse schools in jobs was something that the board of guardians took seriously. In October 1839, they had agreed that boys and girls over 12 could be issued with clothes and a small premium on being 'bound out' as apprentices or domestic servants, providing that they had been workhouse inmates for 12 months and that the people hiring them undertook to employ them for 12 months; the Poor Law Commission did not allow the premium because it would place the workhouse children at an advantage compared with those of independent labourers, but they had no problem with the provision of clothes. Over the next few years, a number of children, including Matilda Kettle in 1849, was recorded as leaving Gressenhall to go into service, with their clothing supplied. In October 1842, the guardians had decided that Bibles and prayer books should also be issued to all who departed from the workhouse in these circumstances; Harriet's sister would have received this parting gift when she went into service with James Clarke in Great Yarmouth.

When George and Rhoda Pinson resigned as master and matron of the workhouse at the end of 1843, the guardians expressed their appreciation of, 'their having prepared upwards of 100 orphan or deserted children for various services whereby they have been rendered useful members of society by having been brought up in habits of cleanliness and industry and who have given very generally great satisfaction to their employers'. Similarly, after the Pinsons' successors, George and Emma Whelan, had resigned their positions at the end of June 1846, 'the visiting committee laid before the board a list of nearly 40 persons who had been rendered fit for permanent service from among the paupers in this union workhouse, and who had obtained situations accordingly through the exertions and management of Mr and Mrs Whelan…since their appointment in January 1844'.

This record of success in placing children in positions outside the workhouse continued in the 1850s. In July 1853, the schoolmaster, Robert Bradfield, gave the board a statement showing the destinations of 88 boys who had left the boys' school since 1845 to take up employment. Twelve had gone into 'farm service' and 11 into 'gentlemen's service'; eight had joined the army; there were five shoemakers, four tailors, four schoolmasters, two carpenters, two printers, a harness maker and an artist. Twenty six had gone into other employments and the occupations of 12 were not known. One of the schoolmasters was William Parke, one of the pupil teachers in the boys' school at Gressenhall, who had been appointed as schoolmaster of the school in the Mildenhall Union workhouse in March 1853. In addition to 'his usual half year's gratuity of ten shillings', the guardians gave him £4 to provide him with 'sufficient and proper clothing…and to pay the expenses of his journey'.

Girls who left the workhouse generally went into domestic service, and by the 1850s the girls' school at Gressenhall had a record of placing its pupils almost as good as that of the boys' school. Data published in 1861 showed that, of the children attending the workhouse schools at Gressenhall for at least two years in the ten years up to the end of 1860, 115 boys and 101 girls had 'left the workhouse for service or other industrial occupation' and only six boys and eight girls had subsequently returned 'by reason of their own misconduct' (another two boys and three girls had returned for other reasons).[14] Some of the adult women also left the workhouse for domestic service and were permitted to leave some or all of their children in the workhouse provided that they paid five shillings per quarter for their maintenance. Thus, on 26 May 1845, Honor Dickerson, 'the laundry woman at the union workhouse' was allowed to go into the service of the former master George Pinson at Norwich Castle, on agreeing to pay 25 shillings a quarter for the maintenance of her five children.[15] This payment was steadily reduced as her children in turn obtained positions and were able to leave the workhouse. Similarly, the former master George Whelan, after his appointment as master of the Haydock Lodge Lunatic Asylum in Lancashire, arranged for three female inmates to go into his service there in July 1846. Domestic service was not the only destination for female inmates, however. In December 1845, the guardians provided £2 to Eliza Dunham, 'to provide her with clothing on her going into a situation as an assistant teacher in the National School, Gorlestone'. This was the school where Eliza Underwood, who was the schoolmistress at Gressenhall from March 1844 until August 1845, had taught, and to which she probably returned after leaving the workhouse. Eliza Dunham's employment there was probably at Eliza Underwood's instigation. As noted above, the 1851 census returns record the two Elizas as fellow lodgers in the house of Phoebe Cooper, schoolmistress, in Gorleston.[16]

That Harriet Kettle did not go into domestic service or regular employment of any kind on leaving Gressenhall may reflect the guardians' reluctance to support her, given her disciplinary record; or it may have been, as the medical officer at the county lunatic asylum quoted Harriet as saying in 1863, that 'she could not earn a living honestly, not being strong enough for service'; or it may simply have been a matter of choice on Harriet's part. Most of the other options theoretically open to her would not have enabled her to escape poverty: prostitution at least offered the possibility of doing so, and that must have been a reason why many girls were drawn into sex work. Although it entailed the risks of abuse and venereal disease[17], prostitution in Norwich also offered Harriet freedom, a release from the constraints of the workhouse and the excitement of life in the city. One authority on the period states that a high percentage of prostitutes had lost one or both parents and notes: 'According to rescue workers and others, a wild impulsive nature, a restlessness, and a desire for independence frequently characterised the young women who moved into prostitution.'[18] That sounds rather like Harriet.

Although direct evidence of Harriet's time in Norwich is limited to the one source mentioned at the beginning of this chapter, it is possible to build up a picture of the kind of life she might have lived there from contemporary reports and newspaper articles.

Norwich, in the 1850s, with a population which would rise to 75,025 in 1861, faced severe economic and social challenges. The textile industry, once the mainstay of the city, had declined and there was much poverty, especially but not exclusively among handloom weavers. Much of the housing in which the poorer people lived was dilapidated, overcrowded and lacking in basic amenities. Despite the passage of Acts of Parliament for, 'better paving, lighting, cleaning, watching and otherwise improving the City of Norwich' in 1806 and 1825, the conditions in the poorer districts remained bad. The water supply and sewage disposal, in particular, were inadequate.[19] The Morning Chronicle

Dutton's Court, Norwich by Catherine Maud Nichols. (Courtesy Picture Norfolk)

A Norwich court in 1910. (Courtesy Norwich Heritage Projects)

investigated the conditions of the poor in 1849 and reported: 'As regards those portions of the city and suburbs where the working classes chiefly reside, the poverty, wretchedness, and vice of the inhabitants, added to the decaying state of the houses, bear witness to the comparatively prostrate state of the manufactures of the town. The houses inhabited by the working classes are generally in the most dilapidated condition. Within the boundaries of the city, you must search for the working classes in narrow lanes, courts, and yards, the entrance to which from the adjoining thoroughfares is through low and narrow openings or archways. Here will be found rows of wretched cottages, built in most cases back to back, ventilation being almost entirely excluded. Where the cottages face each other, in many cases they are not more than three feet apart. Down the centre of these places an open kennel or drain—perhaps not even that—carries off the refuse water.'[20]

In a second article three days later, the same reporter wrote about the conditions of the handloom weavers of Norwich, lamenting that, 'low wages and uncertain employment have reduced this class of operatives to the lowest possible state of wretchedness and misery'. He described the situation of a 17 year old girl who lost her job in a factory, as she put it, 'because a young man kept me out all night,' and then had only irregular 'havel work', preparing yarn for the weavers at home. She had been obliged to supplement her income by 'going on the streets,' commenting, 'I wouldn't do the streets if I wasn't compelled to do it, and then we are obliged to dress nice if we 'go out' and all I can earn at the havel work goes for clothes.' The Morning Chronicle reporter then wrote about the city's lodging houses: 'Many of the low lodging-houses of Norwich are of the most disgraceful character….One, which I visited during the day, was a public-house. The house itself was in the most wretched state of dilapidation…In one of the rooms, used as a sleeping room, were six beds and a "shake-down" or two on the floor…The adjoining room to this was occupied by the landlady…Two other beds, beside that of the landlady, were in this room, and on one corner, on the floor, I observed what seemed to be another bed.'[21] The window of the first room was broken, the holes being stuffed with paper and rags. Fifteen people had slept in the room the previous night—men and women, married and single.

William Lee, who undertook surveys of public health in towns across England for the General Board of Health, reported on Norwich in 1851. He described conditions in the Jolly Drovers public house (in Ber Street): 'This house I understood to combine the accommodation of a lodging house, a beer house and a brothel…It is impossible that any female could retain the least vestige of delicacy or chastity in such places, whatever she might have had previously…'.[22] Harriet Kettle, may well have lived in conditions like these while she was in Norwich.

There was undoubtedly a significant number of sex workers in mid-19th century Norwich, including some, like Harriet, from the surrounding rural area and others, like the 17 year-old quoted in the Morning Chronicle, whose families had worked in the textile industry in the city and who were driven into prostitution by poverty . Shockingly, from the perspective of the 21st century, girls from the age of 12, (from 1875, 13) were regarded as adult women under the law. There were certainly sex workers in Norwich who, like Harriet, were under the age of 16—as was the case for the three girls Elizabeth Frost (15), Elizabeth Smart (13) and Matilda Staff (15) who were brought before the Mayor on 10 January 1859 on a charge of soliciting: 'They all three told a most disgusting story, unfit for publication, of the life they had led, and what houses they frequented.' They were discharged but warned that if they were brought up again they would be punished.[23] It was not until the passage of the Criminal Law Amendment Act of 1885 that sex with a girl under 16 became illegal. Before then, despite prostitution being referred to as the 'great social evil', the authorities had often tended to adopt a laissez-faire attitude. Soliciting was not illegal and, providing it was reasonably discreet, there was a disinclination to interfere in what was seen as a private matter. As one writer puts it, 'the attitude of authority towards prostitutes, like that of society as a whole, was often a rather shame-faced acquiescence in a necessary evil'.[24] In Norwich, however, as elsewhere in

England, attitudes appear to have hardened in the late 1850s and 1860s.

From the 1830s onwards, in Norwich as elsewhere, there were those who, influenced by evangelical Christianity, campaigned for what they saw as the much-needed improvement of public morality. They saw the temptations offered by prostitutes to men as a threat to Christian family life.[25] The Norfolk and Norwich Society for Protecting Young Females and for Preventing the Vice of Prostitution was founded in 1845, on the model of a similarly-named society formed in London (where the issue received much more notice) over a decade earlier. Similar organisations were established in other provincial cities. The success of such societies in securing changes in the law was limited: a Brothels Suppression Bill introduced in the House of Lords in 1844 was withdrawn; a Suppression of Prostitution Bill moved in the Lords by the Bishop of Norwich (who was Chair of the Norfolk and Norwich Society) in 1847 was also withdrawn; and an 'Act to protect women from Fraudulent Practices for Procuring their Defilement' was passed in 1849 but had limited effect.[26]

In Norwich, however, the campaigners began to have some impact by focusing on the implementation of the licensing laws. On 13 September 1845, a deputation from the Norfolk and Norwich Society, including JJ Gurney of the Quaker banking family, invaded the Norwich magistrates' general annual licensing meeting, Gurney stating that the information gathered by the society 'satisfied them, that many public houses were perverted to the purposes of... vice in a most awful degree; and they also knew of many private houses which were used for the same purposes. The extreme youth of many of the unfortunate victims to this vice was pointed out; and Mr Gurney invited the close attention of the magistrates to the subject; earnestly desiring that they would withhold all licenses from persons who were known, through the police, to be in the practice of encouraging prostitution.'[27] The magistrates expressed agreement in principle but cited practical difficulties. They did not want to deprive licensees of their livelihood and could only intervene if they received complaints from two ratepayers prepared to make representations against a house deemed disorderly because it harboured 'thieves and prostitutes'. Few ratepayers, apparently, were prepared to take such a course of action. Nevertheless, the Society's campaign made some headway. In December 1847, its committee sent thanks to the local magistrates at the most recent annual licensing meeting, because they, 'refused licenses to a considerable number of public houses of notoriously immoral character'. Nevertheless, the problem remained.

Six years later, by which time Harriet was in Norwich, it was reported during the magistrates' licensing meeting on 30 August 1853 that the police had filed two reports on the Grapes, in Dove Lane, '...the first stating that the house had been open till three o'clock in the morning, [and] that five or six prostitutes, besides men, were in the house, making a great noise. Another report stated, that this very Tuesday morning, August 30th, the house was open until 2h 30m the company consisting chiefly of girls of the town. Mrs Bowen, the present occupier of the house, in answer to questions, said, she had no explanation to give. She could take no money in the day time, and if she did not keep open at night, she could not take enough money to pay the rent and rates....Mr Springfield—But the police report that you had a lot of prostitutes in the house. Mrs Bowen— Well, Sir, and where's the house that has not?'[28]

In January 1856, a memorial from a group of inhabitants of St Stephen's Parish to the Norwich magistrates adopted a tone of righteous outrage: 'For some time past, we have earnestly endeavoured...to promote a better observance of the Lord's Day, and generally to diminish the grievous amount of local demoralisation, which unhappily exists. But our efforts...have proved almost wholly unsuccessful: in consequence...of the facilities afforded to vice and immorality, by public houses of the lowest description.'

They continued: 'Into these houses, the constant resort of dissolute persons of both sexes, none can enter, without being tempted to sinful courses, and incurring, to a certain extent at least, moral contamination. They form receptacles in which improvidence, depravity and crime are harboured and fostered: the temptations found within their walls, bring misery into families, and ruin to individuals; and the baneful influence, which proceeds from them, affects but too visibly, that portion of the population, more immediately exposed to it. It is unnecessary to dilate upon the scenes nightly occurring in those haunts of iniquity, since their character must be well known to the police...'

The memorialists appealed to the magistrates to take action, by directing the police to keep the houses concerned under observation. The chief constable, however, said that the account was 'highly coloured', adding that, 'there were very few parishes in Norwich in which the public-houses were better conducted.'[29]

Five years later, in 1861, the recorder [resident judge] in Norwich, PF O'Malley, QC[30], addressing the grand jury at the beginning of the city's Michaelmas quarter sessions, reminded them of Queen Victoria's revised proclamation of June 1860 against vice and immorality and urged that more action be taken. The grand jury duly called the attention of the magistrates to the issue. Later in the same week, O'Malley lamented that, 'last sessions, he found that public-houses, whose licenses were regularly renewed by the magistrates, were dens of infamy; and he also found that there were streets in the city along which a decent man could not walk without running the risk of being robbed. There were streets full of brothels...'[31] It would seem that his blandishments did not fall on deaf ears, as the number of cases of refusal of licenses and prosecutions of publicans and lodging house keepers does appear to have increased sharply over the following two years. Norwich was reflecting, and perhaps anticipating, a national trend; as a result of more rigorous implementation of the licensing laws, the number of public houses across the country that let out rooms to prostitutes declined significantly in the late 1860s.[32]

Although there was a general recognition that prostitution was widespread in Norwich, there was a lack of consensus about exactly how many sex workers and how many brothels there were in the city. In Great Yarmouth, the police produced precise statistics in 1863: the town had 130 prostitutes over 16 and

The 1851 Census shows three 'ladies of pleasure' living in Row 32, Great Yarmouth—Mary A Powles, Elizabeth Brewer and Diana Watts (TNA: HO107 1806).

16 under 16; and there were 32 brothels known or suspected, eight 'low lodging houses', five beershops and 13 public houses, 'where thieves and prostitutes assemble'.[33] In Norwich, by contrast, the estimates ranged widely, with higher figures being given by those who wanted to draw attention to what they saw as a serious problem. The Morning Chronicle, in a report on 29 December 1849, had stated that: 'To such an extent is prostitution carried on in Norwich, that out of the 656 licensed public-houses and beer-shops in the city, there are not less than 220 which are known to the police as common brothels. And although the authorities have the power of withholding the licenses, nothing is done to put a stop to this frightful vice.'[34] In July 1853, the chief constable of the city, appearing before a select committee of the House of Commons, had reported the belief that, 'in the city of Norwich there are 200 houses that are used for the purposes of prostitution, and admitted that, 'it is difficult to supervise them… some of these houses are kept by returned convicts, or by men who have been convicted of felony; and in many of those low public-houses crime is fostered…' It was reported later that this statement had 'excited great surprise'. The chief constable had since retired and in September 1853 his successor stated that in the last 12 months police officers had reported only four houses for harbouring prostitutes, 'and in no single case has an information been laid'.[35] On the other hand, a clergyman, quoted in a newpaper article in 1858[36], claimed that Norwich had 1,100 prostitutes. In 1860, the Revd RC Cavell, rector of St Swithin's Church in the city, gave a lecture on 'the great social evil, viewed particularly in relation to Norwich', in which he expressed the belief that, 'the number of prostitutes

known to the police but very slightly represented the real extent of the evil,' and that Norwich had 139 'houses of ill-fame' while Preston, with a slightly larger population, had only 109.[37]

One reason advanced for the large number of brothels and sex workers in Norwich was that they catered for a wide surrounding rural area as well as for the city itself. During his address to the Grand Jury in 1861, the recorder, O'Malley, lamented that: 'It was a very grievous thing, and a very disgraceful thing, for the citizens of this great city, that they should allow their city and their streets to be turned into houses of ill-fame for the accommodation of persons who came to their fairs and markets from the adjoining country; for he believed from enquiries he had made that a great deal more of the vice and immorality of the city arose from the conduct of those who came in and frequented the town on those particular occasions than from the inhabitants of the city itself'.[38] O'Malley stated that the city's brothels were, 'frequented by a countless number of persons, many of them in a higher station of life'. Although blaming outsiders is a time-honoured response to a social problem, local press reports do bear out the claim that some, at least, of the sex workers' clients came into the city from the surrounding countryside and that they included prosperous and outwardly respectable people, like the two gentlemen who, 'were persons in a different station in life from those with whom the bench usually deals', who were fined £1 each for obstructing the efforts of a police constable to arrest two 'well-known and smartly-attired' prostitutes whom they were with (in King Street) at the time.[39]

Many of the public houses and brothels which caused concern to the authorities were clustered around the Market Place, in Goat Lane, Dove Lane, Weavers' Lane (where the Prince Regent public house was particularly notorious), Gun Lane (near Theatre Street), St Giles Street and Bethel Street. Those in St Stephen's Street, Red Lion Street, Rampant Horse Street, King Street, Pump Street (adjacent to King Street and Rose Lane) and Charlotte Street (location unknown) also attracted attention. Some of these public houses had additional facilities that drew in customers. Fiddling and dancing took place at the Curriers' Arms, St Giles Street; the Coach and Horses in Red Lion Street had a popular ninepin ground; and the George in St Stephen's provided 'a long room...where dancing was allowed'. In January 1863, the Alhambra, at St Stephen's Gates, which staged performances of singing, plays and a circus in a wooden structure originally erected for equestrian shows, was presented by the grand jury, at the instigation of the recorder, 'as a common nuisance, on the ground that it attracts a large number of the boys and girls of our city in company with thieves and prostitutes and appears thus to be the cause of much demoralization; that being a slight and temporary building the music can be heard outside, and thus attracts a vast crowd, whose ribaldry and obscene language are constantly heard by passers-by; and that the noise from evening and early morning is such as seriously to affect the comfort of residents in the neighbourhood'.[40] Chapel Field was another notorious area; in 1852, the Norfolk Chronicle reported that it, 'has been for some time infested with thieves and prostitutes and a couple of constables should be stationed there to protect people passing through the field at night'.[41]

One feature of prostitution in Norwich which appears to have really upset the authorities and those who considered themselves respectable was its 'open, bare-faced'[42] and public nature. In 21st century parlance, it was 'in the face' of the city's population, particularly around the Market Place. On 13 May 1857, for example, 'Hannah Colby and Elizabeth Gilbert, two prostitutes, were charged with having made use of obscene language in the Market-place yesterday afternoon, to the annoyance of respectable parties in the vicinity. Col. Beckham stated that he was walking out with his daughters in the Market-place; and the prisoners, who were on the flags, accosted some sailors, saying, "who's your hatter?" and asking them for drink in terms of the most obscene character.' They had to pay a fine of 40 shillings or face imprisonment for 14 days.[43] In May 1863, Hannah Roberts was in St Stephen's Street, using obscene language and, 'shouting at the top of her voice, and there were a great many respectable females passing up and down on either side of the street at the time'.[44]

Later that year, under the heading, 'The Charlotte Street Nuisance'. The Norfolk Chronicle reported: 'Six young females, all prostitutes…were charged…with loitering in Charlotte-street, on the previous evening, for the purpose of prostitution. In consequence of repeated complaints on the part of the inhabitants of this street, which is infested every evening with troops of prostitutes who insult almost every passer by, and make use of the most filthy language, the magistrates have determined, if possible, to abate the nuisance, and instructions have been issued to the police, to take into custody all girls loitering in the locality. The defendants were observed loitering in the street and obstructing the traffic, and upon being ordered to "move on" by the constable, they indecently exposed themselves and defied the officer…'[45] Three of them were discharged with a caution but two were sentenced to seven days, and one to 14 days, imprisonment. There were four other prosecutions connected with prostitution in Charlotte Street in 1863, indicative of the police crack-down in the area that year.

Another concern was the number of robberies that occurred in connection with the sex industry, details of offences of this kind appearing regularly in the pages of the local press, to such an extent that the absence of those accused of 'brothel robberies' before the quarter sessions of January 1863 was in itself worthy of comment. Not all of the robberies by prostitutes actually occurred in brothels; some happened in the street, the woman engaging a potential client in conversation and carrying out the theft while a male accomplice received the stolen item or jumped on the victim to prevent a pursuit. Those cases of robbery by sex workers that came to court were the tip of the iceberg: as the inspector of constabulary noted in 1862, cases were frequently not proceeded with because, 'a great many larcenies from the person were committed by prostitutes on men drunk, who, when sober, were ashamed to appear as prosecutors'.[46] Others, no doubt, were not notified to the police at all. The recorder, speaking after a case heard during the Norwich quarter sessions in October 1862, blamed the landlords of the houses in which the crimes took place more than the sex workers, as they were often complicit in the thefts: 'Experience taught them to discriminate between those who were likely to be afraid of exposure and those who were not; and when they found a married man or anyone else who would be afraid of exposure, indiscreet enough to venture into their houses, the result was, in nine instances out of ten, that the robberies committed escaped detection.'

One case that did come to court, the report on which is worth reproducing in full because, in some respects, it is typical and illustrates the *modus operandi* of the sex workers, is the following: 'Emily Scotter (17) and Georgina Cooper (18), prostitutes, were charged with stealing from the person of Henry Moore, nine promissory notes of the value of £10 each, a bill of exchange, four sovereigns and a half, and other money. Scotter pleaded guilty and Cooper was placed on her trial....Moore is a farmer, residing at Great Hautbois, and on the 14th Jan. last was in Norwich, and cashed a cheque for £100 at Messrs Gurney's bank. He received the money in nine £10 Bank of England notes, and ten sovereigns; and after putting the money in his pocket, he went to the "Old Goat Tavern" in Goat-lane, where he met the prisoner Scotter. He spoke to her, and after some conversation, they proceeded together to the Guildhall Tavern, opposite the Guildhall, where they saw the other prisoner Cooper. The two girls appeared to know each other, and got into conversation; and after having something to drink at the expense of the prosecutor, they all three proceeded together to a brothel in Gun-lane, and went into an upstairs room. After they had been in the room some time, the landlady of the house observed the prisoner Scotter leave in a hurried manner, and thinking that something was wrong, she went upstairs and asked the prosecutor if he had lost anything. The prosecutor felt in his pockets and ascertained that his money had been stolen. Accompanied by the landlord, he at once proceeded to the police station, and an officer went in search of the girls, whom he found in a low house in the Chequers-yard. When the officer entered the room, the prisoner Scotter put her hand into her bosom and took out something, which she dropped upon the ground; and upon the officer picking it up, he found that it was a bundle of Bank of England notes. The officer then desired Scotter to turn her pocket out, which she did, and produced several memorandums, which were identified by the prosecutor as his property. The prisoner Cooper was acquitted. Scotter was sentenced to a year's imprisonment, with hard labour.'[47]

Henry Moore, according to the census returns of 1861, was an unmarried man of 45 who employed five men on his farm. An unusual feature of this case was the amount of money involved: £100 in 1862 would be worth about £10,250 today.[48] This, no doubt, is why Henry Moore was willing to press the prosecution; it may also be part of the reason why the landlord, perhaps hopeful of a reward and certainly anxious not to be associated with the crime, was willing to assist. Most thefts in brothels involved smaller sums or articles such as a pocket-watch. That Henry Moore was unmarried may have made him less concerned that his name appeared in the papers in connection with the case. A more typical feature of the case was that the women, like Harriet Clark and Mary Ann Hubbard in the example quoted at the beginning of this chapter, worked as a pair; many sex workers did so, 'both to protect themselves from abusive men and to overpower and rob tipsy customers'.[49]

Apart from the risk of prosecution, there were other dark sides to the lives of prostitutes in Victorian Norwich. The Revd RC Cavell, in his lecture on 'the great social evil' in 1860, after referring to the number of brothels in the city, added: 'The mere statistics, however, conveyed no idea of the brutality that existed… such a girl, on the average, lived but six years, and very frequently only six months…'[50] That may have been an exaggeration, but sex workers undoubtedly experienced abuse and violence. One example from Norwich in 1860 involved a dealer from Great Yarmouth called Barwell who spent the night with a prostitute, Frances Bidwell, in Weavers' Lane and in the morning accused her of taking money from his trousers. 'The prisoner denied having touched the prosecutor's trousers, and said he treated her brutally both during the night and in the morning…He tore her bonnet and dress to pieces and beat her black and blue.' Frances was then asked if she wished to bring a charge of assault against Barwell, and she replied that she did. The report continued: 'The female searcher stated that she had examined the woman, and found many marks of violence about her person, which corroborated her statement as to the ill-treatment she had received from Barwell.' Barwell was sentenced to three months' imprisonment.[51] No doubt there were other such incidents that did not come to court.

How Harriet Kettle spent her time as 'a girl on the town' in Norwich—where she lived and with whom, and which public or private houses she used for her sex work—is unknown. Nor is it known why she decided to return to Gressenhall workhouse: perhaps she had been a victim of violence, or had become ill, or was pregnant or had had a child. A later source (of 1861) indicates that Harriet had

had no children[52], but in another (of 1863) it is stated that she had had several[53]; there is no way of telling which source is the more reliable. Or perhaps work had become less plentiful. As Judith Walkowitz observes: 'Some women had such difficulty living on the proceeds of prostitution that they had to resort to the workhouse…in off seasons.'[54]

Harriet's motives are unknown, but return to Gressenhall workhouse she did.

Notes

1   The main source for the first dozen paragraphs of this chapter is the MLU minutes; NRO, C/GP14/2, 6-12.
2   TNA: MH12 8478/181.
3   Sixty guardians were elected, or in a few cases continued their service, in April 1851, with three parishes having no representative at that time. Three guardians represented two parishes each. The details of all but one of the elected guardians (or, in two cases, those of their wives) were found in the 1851 census returns; 52 out of the 60 were farmers, including one who was also a landowner and one who combined farming with milling. The analysis of the ages of the 57 guardians whose ages were found, and of the acreages of the farms of those who were farmers, is based on information from the census returns.
4   An analysis by Rose Sheen of the attendance at the weekly meetings of the guardians between 30 May 1859 and 16 July 1860 shows that the average attendance was 18.63, and the range 10 to 40.
5   NM, 18 September 1852; Letter from the clerk of the board of guardians of MLU to the PLB, 17 July 1865. This letter summarises the occasions when Harriet was sentenced to imprisonment between 1852 and 1856.
6   Helen Gordon, *The Prisoner—a Sketch* (1911), quoted by P Priestley (1999).
7   George Laval Chesterton, *Revelations of Prison Life* (1856), quoted by P Priestley (1999).
8   The offence on this occasion was not recorded in MLU minutes.
9   Equivalent to about £2,050 today; Office for National Statistics composite price index, accessed 16/06/2020.
10 NC, 15 October 1853.
11 CLA, case book 1853-1861; NRO, SAH 262.
12 CLA, case book 1861-5; NRO, SAH 263.
13 As illustrated by the biographies of inmates of Gressenhall workhouse produced by members of the Gressenhall workhouse research community.
14 Return relating to Workhouse and District Schools, PP LV, 1861.
15 On 1 February 1841, Honor Dickerson had been in trouble and confined in the 'dungeon' for eight hours for 'throwing some bread over into the able bodied men's ward', presumably to her husband, James. However, there were no further disciplinary episodes. In 1844, she was given £1, 'as a reward for good conduct and for her services as a laundry woman, and the following year she received a similar 'gratuitous remuneration'. Later she lived in London, until 1868, when she was 'removed' to her parish of Little Fransham. MLU minutes; NRO, C/GP14/4, 6, 20.
16 However, Eliza Dunham was back in Gressenhall workhouse in 1859. On 26 December

1859 she and another inmate, Mary Tennant of Shipdham, were charged with disorderly and violent behaviour, and were deprived of their Christmas dinner—which appears to have been served on Boxing Day rather than Christmas Day. MLU minutes; NRO, C/GP14/7, 15.

17 The extent of venereal disease became a national scandal during the Crimean War, when significant proportions of those serving in the British army and navy were found to be affected. Legislation to regulate prostitution in the vicinity of garrison towns and naval ports was introduced 1864, 1866 and 1869, but, following a campaign led by Josephine Butler, was suspended in 1883 and repealed in 1886.

18 J R Walkowitz (1980).

19 John Pound, 'Poverty and Public Health in Norwich, 1845-1880', in C Barringer (1984); R O'Donoghue (2014).

20 MC, 12 December 1849.

21 MC, 15 December 1849.

22 William Lee, *Report to the General Board of Health on a preliminary enquiry into the Sewerage, Drainage and Supply of Water, and the Sanitary Conditions of the Inhabitants of the City of Norwich* (1851).

23 NC, 15 January 1859.

24 K Chesney (1970).

25 J R Walkowitz (1980).

26 T Fisher (2001).

27 NC, 13 September 1845.

28 NC, 3 September 1853.

29 NC, 5 January 1856.

30 He had been appointed Recorder in 1859.

31 NC, 19 October 1861.

32 J R Walkowitz (1980).

33 NC, 24 October 1863.

34 MC, 29 December 1849.

35 NC, 3 September 1853.

36 NC, 20 November 1858.

37 NC, 12 May 1860.

38 NC, 19 October 1861.

39 NC, 28 March 1863.

40 NC, 10 January 1863.

41 NC, 24 December 1852.

42 The words of the Recorder addressing the Grand Jury at the Michaelmas Quarter Sessions, 1861; NC, 19 October 1861.

43 NC, 16 May 1857.

44 NC, 9 May 1863.

45 NC, 25 July 1863.

46 NC, 5 April 1862.

47 NN, 31 March 1860.

48 Office for National Statistics composite price index, accessed 16/06/2020.

49 J R Walkowitz (1980).

50 NC, 12 May 1860.

51 NC, 18 February 1860.
52 Criminal patients' admission register, BM ARD02.
53 CLA, case book 1861-65; NRO, SAH 263.
54 J R Walkowitz (1980).

In Walsingham House of Correction

IT is not clear exactly when Harriet went back to the Gressenhall workhouse, or how long she had been there before her name appeared again in the pages of the minute book of the board of guardians. She may have been back in the workhouse in time to enjoy the Christmas dinner provided on 26 December 1855, and join in the cheers for the guardians. Only 12 days after that, on 7 January 1856, the following appeared in the guardians' minutes: 'Harriet Kettle a person maintained in the workhouse having been refused clothes to leave the same by the board of guardians on her application this day violently refused to perform the task of work ordered by the master and is now accordingly brought before the board and reprimanded by the chairman.'[1] The chairman, as at the time when Harriet had first been imprisoned at Walsingham, was her fellow parishioner the Revd Philip Gurdon, and his response to Harriet's misbehaviour seems mild in the circumstances.

The task refused by Harriet may have been oakum-picking, introduced for able-bodied single women in 1854. Harriet was now 16 or 17, and therefore classified as an able-bodied woman rather than a girl. She would also have been subject to a further sub-classification; in March 1854, it was reported that, of the 67 able-bodied women in the workhouse, 27 were 'of good character', nine were 'of dissolute and abandoned habits' and 31 were 'mothers of illegitimate children but not of dissolute and abandoned habits'.[2] Harriet, undoubtedly, would have come into the second category, the group most likely to have been required to pick oakum. A few years later, in April 1861, the master sent an even more detailed return to the Poor Law Board in which the able-bodied women were listed in no fewer than 20 categories including, for example, 'single women pregnant with their first child' through to 'single women with four or more bastard children' and, by contrast, 'respectable able-bodied women and girls'. As Harriet was not in the workhouse at the time the return was made, there was a nil return for the category, 'prostitute' in which, had she been present, she might have been placed.[3]

If Harriet was required to pick oakum, she was not unique in objecting to it. Male inmates at Gressenhall occasionally refused to do this work or otherwise manifested their dislike of it. So too did a young woman from another workhouse,

Milford & Launditch Union.

APR 1861

A RETURN of all FEMALE PAUPERS of the Age of 16 years and upwards in the Workhouse on the   *ninth*   day of March 1861, classified according to character.

		TOTAL
1.	Single women pregnant with their first child	1
2.	Single women who have had one bastard child	5
3.	Single women who have had one bastard child and are pregnant again	4
4.	Single women who have had two bastard children	3
5.	Single women who have had three bastard children	3
6.	Single women who have had four or more bastard children	3
7.	Idiotic or weak-minded single women with one or more bastard children	
8.	Women whose out-relief has been taken off on account of misconduct	
9.	Women incapable of getting their own living from syphilis	
10.	Prostitutes	
11.	Girls who have been out at service, but do not keep their places on account of misconduct	1
12.	Girls brought up in the Workhouse and who have been out at service, but have returned on account of misconduct	3
13.	Widows who have had one or more bastard children during their widowhood	4
14.	Married women with husbands in the Workhouse	4
15.	Married women with husbands transported or in gaol	
16.	Married women deserted by their husbands	3
17.	Imbecile, idiotic, or weak-minded women and girls	7
18.	Respectable women and girls incapable of getting their living on account of illness or other bodily defect or infirmity	1
19.	Respectable able-bodied women and girls	6
20.	Respectable aged women	7
		63

I certify the above return as correct,

W. N. Scraggs

Master of the Workhouse.

2234.   E. & S.—750,—3/61.

Gressenhall, return of female inmates classified according to character, 1861 (TNA: MH32 84).

where oakum-picking had been introduced earlier than at Gressenhall, who was a prisoner in Wymondham house of correction when it was visited by an inspector of prisons, Mr Hill, in 1850. He reported that the woman, 'had been committed nine times for misconduct in a workhouse; her offence, I was informed, being a refusal to work. The matron of the prison spoke very highly of her conduct in all respects in the prison, and said that she worked very industriously, and was always very respectful. The reason the young woman gave for refusing to work in the workhouse was, that she was set to pick oakum, which she looked on as the labour of a felon; while in the prison she was employed in washing the clothes.'[4] Harriet, who had experience of laundry work, may have had a similar opinion of oakum-picking.

The 'Wash-house' at Brixton Prison from Henry Mayhew and John Binney, The Criminal Prisons of London and Scenes of Prison Life, pub. 1862.

The guardians probably took the view that, if Harriet had no offer of a position, they were justified in not issuing her with clothing. Harriet's fury may have been occasioned partly by the loss of the clothes that she had been wearing on re-admission to the workhouse. According to the General Order (Consolidated) issued by the Poor Law Board in July 1847, the clothes worn by an inmate when admitted, 'shall be purified and deposited in a place appropriated for that purpose, with the pauper's name affixed thereto. Such clothes shall be restored to the pauper when he [sic] leaves the Workhouse.' Harriet, on admission, may have been wearing clothes acquired for, and funded by, her sex work, and no doubt in Norwich as elsewhere, 'the dress code of prostitutes served as a way of advertising themselves and attracting male customers'.[5] It is tempting to speculate that Harriet's clothes were deemed unsuitable to be returned to her and were therefore 'lost'.[6]

The position of a young person in Harriet's situation was referred to in a letter by the master of Gressenhall workhouse, Henry Harrison, to Sir John Walsham, poor law inspector, dated 8 April 1856 and written after two girls had absconded from the workhouse a week previously. 'I hope you will excuse my troubling you,' he wrote, 'but I am placed in rather an awkward position. We have some boys and girls above sixteen years of age: they have made application to the board for a suit of clothes to enable them to leave the house in search of employment, they having been here from ten to twelve years, have none of their own. The board having refused their request two have since absconded. Can I take proceedings against them. When turned of sixteen and they give me notice to leave the house and have no clothes of their own, I cannot turn them out naked and yet I cannot give them clothes…I shall be much obliged if you will advise me how to act.' Sir John asked the Poor Law Board for guidance, and they appear to have advised that, after giving notice, inmates should be able to leave the institution wearing the workhouse clothes.[7]

Only two weeks after the board's refusal to give Harriet clothes to leave Gressenhall workhouse, there was another incident. Harriet was brought before the guardians on 21 January 1856 'charged with great misbehaviour in the workhouse and with threats and violent conduct towards the officers of the house'.[8] It would appear from later sources that her violent conduct on this occasion included an assault on the master.[9] Once again, the guardians ordered that she be taken before a magistrate and this time she was sentenced to 21 days in Walsingham house of correction.

Harriet had already been in Walsingham house of correction on several occasions: twice in the autumn of 1852, once in January 1853 and once in January 1855. Now, in 1856, she was to spend longer there than she would have imagined. After serving her 21 days' sentence Harriet was required to give sureties to keep the peace and was unable to do so—who would have provided such sureties? The result was that she received a new sentence of a full year's imprisonment.

Walsingham house of correction, in the village of Little Walsingham in North Norfolk, was a small local prison. Based on plans for a model prison produced by the prison reformer John Howard, it had been constructed as a 'bridewell' with eight cells in 1787 and became a county house of correction in 1822. Four treadwheels, for grinding corn, were installed in 1823, making the house of correction one of the 54 local prisons in England and Wales which possessed such a facility by 1824.[10] There was a fifth treadwheel for the use of juvenile offenders. A new chapel was built in 1825. In 1836, there were six wards, six day rooms and three solitary cells.[11] Later modifications and further

A 6 bay treadwheel (Walsingham had 5) fitted in Beaumaris Gaol and House of Correction in 1867. It is the last surviving example in a British prison, 1984.

extensions raised the number of cells to 32.[12] An inspector of prisons visiting on 8 October 1857 found that there were separate cells for 24 males and seven females, with room to accommodate up to 20 additional prisoners, including debtors 'in association'; in other words, in communal cells.[13] The thirty second cell may have been a punishment cell, or the padded cell referred to in December 1858, with which Harriet Kettle may have become acquainted.[14] The buildings at Walsingham house of correction appear to have been healthier than those of many other local prisons in England at the time. On 8 December 1853, an inspector of prisons found that although, 'fever had been prevalent in the town of Walsingham', there had been no cases in the prison, which the surgeon attributed to, 'the thorough ventilation and perfect sanitary arrangements'.[15] Efforts to improve the ventilation, noted in an inspector's report of 1850, had clearly paid off.

The provision of separate cells for prisoners received strong official support in the 1830s, and influenced the design of new prisons such as Pentonville, opened in 1842. As a result, across the country, the period 1830-50 saw, 'a sustained effort to reconstruct the prison along separatist lines'.[16] The 'separate system' was believed to be the most effective way of preventing communication among those detained, ensuring that younger inmates would be protected from corruption by the more experienced offenders, and facilitating the reform of the characters of all the prisoners, an undertaking in which prison chaplains played a key role. An alternative approach which, like the separate system, originated in the United States, was the 'silent system' under which prisoners were able to associate but communication among them was forbidden and punished when it occurred. The difference between the two systems was summed up by the Revd Daniel Nihill, governor of Millbank prison, in 1839: 'Under the silent system, the prisoners are collected in masses for work and other purposes, but are forbidden to speak or hold any intercourse; under the separate system they

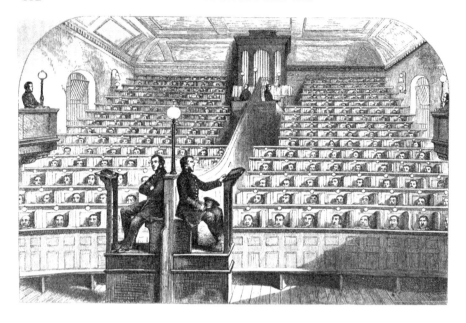

Examples of the two prison systems: above, the chapel at Pentonville under the 'separate' system, below, The work room at Tothill Fields under the 'silent' system. From Henry Mayhew and John Binney, The Criminal Prisons of London and Scenes of Prison Life, pub. 1862.

are precluded from intercourse, by being kept not only in silence, but separation at all times.'[17] The separate system went out of fashion from the 1850s onwards, partly because it was thought to drive prisoners mad; the silent system, however, could lead to a multiplication of disciplinary incidents and it may have been for this reason that reformers like FW Keppel disliked it.[18] In practice, what emerged in many prisons, Walsingham house of correction included, was a compromise, with separate cells for sleeping and eating, and silent association during periods of work, worship and exercise. The regime in prisons across the country became more uniform and harsher after the Prison Act of 1865, which implemented many of the recommendations of the select committee of the House of Lords on gaol discipline (the Carnavon committee) of 1863. Following 'nationaliation' as a result of the Prison Act of 1877, when all prisons were brought under the control of central government, the harshness increased further under the leadership of Sir Edmund Du Cane, chairman of the national Prison Commission, and the emphasis on the reform of prisoners diminished. Deterrence and repression became the dominant priorities. Although she would not have seen it that way, Harriet was, perhaps, fortunate to have experienced prison before rather than after 1865.[19]

The silent system was adopted at Walsingham in 1836 and in 1841 the chaplain expressed the view that it had, 'done much…to diminish the number of reports for misconduct'. A similar note was struck in White's Directory of Norfolk in 1845, where it was stated that at Walsingham, 'the "silent system"… is found to be very beneficial, by preventing the prisoners from instructing each other in their nefarious arts.' However, the chaplain also urged the adoption of, 'better arrangements for every prisoner to have a separate sleeping cell' and an inspector of prisons, reporting in 1842, quoted him, endorsed his sentiments and stated that an addition to the number of separate sleeping cells was contemplated. When an inspector visited in 1850, he noted with approbation that the magistrates had implemented nearly all the recommendations he had made on a previous visit, regarding 'preparing cells to be used for separate confinement (and) a more complete classification of the prisoners with reference to age, previous conviction and general character'.[20]

The number of prisoners in Walsingham house of correction varied from year to year, but there were always more males than females; Harriet Kettle, in 1856, was one of a small minority of women prisoners. The total numbers imprisoned stood at 43 males and 18 females in November 1852, but declined steadily to an average of 20 males and five females in 1859. According to figures provided by an inspector of prisons following his visit on 6 October 1857, most were serving short sentences of up to four months, but a few were awaiting transportation or transfer to one of the national convict prisons, such as Millbank and Pentonville.

He quoted the chaplain's statement: 'we have very few prisoners who are 'habitual criminals'; a large proportion of our offenders are labouring men, who return to their accustomed employment on their discharge from prison, and never return to us again.' A year later, in December 1858,[21] many of those punished were reported to be at Walsingham for short periods of time of up to two months, 'for minor offences by persons committed from the union workhouse'.

Under the provisions of the Gaol Act of 1823, introduced by the home secretary, Robert (later Sir Robert) Peel, at the instigation of the prison reformer Elizabeth Fry, among others, justices of the peace were required to visit the prisons within their areas regularly and send reports to the home office; consequently, oversight of Walsingham house of correction became the responsibility of a committee of visiting justices, or magistrates. The legislation also required that a chaplain and a surgeon should visit the prisoners, that the gaolers should be paid, that male and female prisoners should be kept separate and that the latter should be supervised by female warders. Although it 'marked a dramatically intensified effort to impose uniformity throughout the country,'[22] the Gaol Act was not fully effective until, under the provisions of the Prisons Act of 1835, five paid inspectors of prisons were appointed to enforce its provisions. As has been seen, these inspectors actively promoted the separate system and other reforms in the management of prisons.

From July 1824, the keeper, or governor, of the house of correction was Money Curtis, whose salary was £200 per year, a substantial income. According to the census returns, he was aged 56 in 1851. His wife, Margaret Curtis, was earning £34 per year as matron. She was seven years older than her husband, and had been appointed as matron in May 1835. In the same year, Money Curtis assisted in arresting rioters against the new Poor Law at Bircham in Docking Union and conveying them to Walsingham.[23] Mr and Mrs Curtis were praised by an inspector of prisons following his inspection in 1850, and Money Curtis was again praised after an inspection in 1852, as, 'most zealous and attentive to his duties'.[24] The report of an incident in December 1852, concerning the escape of a prisoner being transported to Walsingham, illustrates his zeal and suggests that Money Curtis still had plenty of vigour and determination, although admittedly the report must have been based on his own account. 'On his way to Walsingham, at a place called Slade Heath, between Gunthorpe and Thursford, the prisoner sprang from the gig, although his legs were strapped and locked on. Mr C. immediately jumped out after the man, when the wheel of the gig, unfortunately, passed over his leg; he, however, closely pursued the prisoner into the wood, came up with him in the midst of a thicket and coming out therefrom; Mr C. demanded his surrender, which he positively refused; and, in the exercise of his just authority, Mr C. struck him on the arm with a stick he happened to have with him. The prisoner then knocked him down and knelt upon his body several minutes; during this time he made an unsuccessful effort to abstract a knife from Mr C's pocket, which the prisoner knew was therein, as it belonged to him. While keeping Mr C. down by kneeling on his body, the prisoner by some instrument (stone or stick) knocked off the locks, and consequently made his escape. Fortunately, Mr C was not much hurt, but suffered great soreness for several days.'[25] The fugitive was caught and brought before the quarter sessions on 9 March 1853. He pleaded guilty to the escape and assault, and was sentenced to six months' imprisonment with hard labour at Walsingham—'but, at the request of Mr Curtis, his place of imprisonment was changed to Norwich Castle'.[26] Perhaps, as he neared retirement, Money Curtis wanted a quiet life. Harriet Kettle, it became apparent four years later, was not the person to give him that.

Like the governor, the 'first turnkey' or warder, William Woodcock, whose salary was £60 per year, was a long-serving employee, having been appointed in February 1837. There was also an assistant turnkey, whose duties included working as the schoolmaster. According to the report on an inspector's visit on 19 November 1852, his day was long, beginning at 6 am and not finishing until 9 pm, with two and a half hours devoted to instruction in the evening.[27] The report following an inspection on 8 October 1857, however, indicated that the evening school was held for only 'about an hour and a half'.[28]

The surgeon, Hugh Rump of Wells, had been appointed in January 1830 and served for 31 years; attending the prison was just part, and probably a very small part, of his work. The chaplain, however, was a full-time employee. From July 1853, the post was held by Henry Kitton, who described his duties thus: 'The chaplain reads prayers and a portion of the scriptures every morning, in the chapel, and lectures on the scriptures read. He sees the prisoners privately in his own room and in their cells; assembles them also in the schoolrooms for religious instruction; superintends the distribution of books; reads prayers twice and preaches twice every Sunday, and devotes all his time in fact to the promotion of the welfare of his prison charge.'[29] Kitton resigned in 1857 and was replaced by NG Pilkington who, like his predecessor, took his duties of 'reforming' and educating the prisoners very seriously.

When Harriet Kettle arrived at Walsingham house of correction in January 1856, she would have already been familiar, from her previous periods of imprisonment, with the governor and first turnkey, and with the reception routine. Had she been carrying personal property, she would have had to surrender it, but it seems unlikely that she had any. Prisoners had to take off their own clothing and, after having a bath, don prison garb, have their hair cut, receive a cursory medical examination and listen while the rules were read to

Rules and Regulations

TO BE OBSERVED IN THE

House of Correction,

AT

LITTLE WALSINGHAM,

In the County of Norfolk.

THE KEEPER of the said House of Correction shall have power to hear all complaints touching any of the following offences, committed by Prisoners of any description: (that is to say) disobedience of any of the Rules of the Prison, assaults by one person confined in such Prison upon another, when no dangerous wound or bruise is given, profane cursing and swearing, any indecent behaviour and any irreverent behaviour at chapel, and also touching any of the following offences committed by any Prisoner under charge or conviction of any Crime: (that is to say) absence from Chapel without leave, idleness or negligence in work, or wilful mismanagement of it; and the said Keeper may examine any person touching the several offences, and may determine thereupon, and may punish all such Offences by ordering any Offender to close confinement in the refractory or solitary Cells, and by keeping such Offender upon Bread and water only, for any term not exceeding three days; and in case any Criminal Prisoner shall be guilty of any repeated Offence against the Rules of the Prison, or shall be guilty of any greater Offence than the Duties of the Keeper is empowered to punish, the said Keeper shall forthwith report the same to the visiting Justices, or one of them, and any such Justice, or any other Justice, shall have power to enquire upon Oath, and to determine concerning any such matter so reported to him or them, and to order the Offender to be punished by close confinement for any term not exceeding one Month, or by personal correction in the Cases of Prisoners convicted of Felony or sentenced to hard labour.

IF ANY PRISONER shall be of a Religious persuasion differing from that of the Established Church, a Minister of such persuasion, at the special request of such Prisoner, shall be allowed to visit him or her at proper and reasonable times, under such restrictions imposed by the visiting Justices, as shall guard against the introduction of improper Persons, and as shall prevent improper communications.

WARDSMEN shall be selected from such of the Prisoners as are most orderly and best qualified for the purpose. They shall sweep the Cells, Work rooms, Day-rooms, Stair case, and Galleries of the Classes under their care once every Morning, and shall wash the Day-rooms and Stair cases, at least once every week, and other parts of the Prison as often as shall be required. They shall in dry weather see that all the Doors and Windows of the night Cells be kept open, and the bedding frequently beat and put out to air. They shall attend to the cleanliness of every part of the Wards and Airing Yards committed to their care, and to the maintenance of decency and good order therein. And shall for the performance of these Duties receive such increased Prison allowance as the visiting Justices shall from time to time direct, and shall be entitled to such share of the earnings of their Classes as the Rules shall respectively prescribe, and they shall not be permitted to receive any fee or gratuity on any account whatever.

NO PRISONER convicted of Felony, or of misdemeanor, and sentenced to hard labour, shall receive any food, clothing, or necessaries, other than the Gaol allowance, except under special circumstances to be judged of by one or more of the visiting Justices. And all convicted Prisoners shall be placed in the Wards allotted for them immediately after sentence.

THE SEVERAL persons who shall be committed to the House of Correction to be kept to hard labour, shall be employed, unless prevented by ill health, every day during their confinement, except on Sundays, Christmas day, and Good Friday, and on any days appointed by Public Authority for fasting or thanksgiving, or as many hours as the day light in the different seasons of the year will admit, not exceeding ten hours, being allowed thereout to rest half an hour at breakfast, and one hour at dinner.

THE KEEPER shall adapt the various employments which shall be directed by the Justices at the Quarter Sessions, to each person, in such manner as shall be best suited to his or her strength and ability, regard being had to age or sex.

THE RULES for Labour among Male Prisoners, shall be applied, as far as the Case allows, to Female Prisoners, who shall be employed in washing, needlework, and other Female occupations under the direction of the Matron.

EVERY PRISONER, unless under solitary confinement by way of punishment, shall be allowed the benefit of fresh air and exercise for the space of one hour at least every day, either altogether or at different times, at the discretion of the visiting Magistrates. Those who are under solitary confinement, from the circumstances of their case, and not especially by way of punishment, such for instance, as persons under charge or conviction of unnatural Offences, shall exercise in Yards, separately, one hour in each day, at a time when such Yards are unoccupied, by other Prisoners.

WARM and sufficient Clothing shall be provided for every convicted Prisoner, consisting of a woollen cap, jacket, trowsers or breeches, linen shirt, worsted stockings, and shoes. No Prisoner before trial, or person convicted of misdemeanor, and not sentenced to hard labour shall be forced to wear a prison dress, unless his or her clothes shall be found insufficient, or improper, or necessary to be preserved for the purposes of Justice.

THE PRISON allowance shall be to each individual, two pounds of white bread per day; and on Sundays, broth made with meat and vegetables; those who undergo severe labour, and those who are committed for trial, or shall be under sentence for capital offences, may be allowed at the discretion of the visiting Justices, one half pound of white bread in addition; in cold weather the Prisoners may have the water which they drink warmed for them, if they desire it, and all those who work at the Mill may claim a handful of Oatmeal to mix with the water when they leave off work.

PROVISION shall be made for the instruction of Prisoners of both sexes in reading and writing; and this instruction, shall be afforded under such rules and regulations, and to such extent, and to such Prisoners, as to the visiting Justices may seem expedient.

GENERAL REGULATIONS.

THE CELLS shall be unlocked at six o'clock in the Morning, from the first day of April, to the thirtieth day of September, and at sun rise during the remainder of the year.

THE PRISONERS shall be locked up in their Cells at such times as the visiting Justices may deem expedient.

CONVENIENT places for washing shall be provided in each Ward for the Prisoners, who shall be allowed an adequate allowance of soap and towels and combs.

SCALES, Weights, and Measures shall be provided by the Keeper, at the expence of the County, open to the use of any Prisoner.

SUCH ALLOWANCE of fuel shall be ordered by the visiting Justices for the different Wards, as experience shall prove to be requisite.

THE HOURS of beginning and leaving Work, of Meals, and of return to labour shall be notified by the ringing of a Bell, fixed in a proper situation for the purpose.

A WARNING BELL shall be rung every Morning half an hour before the Cells are unlocked, and every Prisoner shall be required to leave his or her Cell as soon as it shall be unlocked.

NO TAP shall be kept in the Prison, nor shall spirituous Liquors of any kind be admitted for the use of any of the Prisoners therein under any pretence whatever unless by a written order of the Surgeon, specifying the quantity and for whose use. No wine, beer, cyder, or other fermented liquors, shall be admitted for the use of any Prisoners, except in such quantities and such manner, and at such times, as shall be allowed by the visiting Justices.

NO GAMING of any kind shall be permitted in any Prison, and the Keeper shall seize and destroy all dice, cards, and other instruments of gaming.

NO MONEY under the name of garnish or any other remuneration, shall be taken from any Prisoner on his or her entrance into the Prison or any other occasion on any pretence whatever.

LEGAL ADVISERS whose attendance shall be required by the Prisoners, shall have free access to such Prisoners, between the hours of unlocking the Cells in the Morning and locking them up in the Evening; but if they shall require to be admitted at other hours, they shall obtain the order of a visiting Justice.

FRIENDS of Prisoners shall be admitted by order of any Magistrate to the visiting Room, three to see such Prisoner in the presence of the Keeper, or other Officer, between the Hours of ten and twelve in the Morning, and two and four in the Afternoon; but no friends shall be permitted to see such Prisoners in private, except by the order of a visiting Justice, or in the case of untried Prisoners of the committing Magistrate. No visitor shall be admitted to see any person under confinement on a Sunday without an Order from a Magistrate.

Rules and Regulations to be observed in the house of correction at Little Walsingham.

them. Rules and regulations for Walsingham house of correction[30] survive; they are undated but were certainly issued after 1823 as they refer to 'work at the mill' but may pre-date 1836 as they make no reference to the silent system.[31] Other rules and regulations were approved by the Home Secretary for use in Norfolk's county gaol and houses of correction in 1848.[32] The document of 1823-36 states that all convicted prisoners at Walsingham were to be issued with 'warm and sufficient clothing' comprising (for men) a woollen cap, jacket, 'trowsers or breeches', linen shirt, worsted stockings and shoes. Remand prisoners, and those convicted of misdemeanors rather than felonies, did not have to wear prison clothes. Nothing was said about the women's clothing.

Harriet Kettle would have been allocated to a separate cell. The cells at Walsingham house of correction survive and can be visited. Typically cheerless, they received limited light and their doors had small openings with gratings cut in them, enabling the warders to observe the occupants. As noted above, separate cells were a key element of the system of discipline at Walsingham house of correction.

The daily routine that Harriet would have experienced at Walsingham was dominated by work. Cells were unlocked at 6 am between 1 April and 30 September and at sunrise for the rest of the year. The prisoners had to work for up to 10 hours every day (except Sundays, Christmas Day and Good Friday), starting at 6.30 am. They had breaks for breakfast (half an hour) and dinner (one hour), which would probably have been spent in their individual cells. As at Gressenhall, a bell was rung to mark the times of work and meals, and a warning bell sounded half an hour before the cells were unlocked in the morning. Prisoners in solitary confinement as a punishment were to have an hour of fresh air and exercise every day. In 1842, a prison inspector had recommended that 'the hours of exercise for the female prisoners should be increased,' and one of the visiting justices had responded immediately by ordering that 'the female prisoners should be permitted to take more than one hour's exercise in the course of the day'.

The work done by male prisoners sentenced to hard labour was on the treadwheels, which was not only hard but could be dangerous. They had to work for up to ten hours a day, the equivalent of climbing a sizeable mountain. The Prison Discipline Society recommended that an ascent of 12,000 feet per day should be required on the treadwheel.[33] The rules and regulations for Walsingham house of correction stated that: 'The rules for labour among male prisoners shall be applied, as far as the case allows, to female prisoners, who shall be employed in washing, needlework and other female occupations under the direction of the matron'. Harriet Kettle had been sentenced to hard labour in 1852 and may have been on other occasions as well. However, the inspector of prisons who visited in 1858 noted that it was only male prisoners who were employed on the treadwheels; the women he observed during his visit were employed in needlework and washing. Perhaps 'hard labour' for Harriet meant a lot of laundry, involving strenuous activities such as stoking the boiler and wringing the wet washing. Other work mentioned by the inspectors of prisons in their reports in the 1850s included mat-making, tailoring, shoemaking, knitting stockings, peg-making and picking oakum. The work, notably the grinding of corn with the treadwheels, made money for the prison; for example, according to the Norfolk County Treasurer's accounts for 1854, the prisoners' labours earned over £29 for the county in that year.[34]

The diet stipulated by the rules and regulations for Walsingham house of correction comprised two pounds of white bread per day, with water to drink, which could be warmed in cold weather. On Sundays, broth made with meat and vegetables was to be served. Prisoners undertaking 'severe labour' and those awaiting trial could have an extra half a pound of bread, and 'all those who work at the mill [on the treadwheels] may claim a handful of oatmeal to mix with the water when they leave off work'. In 1842, an inspector had recommended that the diet of prisoners serving terms of more than six months should be increased, for the sake of their health (there had been cases of scurvy and 'occasional dysenteric complaints'),[35] and one of the visiting justices had immediately issued an order that prisoners whose terms exceeded three months 'should be allowed vegetables and milk, in such a quantity as the surgeon shall deem essentially necessary for the preservation of their health'.

For Harriet Kettle, the diet at Walsingham would have been even more sparse and monotonous than it had been at Gressenhall: more bread but no cheese, and vegetables only once a week instead of twice. There was concern at the time that prison diets were too generous, and that crimes were committed to gain access to them, but Harriet's experience at Walsingham would not bear out that view.

The rules and regulations for the house of correction stipulated that 'provision shall be made for the instruction of the prisoners of both sexes in reading and writing,' the detail of the arrangements being left to the magistrates. In 1842, a prison inspector had recommended that 'the means of elementary instruction' should be given to the female prisoners and in 1850 another noted with pleasure that this was happening, and that they were being taught to write as well as read. The school, as has been seen, was conducted in the evenings by an assistant turnkey, under the guidance of the chaplain. Henry Kitton noted of the prisoners in November 1856 that, 'the major part, 73 per cent of the whole, had received some little schooling in their youth, but its imperfect character is shown by the fact that only 63 per cent were able to read, and many of them very imperfectly; and 33 per cent only could write a little beside'. He added that: 'The schoolmaster has attended diligently to his duties, and I find by his books has held school 307 evenings during the year. He instructs the prisoners in reading, writing and accounts; but not many remain long enough under his care to make any very great progress. I have visited the school-room myself from time to time to superintend and direct their proceedings, or to give some simple scriptural lesson.'[36]

Henry Kitton's successor as chaplain, NG Pilkington, reporting in October 1858, gave a much more upbeat assessment of the impact of the education provided for the prisoners on their levels of literacy, indicating that the great majority made good progress in reading and writing, albeit from a low base.[37] The following year, however, he expressed his horror at the prisoners' lack of religious knowledge, reporting that 57 of the 240 committed could not say a word of the Lord's Prayer and that 61 'could not tell me who Jesus Christ was'.[38] It is not clear from the available evidence whether males and females were taught together, and whether the latter were taught by the schoolmaster or the matron. Either way, it would appear that Harriet Kettle's education continued—and may even have progressed—during the six months she spent at Walsingham. Whether the chaplain's ministrations and the services in the chapel rubbed off on Harriet's religious and moral convictions is more doubtful, in the light of subsequent events in her life, but they may have left a trace.

The disciplinary regime in Walsingham house of correction was harsh but controlled, aimed at both deterrence and reform. The governor was empowered to punish prisoners found to be guilty of infractions of the rules (including the rule of silence). 'Profane cursing and swearing', indecent behaviour or irreverent behaviour in the chapel also incurred penalties. Corporal punishment could be used, as it was in 1857 following a repeated assault on the turnkey.[39] As in the workhouse, no alcohol or gaming was permitted. 'Close confinement in the refractory or solitary cells' for any period up to three days could be imposed by the governor, while the magistrates could impose this penalty for up to a month.

'Wardsmen' (no reference was made to 'wardswomen') would be selected, 'from such of the prisoners as are most orderly and best qualified for the purpose'. Their responsibilities included sweeping the floors of the areas they occupied, washing the day-rooms and staircases at least once a week, and airing the cells and bedding. They were also responsible for 'the maintenance of decency and good order' in their parts of the prison. For all this, they could receive any additional food or share of the earnings from the prisoners' work awarded to them by the magistrates. It is unlikely that Harriet performed one of these roles, if indeed they existed for the women.

No details survive, but it can be inferred that Harriet Kettle pushed back against the disciplinary regime and probably 'broke out' on numerous occasions. 'Breaking out' was a recognised response by prisoners in female convict prisons, their behaviour, 'amounting almost to a frenzy, smashing their windows, tearing up their clothes, destroying every useful article within their reach, generally yelling, shouting or singing as if they were lunatics'.[40] Similar behaviour occurred in local prisons. The author of a book on Victorian prisons and prisoners discussed the phenomenon and cited the testimony of two female prison visitors of the late 19th century: Felicia Mary Skene in Scotland and Susanna Meredith in the London area. The former wrote: 'It might seem at first sight as if this system of periodical "breakings out" which is largely adopted by the lower class of female prisoners were a mere unreasoning indulgence in temper; but it is not so, it has a distinct rationale of its own, illogical enough, no doubt, but a well-considered method in the apparent madness. The object of it is simply one of deliberate revenge for the pains and penalties to which their imprisonment subjects them. The women are perfectly aware that

Female prisoner in canvas dress under punishment for tearing her clothes (note the restraints on her arms). From Henry Mayhew and John Binney, The Criminal Prisons of London and Scenes of Prison Life, pub. 1862.

by these paroxysms of violence they give a great deal of trouble and annoyance to the officers, whose duty is to carry out all the unpleasant conditions of the sentences they have brought on themselves by their offences against the law.' Susanna Meredith, referring to a woman prisoner who had 'broken out', commented: 'Finally, she burst into violent fits of weeping, frequently repeating. "They have treated me like a beast and I have become one"…She said: "Well, I did it for variety. Oh, the monotony of prison life! I had to smash the glass of the cell and glass everywhere I could or I should have gone mad."'[41] In Harriet Kettle's case, the prison authorities' judgement was that she had indeed gone mad.

On 11 July 1856, when Harriet had been in the house of correction for nearly six months, the visiting justices reported to the quarter sessions that the prison buildings were in a good state of repair and that the staff 'have performed their respective duties in a satisfactory manner, and the prison throughout kept in a cleanly and excellent order, and the rules duly observed'. The report continued:

'The prisoners generally are in good health and have conducted themselves orderly and respectful, with the exception of Harriet Kettle who stands committed for the term of one year for want of bail to keep the peace, whose conduct has been most violent and refractory', adding that Harriet had, 'lately become a suicidal lunatic'. A medical certificate had been sent to the Home Secretary, so that he could issue a warrant for Harriet's transfer to the county lunatic asylum at Thorpe next Norwich.[42]

Harriet was 'removed' to the county lunatic asylum on 16 July 1856. The surgeon at Walsingham, Hugh Rump, reported to the subsequent quarter sessions that: 'Harriet Kettle a prisoner of very abandoned character after several seizures of temporary insanity, became a confirmed maniac, and was removed to the Thorpe Asylum...' The chaplain, Henry Kitton, reporting to the same meeting, mentioned, 'the homeless occupants of our union houses, to whom prison is no hardship and for whom it has no terrors'. He reported that there had been cases of 'violent and refractory conduct' by 'two...females from Gressenhall Union, of most depraved and outrageous characters. One of these [obviously Harriet] ultimately became deranged and was removed to the Asylum, but we hear she is now recovered and is likely to return to us again...'[43] Despite the forebodings of the chaplain, however, Harriet did not return to Walsingham.

Following their visit to Walsingham in December 1858, the inspectors of prisons commented that: 'The prison was clean, and in good order, and the prisoners made no complaints.' However, the days of the Walsingham house of correction were numbered. It closed on 1 March 1861 after it had been decided that the quarter sessions would no longer be held in Little Walsingham. The closure contributed to a national trend: the number of local prisons in England and Wales fell from 335 in 1819 to 193 in 1862, reflecting not only a desire for greater efficiency and economy but also a fall in crime and a reduction in the length of sentences.[44] The remaining prisoners at Walsingham were transferred, the males to the county gaol at Norwich Castle and a lone female to Wymondham. Today, the building remains virtually unaltered. Money and Margaret Curtis were recommended for pensions; Money, who had 'served the County intelligently and faithfully 36 years' received £150 per year and Margaret, by contrast, only £15. They did not enjoy their superannuation for long: Money died in 1864 and Margaret in 1868. The first turnkey, William Woodcock was awarded £27 per year. The surgeon, chaplain and other staff received nothing, although the magistrates recommended the chaplain for another post in view of 'his high character and excellent services'.[45] Redundancy is never an easy process—not that Harriet Kettle would have felt much sympathy.

As for Harriet herself, on 16 July 1856 she began the first of what would be a series of periods as a patient in the county lunatic asylum.

Notes

1   MLU minutes; NRO, C/GP14/12, 13.
2   PP LV, 1854.
3   TNA: MH32 84.
4   NC, 6 December 1851. Nevertheless, two years later, oakum-picking had been introduced at Wymondham house of correction, alongside laundry work.
5   J R Walkowitz (1980).
6   The guardians received a letter from Money Curtis, governor of Walsingham house of correction, about Harriet's clothes in April 1857, but its contents are unknown.
7   TNA: MH12 8480/200.
8   MLU minutes; NRO, C/GP14/13.
9   CLA, case book 1853-1861; NRO, SAH 262.
10 Randall McGowen, 'The Well-Ordered Prison', in N Morris and D J Rothman (1995).
11 Report on prisons in Norfolk, 19 October 1836, in *Accounts and papers relating to crime; gaols; criminals*, PP XLV, 1837, available via books.google.co.uk.
12 Background about Walsingham house of correction is drawn from historicengland.org.uk; walsinghamvillage.org; and prisonhistory.org.
13 23rd Report of the Inspectors of Prisons, Midland District, PP XI, 1859, session 1.
14 24th Report of the Inspectors of Prisons, Midland District, PP XXXV, 1860.
15 19th Report of the Inspectors of Prisons, Northern and Eastern District, 1856.
16 R McGowen (1995) in N Morris and D J Rothman (1995).
17 The Revd Daniel Nihill, *Prison Discipline in its Relations to Society and Individuals* (1839), quoted in P Priestley (1999).
18 BNP, 8 July 1846.
19 S McConville (1995).
20 15th Report of Inspectors of Prisons, Northern and Eastern District, PP XXXVIII, 1850: NC, 6 December 1851.
21 23rd Report of Inspectors of Prisons, Midland District, PP XL, 1859, session 1.
22 R McGowen in N Morris and D J Rothman (1995).
23 D Adams (2013).
24 18th Report of the Inspectors of Prisons, Northern and Eastern District, PP XXXIII, 1856.
25 NC, 18 December 1852.
26 NC, 12 March 1853.
27 18th Report of the Inspectors of Prisons, Northern and Eastern District, PP XXXIII, 1856.
28 23rd Report of the Inspectors of Prisons, Midland District, PP XL, 1859.
29 19th Report of the Inspectors of Prisons, Northern and Eastern District, PP XXXIII, 1856.
30 Rules and Regulations for Walsingham house of correction, displayed at the Walsingham Shirehall Museum.
31 Thanks to Elizabeth Meath Baker (Walsingham Shirehall Museum) for this point.
32 NM, 29 July 1848.

33 P Priestley (1999).

34 NC, 24 February 1855.

35 7th Report of Inspectors of Prisons, Northern and Eastern District, PP XXI, 1842.

36 NC, 1 November 1856.

37 NC, 6 November 1858.

38 NM, 5 November 1859.

39 NM, 11 November 1857.

40 Lucia Zedner, 'Wayward Sisters: the Prison for Women', in N. Morris and DJ Rothman (1995).

41 Francis Scougal (FM Skene), *Scenes from a Silent World* (1889) and MA Lloyd, *Susanna Meredith: A Record of a Vigorous Life* (1903), both quoted in P Priestley (1999).

42 Quarter Sessions Minutes 11 July 1856; NRO, C/S4/11.

43 Another case of violent conduct concerned, 'a negro, ignorant of our language, who when checked by one of the turnkeys, for doing something wrong, flew into a violent passion, assaulted, and would have seriously injured him, but for the timely aid of another prisoner, who came to the turnkey's assistance'. This black prisoner may have arrived at Wells as a crew member on a ship. Quarter Sessions Minutes 24 October 1856; NRO, C/S4/11.

44 Sean McConville, 'The Victorian Prison 1865-1965', in N Morris and DJ Rothman (1995).

45 NC, 5 January 1861.

In the county lunatic asylum

THE Norfolk county lunatic asylum (later known as St Andrew's hospital, which closed in 1998) was housed in purpose-built premises at Thorpe, a village outside Norwich, on a site between the turnpike road to Great Yarmouth and the River Yare. The building of an asylum was initiated by the Norfolk justices of the peace, using their powers under the 'Act for the better Care and Maintenance of Lunatics, being Paupers or Criminals in England' of 1808, which allowed them not only to build an asylum but also to maintain it from local rates. Norfolk's was one of the earlier county asylums to be erected using the provisions of this legislation.[1] Construction began in 1811 and the buildings were ready for occupation in 1814.

Governance of the asylum was the responsibility of a committee of visiting justices, which met monthly. In the 1850s and 1860s, several members of the committee were clergymen, including the Revd Thomas John Blofeld of Hoveton, who served as chairman throughout the years 1856-1864, when Harriet Kettle was for varying periods a resident of the asylum. Another member, from 1860 until Harriet left the asylum for the last time in 1864, was someone who would already have been familiar to her: the Revd Philip Gurdon of Cranworth. The visiting justices reported on their work to the county quarter sessions and from 1845 onwards[2] their actions were subject to the scrutiny of the national commissioners in lunacy.

The original building at Thorpe comprised a single, long range with an administration block in the middle, dividing the male and female sides where, initially, the accommodation was in individual cells. The number of patients rose steadily, from 62 in the first year, to an average of 71 in 1814-19, 110 in 1820-29, and 159, 185 and 291 in the three following decades.[3] From the 1830s onwards, there were always more women than men. When Harriet Kettle was first admitted, in the summer of 1856, there were 303 patients, of whom 159 were women.

To cater for the increasing numbers of patients, additional buildings were required. Extensions were added to the main building in 1831 and 1840, and a substantial building campaign was undertaken in 1847-9, which included the provision of new dormitories and day-rooms, a chapel and a new kitchen. Improved systems for drainage and sewerage were installed, as a result of which, as the commissioners in lunacy reported in March 1849, 'diarrhoea and

[THE NORFOLK COUNTY LUNATIC ASYLUM.]

The Norfolk County Lunatic Asylum, note the train passing in the middle distance and the river boat in the foreground.

dysentery, formerly so prevalent, are now rarely observed'.[4] In the following decade, additional land was acquired north of the turnpike road, which had to be diverted and bridged.

In contrast with the process taking place in prisons at the time, the individual cells in the original building were largely replaced by wards, although some single bedrooms were retained. At the time of Harriet Kettle's first admission in 1856, the asylum was again full and the women's wards were overcrowded. In 1857, as a temporary measure, a carpenter's shop was converted into an additional dormitory, and work began on further extensions to the buildings.[5] A start had also been made on brightening up the interior of the asylum. The original stone floors were gradually being replaced with floorboards, and bars were removed from the windows, making the buildings less prison-like. Reporting on 1855, the asylum's superintendent noted that: 'During the year, much progress has been made in improving the interior appearance of the wards: fixed seats and tables have been removed and replaced by neat and substantial furniture. The walls of the day-rooms and corridors have been papered and ornamented with a goodly variety of prints and landscapes.'[6]

The visiting justices produced rules and regulations for the asylum in 1814 which, 'reconciled the twin objectives of economy and reforming intent'.[7] Patients (as the inmates were generally, but not invariably, called) were admitted following an order from a magistrate, but there were no fixed criteria for admission. In 1855, the medical officers classified the 'forms of mental disease' suffered by the patients accommodated in the asylum as: mania (acute, chronic or remittent); melancholia; monomania [obsessive behaviour]; dementia; imbecility (congenital); and idiotcy [sic] (congenital), with each class being broken down into general paralysis, partial paralysis, epilepsy and suicidal tendency. By 1863, the categories had been simplified somewhat to: mania (acute, chronic, recurrent, senile or a potu [alcohol-induced]); general paralysis of the insane [caused by tertiary syphilis]; epilepsy (with mania or dementia); melancholia; dementia; and imbecility.[8] About half the patients were classified as suffering from some form of mania, and remittent (or recurrent) mania was the initial diagnosis in the case of Harriet Kettle.

Although relatively small numbers of those with congenital conditions, referred to at the time as imbecility and idiocy, and a larger group of elderly people with dementia, were admitted to the asylum, people in these groups were often accommodated in workhouses, at a significantly lower charge to the rates. FW Keppel, during the quarter sessions of Epiphany 1845, commented of Gressenhall workhouse that, 'there were scarcely any dangerous pauper lunatics; they were chiefly old, deaf and dumb, and dirty people, who being weak-minded or idiots were called lunatics in the returns of the clerks of the unions. There were 13 or 14 in his own union; they did a certain quantity of work, and were he thought very properly treated…'[9] That view was not always shared by the medical officers at the asylum; in the mid-1850s, when space was at a premium, they recommended the discharge of some of the 'harmless chronic patients' but reported, 'we have been deterred from some such recommendations by the consideration of the unfitness of most union houses, without special arrangements, for the reception of lunatics'.[10]

It tended to be those with whom the workhouse authorities could not cope, or who were evidently a danger to themselves or others, who were referred to Thorpe. The earliest known case after 1836 of the transfer of an inmate from Gressenhall workhouse to the county lunatic asylum dated from 18 June 1838 and involved an inmate called William Simmonds, but the reasons were not recorded.[11] In 1843, the poor law commissioners encouraged the guardians to transfer to the asylum two men, 'represented to be idiots dangerous to themselves and residing with friends', so that they would, 'get full benefit of medical care and professional superintendence as well as humanity and sound policy'[12]—which encapsulates the mission of the asylum at the time. By August 1844, there were 13 patients from the Mitford and Launditch Union at Thorpe.[13] By January 1857, the number had risen to 21, with Harriet Kettle's name appearing on the list sent to the Poor Law Board.[14] The weekly cost of Harriet's maintenance in the asylum was 8s 6d (42.5 pence), probably about twice what it cost to maintain an individual in the workhouse.[15]

The staff of the asylum grew and changed over time. Initially, it comprised a master and matron, two porters, two housemaids and a cook, with medical expertise provided by non-resident medical officers. As the accommodation expanded, so did the staff. By the mid-1850s there were 11 male and 11 female attendants, plus laundresses, a cook and three other servants. As required by the Lunacy Act of 1845, a resident medical officer was appointed, although the most senior officer remained the master, now known as the superintendent. From 1843 until his retirement in 1861, this position was held by Ebenezer Owen, formerly the master of a workhouse at Malmesbury, Wiltshire, and a man without medical qualifications.[16] He married the matron, Emma Houghton, the year after his appointment and Emma remained in post for a year longer, until 1862. By then, a medical superintendent, Dr William Hills, had been appointed and his wife subsequently became the matron.

When Harriet Kettle was admitted to the county lunatic asylum on 16 July 1856, there were two medical officers, GW Firth (non-resident) and Edward Casson (resident). GW Firth's involvement, which continued until 1861, may have been occasional, as he had other commitments. He was also the medical superintendent of a 'private hospital for the cure of the insane' ('for the reception of ladies and gentlement of the upper and middle classes')[17] at The Grove, Catton, and was also a surgeon to the Norfolk and Norwich hospital. Harriet was part of the caseload of Edward Casson, whose care for the patients was praised by the visiting justices in their report to the quarter sessions dated 13 October 1856. Casson, the son of a surgeon, had been appointed as resident medical officer at the asylum in September 1854, moving from a similar post in Hull.[18] When Harriet was admitted he was aged 28, and had very recently (on 2 April) married Louisa Houghton, aged 27, sister of the matron and formerly head female attendant at the asylum.[19]

The county lunatic asylum provided a secure place of detention and patients had no choice about being there. A few escapes were recorded in the annual reports of the visiting justices but those who absconded were usually (albeit not invariably) found and returned. The asylum was also, however, a therapeutic institution where, with increasing success, patients were cured. As in other similar establishments in the first half of the 19th century, this aspect of the asylum's role, and the part played in it by medical professionals, grew in significance. More emphasis was given to improving the patients' physical health, by medication, diet and exercise, Disciplinary incidents, and the use of physical restraint and 'seclusion' became rare.[20] Work was considered

William Tuke. Etching by C Callet.
(Courtesy Wellcome Collection)

therapeutic, part of a regime of humane, 'moral' treatment of the kind pioneered by the Quaker, William Tuke, at the York Retreat from the end of the 18th century onwards.[21]

The therapeutic methods used were described by the medical officers in the Annual Report for 1856: 'The treatment of insanity is rather moral than medical—rather hygienic than therapeutic: the moral control and discipline of a well ordered asylum—its amusements of various kinds—and especially its light and voluntary labour,—with their judicious adaptation to various cases and temperaments—these are some of the means of cure, of relief, or of solace, upon which we depend…'[22] Part of the additional land that was acquired for the asylum was farmed so that male patients could be employed in agricultural tasks and part was laid out as pleasure grounds, 'planted with flowers', where female patients (whose work was indoors) could benefit from fresh air and exercise. Through such measures, the percentage of patients who were discharged, 'recovered' increased to almost 50 per cent in the 1850s, although readmissions of discharged patients amounted to roughly a fifth of all admissions.[23]

The 'light and voluntary labour' for women took a variety of forms. In 1857, out of an average daily total of 141 female patients, 23 worked in the laundry and five in the kitchen; 12 helped in the wards; 12 were cleaners in the corridors and elsewhere; a total of 67 were employed in the work room on needlework (51), fancy work (15) or straw bonnet making (1); 20 were engaged in stocking knitting and one in cravat knitting; and one was 'in the establishment', perhaps doing office work.[24] A great variety of articles were made in the work room, including table- and bed-linen, clothing and curtains. As well as working on the farm and in the grounds, the men were gradually given more opportunities for indoor employment as, 'shoemakers, tailors, painters, blacksmiths' as well as 'assisting in the office, engine house, wards, &c'.[25]

The 'amusements of various kinds' included cricket matches and trips on the River Yare in the asylum's own boat, which had room for 13 patients and was kept in a boathouse on the premises.[26] When the commissioners in lunacy visited the asylum in 1855, they reported: 'We are glad to find the patients of both sexes are taken frequently into the neighbouring country for exercise and recreation; twelve of the male patients are now absent playing at cricket, at the Rev. J Blofeld's park, at Hoveton.'[27] Aviaries and a 'vivarium' provided further diversion for the patients. During the winter months, male and female patients could mix at evening 'gatherings…for dancing, singing and recitations'. 'I am happy to add', reported the superintendent, 'that these exercises have uniformly been conducted with propriety and decorum'.[28] Later, the evening gatherings evolved into a fortnightly 'ball' at which the patients could dance to music provided by a brass band formed by the asylum's attendants.[29]

In August 1856, an outing to Great Yarmouth by rail was organised for 130 of the patients, the train picking them up and setting them down immediately outside the asylum. Harriet Kettle may have been a participant; if so, it may have been the first time she had travelled by train. The trip went well: 'The weather was very favourable, and the day passed most pleasantly on the "Denes" where tents had been pitched, and an ample supply of provisions had been provided.' The provisions were consumed to the accompaniment of music by the East Norfolk Militia Band. In each of the next four years, a similar trip was made to Lowestoft, but following Ebenezer Owen's retirement as superintendent, outings to the coast were discontinued and replaced by a (much cheaper) 'harvest treat'.

Reading matter was provided, the superintendent's 1855 Annual Report noting that, 'various publications have been in constant circulation amongst the patients, many of whom derive pleasure from reading. Illustrated publications are in special demand.' In the same year, however, the commissioners in lunacy criticised the 'inadequate' stock of books, and in 1856 they found the 'supply of amusing publications…scanty and insufficient'.[30] The number of books was increased in subsequent years, 200 being purchased in 1859,[31] and in 1861 the commissioners in lunacy found the supply of books and 'entertaining periodicals' to be 'abundant'.[32]

The daily routine was relaxed in comparison with that at Gressenhall workhouse. According to the account provided by Ebenezer Owen in the 1859 Annual Report: 'Both male and female attendants rise at six o'clock every morning throughout the year; but, from the 25th September to the 25th March, the patients' sleeping room doors are not unlocked till half-past six…This half hour is devoted to the lighting of fires, cleaning of hearths, and otherwise preparing the day-rooms for the comfortable reception of the patients when they get up. The patients, immediately after rising, are provided with conveniences for washing themselves; and this practice is enforced or encouraged in those that are averse to cleanliness, and performed for those who may be unable to attend to themselves.' Breakfast was at 8.00, followed, on Sunday, Tuesday and Friday, by a religious service. Employments began at 9.00. 'In fine weather', however, 'all patients capable of taking exercise are conducted to the grounds attached to the asylum; and the attendants encourage and take an active part in their out-door amusements'. At 11 am 'the patients, male and female, who are engaged on any laborious work, receive half-a-pint of beer, one ounce of cheese, and three ounces of bread'. Work then continued until 12.30. Dinner was at 1.00 pm, after which the more active men worked from 2.00 until 6.00 pm, with a break for refreshments at 4.00 pm; the women, presumably, took gentle exercise. At 6 pm, 'supper is served to the patients in their respective day-rooms, after which, 'reading, music, card-playing and other amusements are encouraged until bedtime.'[33] Bedtime was at 7.00 pm in the winter, 8.00 pm in the summer.

This, then, was the pattern of Harriet Kettle's life during the months that she spent in the asylum. She must have appreciated particularly the recreation allowed after supper, which was in marked contrast with the regimes at Gressenhall workhouse and Walsingham house of correction, where cards and other 'games of chance' were strictly forbidden. [34] Harriet would also have enjoyed the dietary for the patients in the asylum, which was considerably more generous than those at Gressenhall and Walsingham, although she may already have been developing the aversion to meat which became pronounced later in her life. Vegetables, grain and meat were produced on the farm established on the asylum's land, whose facilities included a slaughterhouse. Meat and generous quantites of vegetables, with half a pint of beer, were served to both men and women for dinner each day. The men had meat broth or bread and cheese for supper, while the women had bread and butter with three quarters of a pint of tea.[35] The commissioners in lunacy, who always observed (and sampled) dinner, consistently praised the quantity and quality of the food.

As at Gressenhall, the women's clothing was made up on site, but unlike in the workhouse, it was varied. Ebenezer Owen reported in 1855 that: 'The clothing of the patients…has been undergoing change, from uniformity in colour and form, to the variety in both these respects which ordinarily prevails among the labouring classes in this county.'[36] In the same year, the commissioners in lunacy noted that, 'the women were well dressed; the dresses of the patients are now various, both as to colour and texture'.[37] The following year, they commented: 'We think it would increase the comfort of the inmates [sic], if looking glasses were placed in the lavatories, and a few also in some of the day rooms, dormitories and single sleeping rooms on the female side'[38]—and, in due course, looking glasses were installed. For Harriet Kettle, being able not only to choose her clothes but also to check her appearance in a mirror must have been a new and agreeable experience.

When Harriet was admitted to the asylum, on 16 July 1856, Edward Casson recorded her age, inaccurately, as 22. In the admission register, Harriet's bodily condition was recorded as 'thin', probably a reflection of her diet at Walsingham.[39] In the case book, Casson described her as: '…of moderate habit of body and lymphatic temperament. Rather excited countenance. Nothing particular about the head. Viscera appear healthy. No epilepsy, etc. Pulse, tongue and skin normal. Case of re-mittent mania which has been coming on for an uncertain time and is ascribed solely to a naturally bad temper and from her irregular life she having been a girl on the town in Norwich for some time previous to her committal to prison for having asaulted [sic] the master of a workhouse during her abode there for a time. No hereditary taint known. She seems to have no settled delusions so far meerly [sic] paroxysms of maniacal excitement. At others quiet. She seems to have a strong suicidal tendency have [sic] attempted it more than once.'[40]

Close observation of patients, and the keeping of case notes, were practices that had originated in French hospitals in the early 19th century and were indicative of a pragmatic, open-minded approach to the management of mental illness.[41] The attention given by Edward Casson to Harriet's physical health reflects the thinking at the time about the origins of mental illness; increasingly, disturbances of the brain were thought to have physical causes. His note, 'nothing particular about the head', shows that phrenology, the study of the shape of the human skull to identify mental characteristics, still had some influence, although it had been losing credibility by the end of the 1830s.[42] The reference to attempted suicide may have come from Harriet herself or it may have been reported by the surgeon to Walsingham house of correction, where it was claimed that she had become a 'suicidal lunatic'.[43] It was probably for this reason that, although placed in ward number 6, Harriet was to sleep in the infirmary, 'where the night nurse is'.

The first two months of Harriet's confinement in the county lunatic asylum were eventful, as the entries in the case book testify. She was quiet and orderly at first; then, on 6 August, she 'behaved not nicely'. Harriet and another patient had, 'been setting their heads together and been conversing in a most shameful manner and because reproved they both acted disgracefully but Kettle attacked one of the attendants and kicked and bit and became so violent as to require 7 nurses to overcome her. I ordered her a ticking dress on and to be put in seclusion. She managed to get it off once or twice and was very violent and abusive in her language to myself and others. She knocked the door and screamed with all her might.'

Harriet continued to make a lot of noise, including throughout the night of 7-8 August, but she was released from seclusion on 9 August after 'promising to behave herself' and was placed in a different ward. Seclusion, for which a 'padded room' was available, was only used very occasionally at Thorpe by the 1850s. According to the annual report of the visiting justices, Harriet's was the only case in 1856; she was referred to as a 'subject of homicidal mania'.[44] On her release from seclusion, Harriet was prescribed milk and an extra egg daily, and medication including, 'an anodyne pil [sic] at night'.

Despite Harriet's promise, there were further incidents. On 26 August, Casson wrote in the case book: 'Though treated with the greatest kindness, she has once or twice broken out threatening to give us some trouble. Today she is tranquil but she is thoroughly bad and swears she won't leave this place (for she knows she would have to go to prison again) and if I do discharge her she'll kick up a devil of a row. Her language is filthy and blasphemous in the extreme and I find as she owns herself, "she is a d_____d sight more rogue than fool"!!!' It is interesting that Casson used the phrase 'broken out'. As noted previously, 'breaking out' was a recognised feature of the response of some women to prison, and characterisations of the phenomenon accord remarkably well with Harriet's behaviour as recorded not only in the asylum but also in Gressenhall workhouse and Walsingham (and later Wymondham) house of correction.

About a fortnight later, Harriet smashed three windows 'because her sister did not come and see her'. This is the first evidence of a continuing relationship between Harriet and Matilda Kettle. Matilda may have known that Harriet was a patient because she had been informed by the asylum, as Harriet's next of kin, or possibly because Harriet had written and told her. Matilda probably lived in Norwich and, if this was the case, visiting Harriet at Thorpe would not have been too difficult. Although she did not come on this occasion there may well have been others when she did. The asylum appears to have had a relaxed attitude to visiting, a later report noting that many patients were, 'allowed to pass the day with their relatives and friends'—another contrast with Gressenhall workhouse, where visitors were allowed to stay for only one hour, or for two separate hours on Sundays.[45] For her misdemeanor in smashing the windows, Harriet was moved back to ward number 6 and put on a low diet for a week, but this ended when she promised to behave well again.

After another two weeks, on 26 September 1856, it was noted of Harriet that 'she fears committee day [no doubt because she did not want to be sent back to Walsingham house of correction] and manages to fly into a passion a few days before, today she was in a bad humour and began abusing one of the nurses and tore her hair from her head and hurt her severely'. She was put on a low diet again and on this occasion also the 'shower bath [was] administered, 1 minute, 2 and 3 minutes duration with 5 seconds interval between each shock'.

The shower bath was a recognised form of treatment for those suffering from mania. In the visiting justices' annual report for 1856, the asylum's medical officers wrote: 'As a means of medical treatment, the shower

Photograph of a typical 'shower bath' used to treat patients.
(Courtesy Wellcome Collection)

bath has been occasionally employed, for the most part with signal benefit, in cases of maniacal excitement: the apparatus in use here is a powerful one, the content of the cistern being twenty-four gallons; its height from the floor eight feet six inches; the tubes which discharge the water have 1/4th inch diameter, and there is to the cistern an inch and a half supply pipe; the most forcible manner in which it is ever used by us, is by raising the valve (the supply pipe being at the same time opened) for one minute, then closing the valve for five seconds, raising it again for two and three minutes with a similar pause between…The cases in which we have prescribed its use has [sic] been for maniacal patients whose physical powers were not depressed.'

After this experience, Harriet had a day or two in bed. On 30 September, surprisingly, in view of what had happened a few days previously, Edward Casson, the medical officer, 'reported to the committee of visitors…that Harriet Kettle was sufficiently recovered to be discharged'.[46] The visiting justices at the county lunatic asylum wanted Harriet to be moved back to Walsingham house of correction and their clerk wrote to his opposite number in Walsingham requesting that 'the necessary steps may be taken for her removal…to your prison again, for the remainder of the term of her imprisonment'. But the prison authorities, no doubt recalling Harriet's previous behaviour, were in no hurry to receive her back. The clerk to the visiting justices at Walsingham replied that it was for the asylum to contact the Secretary of State for authority to return her. This does not appear to have happened, and Harriet remained at the asylum. On October 20, she was 'going on very quietly and is employed regularly. Much better tempered since the bath'. Two months later, she was 'better on the whole' but 'requires great humouring to keep her at all quiet…Subject to spasms which a sedative and stimulant combined generally relieve.' At the end of December, Edward Casson noted that Harriet was 'well mentally and bodily, to which I have certified and hope to have her removed soon'.

On 9 February 1857, immediately before Harriet's 12-month sentence at Walsingham house of correction was due to expire, Casson wrote to the overseers of the poor in Cranworth and, either with that letter or shortly afterwards, sent a certificate concerning Harriet's sanity. His letter of 9 February was referred by the parish to the board of guardians at Gressenhall, who considered it at their meeting on 16 February. Casson had enquired about outdoor relief being provided for Harriet on her discharge from the asylum, presumably on the ground that returning to the workhouse would be harmful to her mental health. The guardians decided to refer the matter to the Home Secretary, 'for his opinion and directions'. They instructed their clerk to make him aware of all the circumstances and to, 'express the unanimous feeling of the guardians that although apprehensive of further violence and misbehaviour on the part of Harriet Kettle if again admitted into the workhouse they do not feel justified in holding out an incentive for such misconduct by an allowance of out relief'. This was really a matter for the Poor Law Board; the reply from the Home Office merely stated that if a certificate was received attesting to Harriet's sanity she must be discharged from the asylum.[47]

The clerk was also instructed to write to Edward Casson informing him of the action taken by the guardians but may have omitted to do so, as on 11 March the latter noted that, 'we have heard no more from the parish to whom a certificate was sent'. The asylum decided to send a certificate of Harriet's sanity directly to the Secretary of State, 'and trust to get rid of her as she is a good-for-nothing creature. Says now she wishes to go'. This, no doubt, was because she would no longer have to return to Walsingham house of correction. In response to the asylum's application, the Home Secretary authorised Harriet's discharge as she was, 'now of sound mind, and the term of imprisonment to which she was sentenced having expired'.[48]

On 31 March 1857, Harriet was discharged from the county lunatic asylum, 'recovered'. It would appear that the parish of Cranworth had accepted responsibility for her as, after appearing before the committee of visiting magistrates, Harriet was 'delivered to the care of Edward Webster, overseer of Cranworth'.[49] It is not known whether, on being told that she would not be given outdoor relief but would be served with an order for admission to Gressenhall workhouse, she decided to fend for herself and resume her sex work in Norwich. However, she was certainly back in the workhouse by December 1857.

Notes

1 Local authorities were not compelled to built suitable facilities for their pauper lunatics until the passing of the County Asylums Act of 1845.
2 Under the provisions of the Lunacy Act passed in that year.
3 S Cherry (2003).
4 NM, 24 March 1849.
5 NM, 11 April and 8 July 1857.
6 CLA, annual report 1855; NRO, SAH 28.
7 S Cherry (2003).
8 CLA, annual reports, 1855 and 1863; NRO, SAH 28.
9 BNP, 8 January 1845.
10 CLA, annual report 1855; NRO, SAH 28.
11 MLU minutes; NRO, C/GP14/3.
12 TNA: MH12 8477.
13 TNA: MH12 8477.
14 MLU minutes; NRO, C/GP14/13.
15 TNA: MH12 8480.
16 S Cherry (2003).

17 NC, 15 September 1855, advertisement.

18 NC, 16 September 1854.

19 Freereg.org.uk, accessed 11 June 2020; Cherry (2003).

20 Attendants were not allowed to strike the patients, and in 1856 one was dismissed for doing so: NM, 16 April 1856.

21 A Cherry (2003); A Scull (1991); L Appignanesi (2008).

22 CLA, annual report 1856; NRO, SAH 28.

23 S Cherry (2003).

24 CLA, annual report 1857; NRO, SAH 28.

25 CLA, annual report 1863; NRO, SAH 28.

26 NM, 16 April 1856.

27 NM, 24 October 1855. Revd J Blofeld was the chairman of the committee of visiting justices responsible for the asylum.

28 CLA, annual report 1855; NRO, SAH 28.

29 CLA, annual reports 1861 and 1862; NRO, SAH 28.

30 NM, 11 July 1855, 16 April 1856.

31 CLA, annual report 1859; NRO, SAH 28.

32 CLA, annual report 1861; NRO, SAH 28.

33 CLA, annual report 1859; NRO, SAH 28.

34 On 9 June 1845, it was reported that four male inmates had been guilty of card-playing in the workhouse and it was ordered that they be taken before a magistrate to be punished. The master and porter were reprimanded for their negligence in allowing it to happen and the workhouse's tailor, who had witnessed but not reported it, was dismissed. NRO, MLU minutes, C/GP14/6.

35 CLA, annual reports. An allegation in the Norfolk Chronicle in January 1853 that the patients were poorly fed received a robust response from the visiting justices; NC,19 February 1853.

36 CLA, annual report 1855; NRO, SAH 28. The CLA was in the forefront of a national trend in this respect: see V Richmond (2013).

37 NM, 24 October 1855.

38 NM, 16 April 1856.

39 CLA, admission register 1845-61; NRO, SAH 175.

40 CLA, case book 1853-1861; NRO, SAH 262.

41 L Appignanesi (2008).

42 A Scull (1991).

43 See above, p. 87.

44 CLA, annual report 1856; NRO, SAH 28. The padded room is referred to in the Annual Report for 1861.

45 CLA, annual report 1863; NRO, SAH 28; MLU minutes, 31 May 1847; NRO, C/GP14/7 and 25 October 1852; NRO, C/GP14/10.

46 Letters from the clerk to the visiting justices of the CLA to the clerk to the visiting justices of Walsingham house of correction, 1 and 8 October 1856; NRO, SAH 38.

47 TNA: HO13/105, p.85.

48 CLA, reception orders 1857-60 and 1860-63; NRO, SAH 168/3.

49 CLA, minutes of the visiting justices 1856-62; NRO, SAH 8.

Attempted arson, remand and trial at the assizes

THE first evidence of Harriet Kettle's return to Gressenhall workhouse is in the minutes of the guardians' meeting on 28 December 1857. Harriet appeared before the board charged with 'violent and abusive conduct towards the porter'. On this occasion, she was merely 'admonished by the chairman [still her fellow-parishioner the Revd Philip Gurdon of Cranworth] and promised to behave better in future'.[1] Harriet was now 18 or 19. As during her previous stay in the workhouse, she would have been classified as an able-bodied woman and would have been accommodated with those considered to be of bad character.

There were changes among the officers of the workhouse in 1857-8. In December 1857, the master and matron were still Henry and Margaret Harrison but in July 1858 Henry Harrison died and his wife had to leave Gressenhall as she was not allowed to continue as matron in his absence. The new master and matron were Robert William Scraggs, aged 44, formerly an attorney's clerk, and his wife Mary Ann, aged 46. They took up their posts on 25 September 1858.[2]

The porter and assistant matron, William Owen and his wife Ada, had left Gressenhall in November 1857 to become master and matron of the Wayland Union Workhouse. Thomas Butcher, aged 54, formerly an innkeeper, and his wife Mary Ann, aged 40, were appointed to the vacancies at £20 and £5 per year respectively.[3] They had been unsuccessful applicants when William and Ada Owen were appointed in September 1855 and on this occasion were the only candidates. They were appointed despite the objections of some of the guardians, who considered that Thomas's age and Mary Ann's (unspecified) infirmities, 'are such as will probably render them incapable of performing the required duties satisfactorily'. They were, in fact, to remain at Gressenhall for over five years, until March 1863, although their period of service was not untroubled, and Harriet Kettle appears to have nursed an intense dislike of them, first expressed in her 'violent and abusive conduct' towards Thomas Butcher in December 1857. The relative mildness of her punishment for that offence may suggest that the guardians were aware of some provocation from the porter's side. Subsequent entries in their minute book indicate that Thomas Butcher was not a model employee.

In April 1858, Thomas was instructed by the guardians to, 'enter in a proper book…the several quantities of coals and coke daily taken from the store for the use of the workhouse…and such book…be laid before the board at the commencement of each weekly meeting,' suggesting that coal may previously have been misappropriated. A year later, on 28 March 1859, Butcher narrowly escaped dismissal: 'A complaint having been made to the guardians of the use of bad language by Thomas Butcher the porter towards the pauper Inmates of the workhouse and on investigation of the circumstances it appearing that such complaint is well founded, it is proposed…that Thomas Butcher be forthwith dismissed. Amendment proposed…that Thomas Butcher be reprimanded for his conduct on this and similar occasions and that such reprimand be entered on these minutes with a view to his immediate dismissal in the event of any repetition of such offence.' The amendment was carried, by five votes to three. Thomas Butcher was called before the board and, 'admonished accordingly when he expressed his regret and promised not to offend again'. Unabashed, in June 1860, Thomas and Mary Ann Butcher applied to the guardians for an increase in their combined salary and, if that was refused, permission to apply for other jobs. Unsurprisingly, the board turned down the request for a rise, and allowed the Butchers to apply elsewhere, but such applications, if they were made, came to nothing.

Meanwhile, no references to Harriet Kettle had occurred in the guardians' minute book between December 1857 and October 1858, and it is possible that Harriet spent at least part of that period in Norwich. However, she was certainly in Gressenhall workhouse on 1 November 1858, when she was accused of 'insubordinate conduct' (to whom was not disclosed) and was once again reprimanded by the chairman, the Revd Philip Gurdon.

Under three weeks later, on Saturday 20 November, Martha Craske and Harriet Kettle assaulted Mary Ann Butcher in the dining hall. Immediately after that, Harriet tried to set fire to the workhouse. This action was to determine the course of her life for the next three years.

The incident was reported to the guardians at their meeting on Monday 22 November. According to the minutes of the meeting (reproduced on page viii): 'Martha Craske a poor person maintained in the union workhouse is brought before the board in custody charged with assault upon Mrs Butcher the assistant matron and with gross misbehaviour and is ordered to be taken before the magistrates. Harriet Kettle a poor person also maintained in the said workhouse is likewise again brought before the board charged with the like offences and with having destroyed her bed and bedding and attempted to set fire to the workhouse. Ordered that she also be taken before the magistrates and dealt with according to law.'

Martha Craske has already featured in this narrative; in January 1853, after a sequence of misdemeanors, she and Elizabeth Craske, her sister, along with Harriet, had been charged with a variety of offences. Martha had continued to receive punishments for assorted incidents of misbehaviour in the years since then. Now Martha and Harriet were almost five years older than in 1853 and were still in alliance and in rebellion against the workhouse authorities.

They were handed over to the police and 'brought up by superintendent Parker', the same police officer who had been shot in the face by poachers at Letton in 1851. Martha and Harriet appeared before the magistrates in Petty Sessions, who included FW Keppel, former chairman of the board of guardians at Gressenhall, on the same day as the guardians' meeting, Monday 22 November 1858. Of Martha Craske, the Norfolk News reported: 'This not being the first time the prisoner had been up for misbehaviour, she was ordered to find sureties for her good conduct for the next 12 months and, in default, she was committed to Walsingham prison, of which place she has been an inmate several times.' Of Harriet, it was noted that she had already been in prison five times for insubordination. The paper commented that: 'Her conduct…before the magistrates was of the worst description. She swore that if ever she had the chance, she would do Mrs Butcher's business and set fire to the union.'[4] She also, according to a later report, said, 'she hoped she should be transported'.[5] Given everything that had happened over the previous two years, the prospect of a new life in Australia, even as a convict, must have held some appeal. Perhaps she even thought that she would find her father there.

After her appearance before the magistrates, Harriet was detained, not in Walsingham but in Wymondham house of correction, pending her trial at the assizes in Norwich on a charge of arson. This was not just to separate her from Martha Craske; Wymondham was much nearer to Norwich than Walsingham and catered for prisoners on remand.

Harriet's reaction to Wymondham house of correction was similar to what it had been at Walsingham. According to a later note by the medical officer at the county lunatic asylum, she was, 'very unruly, broke the windows and would do nothing but scream and swear'.[6] In their report to the Easter 1859 quarter sessions, the visiting justices of the house of correction reported that, 'Harriet Kettle, a prisoner in custody for trial upon a charge of arson, having been reported by the surgeon as of unsound mind, was on the first day of February last removed by order of the Secretary of State to the lunatic asylum at Thorpe.' The warrant for her removal, issued by the Home Secretary on 29 January 1859, referred to a certificate signed, as the law required, by two justices of the peace and two surgeons, and stated that the asylum had been 'recommended to me as a fit and proper receptacle for the said lunatic'. This time, the cost would be chargeable to the common fund of the Mitford and Launditch Union;[7] no small matter, as the charge for Harriet's maintenance in the asylum was over £5 per quarter.

And so, on 1 February 1859, having spent just over two months at Wymondham house of correction, Harriet Kettle was transferred to the county lunatic asylum for her second spell there.

Changes had taken place at Thorpe since Harriet's previous period in the asylum in 1856-57. Substantial extensions to the buildings had been completed, providing 120 more beds, day rooms, a dining hall and a larger chapel, and new laundries with steam-driven washing and wringing machines.[8] The medical officers reported that: 'During several months [in] 1858, the tranquility of the wards was disturbed by the extensive works which were going on. The inevitable access of workmen caused much excitement, particularly among the female inmates [sic]; and for some time, the transfer of the two sexes, from one side of the house to the other, though got through in a single day, unsettled the establishment.'[9] By the time Harriet arrived, however, calm was being restored. As a result of the changes in the building, her living conditions would have been less crowded than during her previous spell in the asylum. She would have eaten dinner in the new dining hall, used for the first time on Christmas Day 1858, and may, along with the majority of the patients, have attended services in the chapel, which came into use shortly after her arrival and for which a harmonium was acquired. The demeanor of the patients during the services was described by the superintendent as, 'orderly; and in many instances apparently devout'.[10]

Harriet might also have noticed changes to the interior of the asylum buildings. The process of replacing the stone floors with floorboards was now complete in nearly all the dormitories and single bedrooms and in most of the day-rooms. Additionally, as noted by the superintendent: 'The small prison-like windows throughout the old portions of the building, numbering about 200, have been removed, and their places supplied with windows similar to those of private houses.' Flowers, prints and bird-cages continued to enliven the accommodation. Each ward was now provided with 'water closets, baths and lavatories,' although it appears from a later reference that patients were still having to share bathwater.[11] The beds were improving: 'trough' beds were being phased out, pillows were filled with oat chaff rather than straw and horsehair was very gradually replacing straw as the filling for mattresses, a process encouraged over several years by the commissioners in lunacy although still incomplete five years later. Each bed was provided with two linen sheets, four heavy blankets for the winter and three for the summer and a cotton counterpane. The combined effect of all this provision, in the view of the medical officers, was that the, 'furniture and adornment of the interior...may almost be called sumptous'.[12]

When Harriet was admitted to the asylum at the beginning of February 1859, the information recorded by Edward Casson, the medical officer, was terse: '24 years. Single. Prostitute'. There was a reference back to her earlier spell in the asylum, with the comment, 'a history of her case answers exactly to her present symptoms'. On arrival at the asylum, Harriet, 'became very quiet and only complained of haemorrhoids'. Medication and tonics were prescribed. A fortnight later, she was reported to have 'gone on quietly and can behave as well as anyone if she pleases, which shews it is merely temper'. There were no incidents in March. In April, 'she...once threatened to be noisy but on being warned that she would be treated with low diet, etc, she behaved well and is going on nicely so far'. On 27 May, however, Casson wrote that Harriet 'has been very quiet until lately when the other day she broke out suddenly without seeming cause and became violent and abusive and required removing from the laundry [where, presumably, she was working] to her ward and a shower bath of 1, 2 and 3 minutes' duration, and to be on low diet for 3 days. This had the desired effect and she has continued quiet again of late'.[13]

The quietness evidently continued. On 16 June 1859 the county lunatic asylum was visited by two commissioners in lunacy, BW Proctor and Robert Nairne. On that date there were 319 patients (175 female) in the asylum. The commissioners reported that: 'The patients are very tranquil' and that cases of seclusion were, 'very rare'. As usual, their visit must have coincided with dinner time, as in their report they stated: 'We tasted the food which was very good, & saw all the rations served, which were ample. The dinner consisted of roast beef, vegetables & bread, with half a pint of good beer for each person.' They reported approvingly on all the improvements that had been made, but noted that more washing equipment was still required in the dormitories. They also reported that, 'the body linen is now changed twice a week' (reflecting the beneficial impact of the new steam laundry), but then found on their next visit that it was only being changed once a week.[14]

On 28 July, Harriet was transferred back to Wymondham, preparatory to her trial at the summer assizes. She was 'very quiet until getting there but when she found out she was to be placed there and take her trial, she began swearing directly'.[15]

The guardians at Gressenhall were keen to see the prosecution of Harriet proceed, and directed their clerk, Charles Wright (who was a solicitor), to conduct it and to bring the judge's attention to, 'the frequent punishments she has undergone for misbehaviour in the workhouse and the difficulty the guardians experience in dealing with her and other apparently irreclaimable women of her class'.

But Harriet's trial did not go ahead—not yet. Her appearance at the county summer assizes on 28 July 1859 was brief. Robert James Tunaley, the surgeon employed at Wymondham house of correction, reporting to the quarter sessions in October 1859, recalled that, 'Harriet Kittle [sic], whose mental delusion and violence rendered it necessary to remove her to the asylum, was returned into the custody of the matron for trial at the assizes, but her demeanor was such, the judge would not allow her to plead, and she was again brought back to this prison, and subsequently removed to the asylum.'[16]

The Norfolk Chronicle and Norfolk News carried almost identical reports of what occurred: 'Harriet Kettle, a young gipsy-looking woman, was charged with setting fire to Gressenhall workhouse. The prisoner had previously been in the asylum and when brought up in the custody of the governor, Mr Pinson, she made the court resound with her shrieks. Mr Masters, surgeon, stated that the prisoner was not in a fit state to plead, as she was perfectly crazy, and she was accordingly removed uttering the most fearful cries and execrations. Such a scene was perhaps never before witnessed in this court.'[17]

The description of Harriet as 'gipsy-looking' provides a new insight into her physical appearance, and the scene in the courtroom can be readily imagined. The Norwich Mercury, in a briefer notice, reported that Harriet was 'screaming with all the fury of madness'.[18] Mr Pinson, of course, was the former master of Gressenhall workhouse.

An account of what had happened in court was also recorded in the case book of the county lunatic asylum. According to Edward Casson, Harriet, 'was taken to the assizes and placed at the bar to plead to the indictment for felony, when she set to screaming and shouting and calling the judge the most vile and filthy names, which had the effect she wished, and she was sent down so that the gaol surgeon might examine her and report to the court her state of mind when he came to the conclusion that she was not in a fit state to plead and himself and another surgeon having certified that she was insane she was again placed here by Secretary of State's warrant and thus one's efforts to get rid of a character not at all fitted to be in an asylum for the really insane and not a place for such bad characters as her to be retained in, was [sic] again frustrated'.

The county lunatic asylum was unable to 'get rid' of Harriet because Wymondham house of correction was determined to get rid of her. There can be little doubt that Harriet's preference was for the asylum.

And so, a week after being discharged from the asylum, Harriet was readmitted to it. This time, she was allocated to 'the best room used by patients, viz the work room No 3'. She remained at Thorpe for nearly nine months, from 6 August 1859 until 27 March 1860, with no untoward incidents of any kind being recorded. Edward Casson commented on 27 September 1859 that she 'has gone on perfectly quietly and employs herself at knitting, etc, and has not put on any temper, as she knows full well that the shower bath would be used and this she has no relish for, and behaves as well as she could, always if she chose'.

However, despite being considered fit to do so, Harriet did not appear for trial at the winter assizes in December 1859, to the evident irritation of the guardians at Gressenhall, who had made preparations for the prosecution. On 13 December their clerk wrote to the visiting magistrates of the asylum asking why Harriet had not appeared and why the guardians had not been informed, 'which might have saved loss of time and expence'.[19] His opposite number, FJ Blake, clerk to the visiting magistrates at Thorpe, replied stiffly that, 'it does not appear that there has been any irregularity in the proceedings in the case as regards the officers of this establishment'. He added that, before Harriet could appear before the assizes, a certificate testifying to her sanity, signed by two medical men, would have to be forwarded to the Home Office. His letter continued: 'I am also directed to inform you that these proceedings are generally three to four weeks in progress, and had the thing been contemplated, there was no time to have Harriet Kettle removed to Wymondham so as to take her trial'. Blake concluded, cuttingly, that 'the prosecutor and witnesses were most needlessly taken to Norwich—inasmuch as it was publicly advertized that no prisoner would be tried at those assizes, but such as were in prison and committed for trial at the assizes, a circumstance of which you could scarcely have been ignorant.'[20]

But why was 'the thing' not contemplated, given the belief of the medical officers that Harriet was sane? It appears that the visiting magistrates and their clerk had simply overlooked the need to send the requisite certificate to the Home Office. That impression is reinforced by a note in the minutes of the visiting magistrates for 28 February 1860, when: 'The attention of the medical officers was drawn to the case of Harriet Kettle, whose trial should take place at the ensuring assizes and upon the receipt of their certificate as to her sound state of mind, the clerk was directed to forward the same to the Secretary of State for the Home Department and to request that the necessary steps may be taken for her removal from the asylum and at the same time to forward a copy of the certificate to Charles Wright, the clerk to the magistrates [sic] of the Launditch [sic] Union.'[21] Clearly, the visiting magistrates of the asylum did not want the same oversight to happen again. Nor, it seems, did they want Harriet to be transferred to Wymondham house of correction only to be declared insane and sent back to the asylum. At the end of December, Edward Casson noted that, at the coming of the next (Lent) assizes, Harriet would be 'taken direct from here to the court instead of being sent to Wymondham first'.

As the date of Lent assizes approached, the board of guardians at Gressenhall several true bills.

TRIALS OF PRISONERS.
ARSON BY A SUPPOSED LUNATIC.

Harriet Kettle, (26), pauper, who was indicted at the summer assizes, 1859, and upon her arraignment being found insane, was ordered to be kept in custody until her Majesty's pleasure was known, and was, on the 26th of March, 1860, received back into custody from the county lunatic asylum, by order of a Secretary of State's warrant, under 3 and 4 Victoria, c. 54, was again placed in the dock. Mr. Bulwer prosecuted.

The prisoner exhibited the utmost excitement, and evidently acted as though she was insane. She declared she would take her own life, and that " no man should conquer her."

The prisoner was charged with attempting to set fire to the Mitford and Launditch Union-house, at Gressenhall, on the 20th of November, 1858.

Robert W. Scraggs, the master of the union, stated that on the day named his attention was called to the prisoner's beating the assistant matron, in the dining-hall. He assisted in removing the prisoner, and put her into a separate apartment. She then declared that she would burn down the " b——y building," and soon after he (witness) went into the room, and found some straw on the floor which had been ripped out of a bed in the room. The straw had just been set fire to. Witness put the fire out. The bedding had all been destroyed. She was subsequently taken before a magistrate, when she said that she hoped she should be transported. She was very violent. Witness did not, however, think that she was insane.

Mr. Owen, the master of the Thorpe Lunatic Asylum, deposed that he did not think the prisoner was insane, but that she was subject to violent fits of passion, especially when thwarted.

Mr. Masters, surgeon to the gaol, (who had had a very brief interview with the prisoner) deposed that he thought her insane, but he had not had a fair opportunity of testing the accuracy of his opinion.

The learned JUDGE having summed up, in which he said it was quite possible for the prisoner to behave in this violent manner for the purpose of escaping punishment,

The jury found her guilty, being of sound mind when she set fire to the room.

Prisoner was sentenced to eighteen months' hard labour, and was removed uttering violent language and declaring her innocence.

Report of Harriet's trial in the Norfolk Chronicle. 31 March 1860

checked with the Home Office that the prosecution of Harriet would be taking place. The answer was in the affirmative.[22] This time, the trial did go ahead.

Harriet Kettle's trial took place on 28 March 1860. Afterwards, on 31 March, similar reports appeared in two of the local weekly newspapers, the Norwich Mercury and the Norfolk Chronicle. According to the Norwich Mercury:

'Prisoner, on being placed in the dock, and asked if she were guilty or not, stated first that she was not guilty, and then for a minute or two poured forth a torrent of words, the purport of which was that she did not wish to burn the union, but to kill herself, that she had been very badly treated by the authorities at the workhouse, and by everyone else, and that she would kill herself whatever they might do to prevent her, for she would be ill treated or conquered by nobody.'

The Norfolk Chronicle provided a shorter summary:

'The prisoner exhibited the utmost excitement, and evidently acted as though she was insane. She declared she would take her own life and that "no man should conquer her"'.

So did Harriet say 'nobody' or 'no man' and, if the latter, what significance did the statement have? She was prepared to defy men, departing from the submissive behaviour expected of women in Victorian times, but she was as likely to commit violent acts against women. In her rage, she did not discriminate.

The Norwich Mercury continued:

'R Bulwer was for the prosecution; prisoner was undefended.—Robert William Scraggs, master of the Mitford and Launditch Union, stated that on the 20th November, 1858, prisoner was an inmate of that workhouse. On that day, his attention was called to a disturbance in the dining-room of the establishment. He went there, and found prisoner beating the assistant matron. She was removed to a dormitory, and when she had been in about ten minutes witness heard a noise like the striking of a match. He immediately went into the room, and found a quantity of straw, which had been taken out of the bed in the apartment, had been set on fire. The prisoner must have set it on fire, for the bed was in a proper condition when she was placed in the room, and nobody had been in but herself from that time to the time witness went in. Witness had frequently seen her in ungovernable passions, but he thought she was not mad, but that these fits of rage were the result of the pure badness in her.'

The Norfolk Chronicle reported that after Harriet had been removed from the dining room she was put 'into a separate apartment' where 'she then declared that she would burn down the "b----y building"'. As well as setting fire to the straw, she had destroyed the bedding. The report added that, 'she was subsequently taken before a magistrate, when she said that she hoped that she should be transported'.

It is noteworthy that the Norwich Mercury's report referred to Harriet striking a match. In doing so, like those who set fire to stacks of hay and straw on farms, she was making use of a relatively recent invention. As one writer has put it, "Lucifer' [friction] matches, as sold in every village store, only came onto the market in 1830. This proved an absolute boon to would-be incendiaries'.[23]

Ebenezer Owen, master of the county lunatic asylum, was called to give evidence[24], and stated his opinion that Harriet was not insane but was subject to 'paroxysms of rage' (Norwich Mercury) or 'violent fits of passion, especially when thwarted' (Norfolk Chronicle). Mr Masters, surgeon to the gaol at Norwich Castle, was called and stated his view that Harriet was insane, while admitting that he had only been with her for a short time. The judge summed up, in which, according to the Norfolk Chronicle, 'he said it was quite possible for the prisoner to behave in this violent manner for the purpose of escaping punishment'.[25]

Finally, according to the Norwich Mercury:

'…the jury, after a brief deliberation, found the prisoner guilty. She was sentenced to 18 months imprisonment. Prisoner immediately became very violent, and was about to make some statement of her innocence, but she was removed, though not without some resistance, and a great deal of bad language on her part.'

For Harriet, it could have been worse. Arson of any kind was a capital offence until 1837 and arson to a dwelling house continued to carry the death penalty until 1861, although the sentence was never carried out. Until the 1850s, those convicted of arson were often sentenced to transportation (which Harriet had said she wanted), after which imprisonment became the normal punishment.[26]

Three months after Harriet's trial, the guardians took the sensible precaution of paying £16 9s 9d (£16.49) to Eliza Leatherdale, widow, bookseller and stationer in Litcham and agent of the Norwich Equitable Insurance Society, for 'one year's insurance of the workhouse against fire to midsummer 1861'.[27] But no further arson attempt was recorded.

Notes

1   A main source for this chapter is the MLU minutes; NRO, C/GP14/5, 11, 12 and 14.
2   Robert Scraggs' father had been the vestry clerk in East Dereham.
3   TNA: MH12 8480/424.
4   NN, 27 November 1858.
5   NN, 31 March 1860.
6   CLA, case book 1853-61; NRO, SAH 262.
7   CLA, reception orders 1857-60 and 1860-63; NRO, SAH 168/3.
8   CLA, annual report 1858; NRO, SAH 28; Cherry (2003). Later, in 1876, new buildings were erected north of the road to Great Yarmouth and male patients were transferred there.
9   CLA, annual report 1858; NRO, SAH 28.
10 CLA, annual report 1859; NRO, SAH 28.
11 In 1863, the Commissioners in Lunacy expressed the 'hope that it will be found practicable in future to give a fresh supply [of water] to each patient', CLA annual report

1863; NRO, SAH 28.

12 CLA, annual report 1859; NRO, SAH 28.

13 CLA, case book 1853-61; NRO, SAH 262.

14 CLA, reports of the commissioners in lunacy 1844-1925; NRO, SAH 141.

15 CLA, case book 1853-61; NRO, SAH 262.

16 Quarter sessions minutes 1857-62; NRO, C/S4/12.

17 NC, 30 July 1859.

18 NM, 30 July 1859.

19 MLU minutes; NRO, C/GP14/15.

20 CLA, minutes of the visiting justices 1856-62; NRO, SAH 8.

21 Ibid.

22 TNA: HO13/106 p.106.

23 J E Archer (1990).

24 As stated in NC. According to NM the witness was Mr Holl, a surgeon, but that was
    clearly incorrect, as there was no officer of that name at Thorpe.

25 It was not unknown for prisoners facing trial to do this. An inspector of prisons, when
    visiting Swaffham house of correction in 1857, commented on a prisoner, 'who was
    acquitted of arson on the ground of insanity, in March 1856, and ordered to be confined
    during Her Majesty's pleasure. The surgeon states: "I have not seen in the prisoner
    a single instance of aberration of mind…"' 23rd Report of the Inspectors of Prisons,
    Midland District, PP XI, 1859 (session 1).

26 JE Archer (1990).

27 MLU minutes, 2 July 1860; NRO, C/GP14/15; 1861 census returns.

Punishment: Wymondham House of Correction, Norfolk Lunatic Asylum and Bethlem Hospital

A FTER her trial, Harriet was again imprisoned in Wymondham house of correction, where she had been detained previously after her arson attempt at Gressenhall, and from which she had been transferred to the county lunatic asylum. Wymondham, at this time, was the place of imprisonment for all women in Norfolk whose sentences exceeded three months.[1]

The house of correction in Wymondham had a long history. Recent investigations have established that there was a structure on the site in the 14th century, which developed into a manor house in the 15th and 16th centuries.[2] This building became a bridewell (local prison) in the early 17th century, with underground cells in the basement. It was still serving this purpose when visited by the prison reformer John Howard in 1779. He described it as, 'one of the vilest prisons in England'. The impact of his criticism was such that a new gaol was created by adding two wings, one on each side of the original building, the latter becoming the accommodation for the gaoler, or keeper, and his family. The new bridewell had 21 separate cells, four workrooms, two side wards and a mill where hemp was dressed. For its time, it was innovatory, one of the earliest examples of the separate system in practice; visitors were received from other parts of England and even from the United States. The keeper's house was demolished in 1810 and replaced by a new edifice 20 feet nearer the road that runs past the site.

The history of the prison in Wymondham could have ended in 1825, as in that year the county magistrates, meeting at their quarter sessions, decided to close it and sell the premises. However, there was no buyer, and in 1831 the building was repaired and re-opened as a county house of correction for women, one of only a few in England and a progressive development for the period. As one authority has written: 'The segregation of women by sex was one of the major achievements of nineteenth-century penal reform. More than any other single aspect of reform, it rescued women from the degradation and exploitation

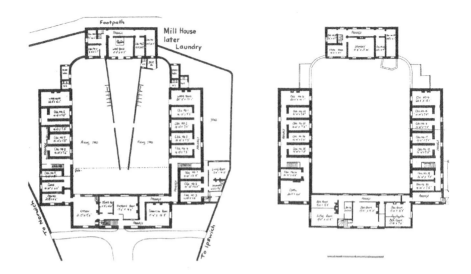

Plan of Wymondham House of Correction, 1865.

of eighteenth-century prison life'.[3]

Wymondham house of correction also accommodated male remand prisoners but this posed a problem because the law required that they should be supervised by a male gaoler and the magistrates were reluctant to contemplate the expense of employing an additional officer. The solution was to create a separate 'lock-up house' and residence for a male police officer on the site, and these had been completed by 1850.[4] Meanwhile, the mill had been converted into a laundry, which can probably be identified with the wash house of which one of the magistrates commented in 1845 that it, 'reminded him of the black hole of Calcutta; he was only surprised that it did not kill half the women'.[5]

An inspector of prisons, Mr J Hill, visited Wymondham in 1850. As at Walsingham, he found that: 'In accordance with the inspector's recommendations, steps had been taken towards having the cells used for separate confinement brought within the provisions of the statute [the Gaol Act of 1823]'. The newspaper report on his visit recorded his view that: 'The system of discipline in use here was, in his opinion, calculated to deter people from the commission of crime, and decidedly to improve the character of the prisoners.'[6] As at Walsingham, the provision reflected the priorities which now informed the management of prisons across the country: deterrence and reform. For women in prison, reform entailed restoring their respectability and 'womanliness'.[7]

However, further improvements were needed. The inspector noted that, 'as an artificial light had not been introduced, far too much time was passed in bed'. As a result, the visiting justices decided to use gas to both light and warm the cells and by 1851 the necessary equipment had been installed and was in use, allowing what was referred to in 1854 as the 'solitary system' to be implemented fully.[8] Following a further inspection on 17 November 1852, it was reported that: 'The ventilation is better than it was, but some of the cells were still very close. The pipes for the escape of the smoke and unconsumed gas is [sic] merely carried through the window, consequently, on the side exposed, to the wind, the noxious air is forced back into the cell when the window is opened. These pipes should be carried to the roof of the building, as at Norwich Castle, where the system of warming the cells with gas has been very successful.'[9] When the prison was inspected five years later, on 6 October 1857, the work had been done. The inspector quoted the surgeon's comment that, 'the ventilation, drainage and sanitary condition of the prison [are] now very good'.[10]

In 1861, the inspectorate reported that the house of correction had 36 cells for individuals and four capable of containing a larger number, together with two day rooms and a punishment cell.[11] Throughout the periods of Harriet Kettle's confinement at Wymondham, the number of prisoners was generally lower than the number of cells. There had been 26 inmates at the time of the inspection in 1852, a large proportion of whom were domestic servants who had robbed their employers. The inspector quoted the matron: 'It is the great love of dress that leads to crime; they dress far above their situation in life. Some few follow crime as a profession, and some through poverty.' At the inspection of 1857 there were 25 prisoners. The inspector noted the case of, 'one girl, stated to be 18 years of age, but apparently much younger, sentenced to two years' imprisonment, for breaking into her master's room and stealing nine £10 notes, with which she absconded, and, disguising herself in boy's clothes, went to Edinburgh, where she spent the money in three weeks.' He continued: 'In her case, I believe a restless disposition, and love of a wandering life, induced her to rob her employer; but all the other cases [of larcenies by servants} appeared to proceed from an inordinate love of dress.'[12] In 1858, the year when Harriet Kettle arrived at Wymondham for the first time, the average number of prisoners was 23, most of whom were serving sentences of under six months. Some, like Harriet, had been imprisoned for offences committed in workhouses, and a significant proportion, again, were domestic servants who had stolen clothes or other items from their employers. Once they were in the prison, the dress code (as described in 1836) was basic: 'shift, jacket, petticoat, apron, handkerchief, cap and stockings'.[13]

As at Walsingham, following the passage of the Gaol Act in 1823, a committee of visiting justices became responsible for the supervision of Wymondham house of correction.[14] The chief officer was the matron, who at the time of Harriet Kettle's detention there was Emily Greenfield. Originally

Wymondham Bridewell, c1904. (Courtesy Wymondham Heritage Museum)

from Sussex, she had obtained the position of turnkey (warder) at the prison in 1847. In April 1853, the visiting justices agreed to raise her salary from £35 to £40 per year in view of her 'arduous duties'.[15] The previous matron, Martha M Bryant, who had been recruited from Coldbath Fields prison in London in March 1846,[16] earned £60 per year. She died on 28 August 1854 after over eight years' service, the newspaper notice referring to her as 'the respected matron of Wymondham Bridewell'.[17] Two months later, Emily Greenfield was appointed to the vacancy, on the strength of 'having discharged the duties of turnkey in a satisfactory manner'.[18] She remained in the post for almost a quarter of a century, receiving an increase in salary in 1875 on account of her long service. When the magistrates discussed the matter, the Earl of Kimberley remarked that, 'the matron was fully deserving of the increase, she having long been a servant of the county, and the prison having been exceedingly well managed by her'.[19]

Emily Greenfield was assisted by a turnkey, who at the time of Harriet Kettle's imprisonment at Wymondham was Elizabeth Critolph; she left at the end of 1861 and was replaced by Mary Ann Goss, a bricklayer's daughter from Shipdham.[20] Mary Ann's salary was increased in 1863 owing to her increased duties in the laundry. A cook and housemaid were employed but there was no schoolmistress, as one of Emily Greenfield's duties was to instruct the prisoners in reading and writing and, apparently, she performed this role effectively. She was praised by the prison's chaplain, who in 1857 noted that: 'The matron, who took great interest in the prisoners, had been very diligent in teaching them to read and write.'[21] There was said to be a good supply of books for the prisoners

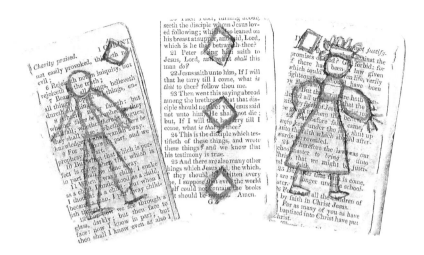

Wymondham Bridewell: playing cards made from pages of the New Testament. (Courtesy Wymondham Heritage Museum)

to read.

The surgeon, Robert James Tunaley, had been appointed when Wymondham house of correction reopened as a women's prison in 1831; he was also the medical officer for the Wymondham district of Forehoe Union.[22] The chaplain, the Revd David Jones, was appointed in January 1840 and, like his peers at Walsingham (and unlike his predecessor, who suffered from 'mental derangement which had rendered him altogether incompetent to the discharge of his duties'[23]), appears to have been an active and dedicated minister. In 1857, an inspector reported that the chaplain gave the prisoners religious instruction in class three times a week and visited them individually in their cells once a week, while a report in 1861 expanded further on his duties: 'The chaplain reads prayers in the chapel every morning and twice on Sunday, with a sermon; he visits every prisoner individually in her cell once during the week, hears them read, repeat their lessons and portions of scripture, questions them thereupon. When a prisoner comes into or leaves the prison he especially visits and admonishes her'.[24] The chaplain, again like his counterparts at Walsingham, thought that his admonitions had some effect in 'reforming' the prisoners, reporting in 1860 that: 'Many of the prisoners had left the prison with the apparently sincere resolution to act uprightly for the future, and thus endeavour to retrieve their lost character.'[25]

Whether his words had any impact on Harriet Kettle is unknown, but they appear not to have influenced all the women detained in the prison. Copies of the New Testament were issued to the prisoners, and during a recent renovation of the building, some torn-out pages were found hidden behind a window frame.

Wymondham House of Correction, 2020.

They had been made into playing cards, with blood used for the red suits and charcoal for the black.[26] It must have taken some ingenuity on the prisoners' part to subvert the separation and silence imposed by the authorities and organise a game of cards.

After Wymondham prison had reopened in 1831, the visiting justices agreed that the women detained there would undertake washing for the county gaol at Norwich Castle. In 1831, it was reported that the prisoners were washing and mending 200 articles weekly and that the arrangement, as well as saving money for the county, 'afforded a means of providing hard labour for the female convicts'.[27] A new contract for the work of washing and ironing, and making and mending of clothing, was agreed in 1851.[28] The following year, an inspector reported that oakum-picking and mat-making had also been introduced; the oakum-picking, which was probably regarded as lighter labour than the washing, continued in subsequent years but the mat-making appears to have been dropped.

During Harriet Kettle's first period of detention at Wymondham, in December 1858, the inspectors of prisons arrived. They reported that there were 26 prisoners and stated that the general health of those confined had been good. The food, they said, was good and sufficient, and the prisoners made no complaints. The report continued: 'The duties of the chaplain and surgeon are performed with regularity, and the prisoners make considerable progress under the instructions of the chaplain and matron. When not in school they are employed washing, knitting and picking oakum.' Over the year, there had been 55 punishments for offences committed within the prison, 'principally for talking to each other from cell to cell'.[29] Clearly the silent system was being enforced rigorously.

After her trial on 28 March 1860, Harriet spent barely a month in Wymondham house of correction before, once again, being transferred to the county lunatic asylum. On 5 April, the visiting justices at Wymondham reported to the quarter sessions that Harriet 'was after her conviction at the recent assizes again received into this prison. ...She was at the time she arrived here in a most violent and excited state and now remains in the same state, and from the report of the surgeon it appears an application must again be made for her removal to the lunatic asylum'. The matron, Emily Greenfield, in her report added that, 'the prison is clean and in good order until the last few days having received a lunatic prisoner who is noisy and violent'. On 26 April, Harriet was removed to the asylum.

The medical officer of the asylum remained convinced of Harriet's sanity. So did the board of guardians at Gressenhall, who had sustained legal expenses of £9 16s 6d in prosecuting Harriet and wanted her to be punished and 'reformed'. Their clerk contacted Emily Greenfield, having heard about the steps taken to transfer Harriet to the asylum. On 16 April the guardians discussed her reply and 'such reply not being deemed satisfactory', the clerk was instructed to write to the Home Office on 16 April, 'to express the feelings of the guardians against a commutation of her sentence on slight grounds of insanity, the guardians being desirous that if the prisoner should be again removed from custody in the present place of her confinement she should be placed in such a situation as to encourage a hope of her ultimate reformation'. The reply from the Home Office, dated 24 April 1860, was bland: Harriet had been certified to be insane and therefore must be removed to a lunatic asylum.[30]

The warrant for Harriet's transfer to the asylum stated that the parish of Southburgh (which bordered Cranworth), 'in which the said lunatic has been adjudged to be settled' would be required to pay for her maintenance in the asylum, a covering note again emphasising that the government would not pay.[31] As has been seen, the cost would amount to over £5 per quarter and Southburgh objected. Two magistrates investigated and decided that Harriet, after all, was 'chargeable' to Cranworth. Their adjudication did not come cheap, no doubt because they needed to be maintained in the manner to which they were accustomed while carrying out their investigation: the Mitford and Launditch Union received a bill for £9 4s 0d, equivalent to over £943 today.[32] Cranworth was ordered to pay for Harriet's maintenance together with the expenses arising from 'the investigation of her sanity'. The Home Office issued a revised warrant on 4 August, this time giving Cranworth as the place of Harriet's settlement.

Edward Casson, the long-suffering medical officer at the asylum noted of Harriet that, 'on admission she was…very much the same as when she last entered the asylum and I may add left it', and recalled that after her trial she 'made a disturbance and was certified as insane (which I think she certainly is not)… and removed here'. Harriet's bodily condition was recorded in the admission register as 'weakly'.[33] She had a stomach upset and was prescribed medication which included tincture of opium, or laudanum. Harriet seems to have behaved in an orderly manner throughout this fourth stay at Thorpe. On 22 June she was reported to have 'gone on very quietly and employed herself at needlework. Suffers from dyspepsia and requires tonics, generally. Mentally sane'. On 30 July, she had 'had no outburst of passion since the last entry. She has taken the entire charge of an idiot child aet [aged] 7 years lately sent here and makes an excellent nurse to it. Continues quite rational and free from delusions'. Finally, on 25 August 1860, 'She was on this day removed from the asylum to Wymondham gaol…Discharged recovered'.[34]

Meanwhile, while Harriet was a patient at the asylum, the board of guardians at Gressenhall had remained dissatisfied with the situation. After receiving the reply from the Home Office dated 24 April, stating that Harriet would be removed to a lunatic asylum, they ordered the clerk to find out where Harriet had been sent and 'to call the particular attention of the medical and other officers of that establishment to the circumstances under which Harriet Kettle was recently convicted and as to the questionable state of her mental health'. The clerk must have found out quickly enough that she had been sent to Thorpe. At their meeting on 21 May, the guardians noted a letter from Ebenezer Owen, master of the county lunatic asylum reiterating his and the medical officer's opinion that Harriet was sane. They decided to ask him for 'the necessary certificates of her sanity in order that they may be prepared to take the required steps for her removal to a proper place of confinement'[35]but these appear not to have been forthcoming; in their absence, as the Home Office reminded the guardians on 13 June, Harriet could not be discharged from the asylum.[36] The clerk to the guardians wrote to the asylum's visiting magistrates again on 16 and 23 July, reminding them of the case, 'which they consider not only of pecuniary importance to the parish chargeable with her maintenance…but as tending to frustrate the ends of justice and destroy every hope of the unfortunate woman's ultimate reformation'. He continued, 'it is sufficient to remind you that your medical and other officers have always deemed her sane.. and they have recently certified her sanity to the commissioners in lunacy'. The letter concluded: 'Under these circumstances it is not unreasonable that the guardians should express the hope and expect that the necessary steps will immediately be taken for her removal to some proper receptacle for such persons. The guardians will feel obliged by your informing them when these measures are adopted.' Their frustration with the situation was now ill-concealed.

A certificate as to Harriet's sanity, signed by GW Firth and Edward Casson, was sent to the board of guardians on 7 August, accompanied by a letter from the visiting justices' clerk stating that the certificate was being sent, 'that the guardians of the Mitford and Launditch Union may take such further proceedings as they think advisable'.[37] The letter and certificate were received by the board on 13 August, when the clerk was ordered to send them to the Home Office with a letter 'particularly requesting that on removing Harriet Kettle from the Asylum she may be imprisoned in some other place than the house of correction at Wymondham in order to avoid a repetition of the proceedings which have hitherto been adopted in her case'.[38]

However, this cut no ice with the Home Office, from which a reply was sent to the clerk on 23 August stating that, as Harriet had been convicted of a serious offence, the Home Secretary had, 'no alternative but to order her removal back to the prison from which she was sent'.[39] Therefore, it was to Wymondham house of correction that Harriet was again transferred on her discharge from the asylum on 25 August 1860.

Although their view of Harriet Kettle's sanity was different, the visiting justices at Wymondham house of correction had been thinking along not dissimilar lines about what should happen to her. In their report to the summer quarter sessions on 4 July 1860, they noted that they had obtained an order for her removal to the county lunatic asylum but added that she 'on two separate occasions previously to taking her trial, has been removed from this prison to the asylum at Thorpe…in consequence of her having been certified by two medical men as being insane, and not having on her return manifested the least symptoms of improvement, your committee would suggest that steps be taken to obtain, if possible, her removal to some criminal lunatic asylum'.[40] When the report was discussed, one of the magistrates, Mr Edwards, commented that, 'it was very generally supposed that she was not insane, but, preferring the comforts of Thorpe asylum to the prison treatment, and having a very violent temper, she occasionally broke out into such paroxysms of passion as induced those in whose custody she was to think her mad, and consequently get her transferred to the lunatic asylum. He understood that she was not the only prisoner who did this.' The chairman remarked that: 'As this woman would move in a sort of charmed circle between Thorpe asylum and Wymondham bridewell, he did not think the court could do anything.'[41]

The authorities at Wymondham house of correction were not thrilled to receive Harriet on her discharge from Thorpe in August 1860. The report of the surgeon, Robert James Tunaley, dated 16 October 1860, stated that Harriet re-entered the prison on 28 August by order of the Secretary of State, 'it having been certified to him, she was perfectly sane, but the very circumstance of being guarded by two male and one female attendant rather belied the probability of her sanity, which her subsequent behaviour confirms'. In her report, the matron, Emily Greenfield, added that, 'the prison is clean and in good order considering having Harriet Kettle who is a lunatic, and not in a proper state of mind to be in a prison'. However, the chaplain, David Jones, paid tribute to Emily Greenfield's management of Harriet in his report: 'The chaplain regrets to add that the conduct of the poor girl, Harriet Kettle, who was brought back from Thorpe lunatic asylum interferes very much with the proper discipline of the prison. The matron, however, who acts with kindness and firmness towards her, has, at times, great influence over her'.[42] There were not many people of whom that could be said.

Emily Greenfield was to remain in her position until her resignation in 1878 when, under the provisions of the Prison Act of the previous year, the national government took control of all prisons from the local authorities and Wymondham house of correction, along with many other small local prisons, was closed. Mary Ann Goss, who had worked as turnkey with Emily since 1861, resigned at the same time. The visiting justices recommended that they be granted 'retiring allowances' of £90 and £25 per year respectively.[43] When the census was taken three years later, the two women, in retirement, were sharing a house in Norwich Road, Wymondham. Emily, the head of the household, now aged 64, was described as an annuitant and Mary Ann's relationship to her was stated to be 'companion'. Mary Ann Goss died in 1883, aged 48; Emily Greenfield outlived her, dying in 1886, aged 70.[44]

Back at Gressenhall, the board of guardians, at their meeting on 10 September 1860, considered a letter addressed to them from the Home Secretary, acknowledging their request that Harriet be moved to a prison other than Wymondham house of correction and asking the guardians if they could suggest somewhere else. The Clerk was instructed to mention Walsingham, which had not yet closed and had male staff, who were considered more effective, but to say that the guardians thought that Harriet's removal to a prison outside Norfolk, 'would be much more conducive to the ends of justice and to the reformation of the prisoner'.[45] The Home Secretary replied on 25 September, contradicting his previous request and stating that he did 'not think it necessary to remove Harriet Kettle from Wymondham house of correction'.[46] So that, for the time being, is where Harriet remained.

On 2 January 1861, Emily Greenfield reported to the quarter sessions that: 'the prison is clean and in good order in consideration having a lunatic prisoner', while the visiting justices noted that, 'the prison was recently visited by Captain Voules Her Majesty's Inspector of Prisons who considered the prison to be in an efficient and satisfactory state with the exception of one prisoner (Harriet Kettle) upon whose case he undertook to make a special report to the Secretary of State'.[47] In his report, published in 1861, Voules wrote that, 'one insane person who had been in a lunatic asylum three times was brought to the prison during the year from the county lunatic asylum, and was afterwards removed by order of the Secretary of State to Bethlehem hospital'.[48]

And, perhaps as a result of Captain Voules' intervention, that is how the situation was resolved. As the visiting justices for Wymondham reported to the Easter quarter sessions on 4 April 1861, 'Harriet Kettle…having never in the opinion of this committee…been a fit subject for a prison having constantly when here by order of the surgeon been attended by a nurse and treated in every respect as the patient of an hospital, the committee on 23rd of February called to their aid Dr Ranking and Mr Gibson[49] and those gentlemen having certified the prisoner to be insane, a report of her case with the certificate was duly forwarded to the Secretary of State on the 6th March instant, such prisoner was removed by his order to the criminal lunatic asylum at Saint George's in the Fields, Surrey.'[50] The visiting justices and the officers of Wymondham house of correction were clearly relieved when Harriet, 'whose excitability and violence caused so much trouble and expense' (according to the surgeon) had gone.

Harriet was escorted to London. The journey, by train, would have taken at least four or five hours, or more, as she and those accompanying her would probably have been travelled on the statutory 'parliamentary' train rather than a more expensive express service. With the exception of her possible participation in trips to Great Yarmouth and Lowestoft with the asylum in 1856, 1859 and 1860, Harriet was leaving Norfolk for the first time in her life. Arriving in the huge metropolis must have been a very strange experience for her.

The asylum at St George's Fields (not 'St George's in the Fields', as the visiting justices had called it) in Southwark, also known as the Bethlem or Bethlehem hospital, occupied the building on the South Bank that now houses the Imperial War Museum. The original Bethlem hospital in London (from which the term 'bedlam' is derived), dated back to 1247. Originally part of a priory in Bishopsgate, it was granted to the City of London in 1547, after the dissolution of the monasteries by Henry VIII, and moved into a new building in Moorfields in 1676. When those premises became dilapidated and unsafe, the decision was made to move to the new site at St George's Fields. The new hospital opened in 1815.

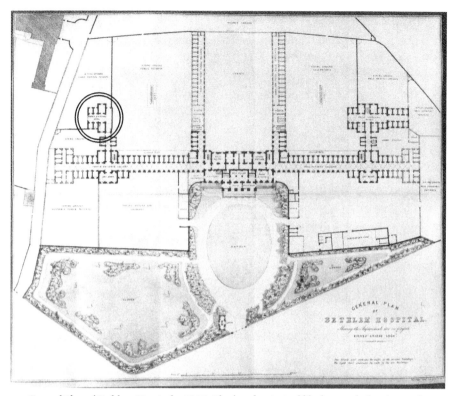

General Plan of Bethlem Hospital, c1847. The female criminal block is marked with a circle.
(Courtesy Bethlem Museum of the Mind)

Behind the imposing main building with male and female wings, to which a dome was added in 1845, were detached blocks for male and female criminal patients, opened in 1816 and expanded in 1838.[51] Their occupants were originally people who had been acquitted or found unfit to plead in their trials on the grounds of insanity. Later, those, like Harriet, who were certified to have become insane while serving their sentences, were also admitted. Unlike the rest of the patients, who were charged fees, those in the criminal wings were maintained by the Home Office.

The internal layout of the criminal lunatic blocks was similar to that in the main male and female wings. Patients occupied individual sleeping rooms which faced spacious corridors which served as day rooms. Illustrations of the female and male wards in the main (non-

Dr William Charles Hood by Charles Frechou, 1851.

The Royal Hospital of Bethlehem—The gallery of women.
(Illustrated London News, 24 March 1860)

criminal) block, accompanying glowing articles in the Illustrated London News in March 1860, depicted corridors containing flowers, caged birds, paintings and sculptures.[52] However, it appears that these enhancements did not reach the criminal lunatic blocks, which remained gloomier and more prison-like. According to the Quarterly Review (referring mainly to the male block): 'These dens, for we can call them by no softer name, are the only remaining representatives of old Bedlam. They consist of dismal arched corridors, feebly lit at either end by a single window in double irons, and divided in the middle by gratings more like those which enclose the fiercer carnivora at the zoological gardens than anything we have elsewhere seen employed for the detention of afflicted humanity.'[53]

In 1863 and 1864, shortly after Harriet's sojourn there, all the criminal patients at Bethlem hospital were transferred to the new state criminal asylum at Broadmoor and the criminal wings at Bethlem were then demolished. [54]

While Harriet was at Bethlem, she came under the care of Dr Charles Hood, who had been appointed as the first resident physician superintendent at the hospital in 1852, at the age of 28. His appointment was part of a programme to reform Bethlem after a series of scandals involving allegations of negligence and ill-treatment and an unfavourable report by the commissioners in lunacy. Hood was responsible for brightening up the wards for the non-criminal patients. He also raised the status of the attendants and provided occupations and recreational

19th century photograph of the rear of Bethlem hospital, showing the female criminal wing on the right. (Courtesy Bethlem Museum of the Mind)

activities both inside and outside the hospital. Dr Hood resigned from his post in 1862, after Harriet had departed, and became the Lord Chancellor's 'visitor in lunacy'. He was knighted in 1868 and died two years later. [55]

When Harriet Kettle was formally admitted to Bethlem hospital, on 7 March 1861, her age was given as 25. She was said to have no children. Her 'degree of education' was recorded as 'moderate' and her religious persuasion was stated to be Church of England. The responses given to the questions, 'whether suicidal' and 'whether dangerous to others' were 'yes' in both cases. To the question, 'state of bodily health' the response was 'Bad. Cannot eat animal foods'. A purgative (aloes) was prescribed, which had been a common practice at Bethlem for many years. Surprisingly, and questionably, as it had never been mentioned previously and was denied by Harriet herself, the response under, 'peculiar delusions, or the way in which the insanity is manifested' was 'being possessed of property'. The question, 'has the patient been of sober habits' was answered, 'it is thought not'.[56]

According to a report of June 1861, Harriet was one of only 20 female criminal patients. There were 133 male criminal patients, including Richard Dadd, the noted artist, who had been admitted in 1844 after murdering his father. However, as he and Harriet were confined in the separate male and female blocks, they would not have met.[57]

The first entry in Dr Hood's case notes relating to Harriet, dated 4 April, was:

'This girl is reported to have lived a profligate life and to have been confined several times in an asylum....She has little or no controul [sic] over her temper and her disposition is bad and naturally vicious. She renders herself very obnoxious to her fellow patients by her quarrelsome ways and jealous character, but in no other way does she show any indication of a disordered mind nor does she allow that there is any delusion about property occupying her mind. She takes very little food and is not able to touch meat. She is sometimes industrious, but so fitful that she cannot be depended upon.'[58]

Little changed over the succeeding months. On 19 May, it was noted that 'she has lately been more quarrelsome and disagreeable with her fellow patients'. There was no improvement by 16 July, but 'the catamenia [periods] which were suppressed have returned'. On 31 August, it was noted that, 'she continues very bad tempered and badly behaved and latterly [has] shown great obstinacy in refusing food. On two occasions it was necessary to feed her with the stomach pump, but now she takes food well again'. Harriet's refusal to eat, and the suppression of her periods, might now be interpreted by psychiatrists as expressions of her rejection both of the institutional regime and of her own past experiences, in her childhood and subsequently.[59] On 8 October, however, Hood wrote of Harriet that, 'she is well behaved again and appears quite sound in her mind'.

The final note was on 23 October 1861: 'The period of her sentence has expired and an order has been received for her discharge. An attendant has taken her to E. C. [Eastern Counties] Railway and started her off for Norwich.' As when she arrived in the city, the journey across London to Bishopsgate Station (the predecessor of Liverpool Street) must have been an eye-opener for Harriet. After another long train journey, probably unescorted this time, she must have been glad to be back in Norfolk. Perhaps, like Michael Davitt, the Irish Fenian, she experienced, 'the wild, ecstatic, soul-filling happiness of the first day of freedom'.[60] Somewhat belatedly, on 1 November, a letter was sent from the Home Office to the board of guardians at Gressenhall informing them of Harriet's release.[61]

Harriet found her sister Matilda in Norwich. Matilda was still single; at the time of the census in April 1861 she had been working as a domestic servant in Colegate, but she had probably left her position by the time Harriet arrived in the city. When Matilda married William Pank in Norwich on 14 January 1862,[62] both she and the groom were said to be resident in New Catton, the growing suburb north of the city centre. William Pank was recorded in the 1861 census as an 'attendant and gatekeeper', aged 30, at the Norwich city asylum in the parish of St Clement's.[63] On the marriage certificate, his occupation was given as 'keeper of lunatics'. It is ironic that Matilda's husband-to-be was working at a lunatic asylum, albeit not the one in which Harriet had been a patient.

Matilda, like Harriet, was literate, and it would appear that she was a better writer than her sister. On 27 October 1861, a letter written by her was laid before the board of guardians of Mitford and Launditch Union by the chairman, the Revd Philip Gurdon. Perhaps the letter had been sent directly to him. Matilda reported that Harriet had been discharged from Bethlem and requested outdoor relief for her.[64] The clerk to the guardians wrote to the Poor Law Board in London on 5 November. The letter began, 'It may possibly be in your recollection that a young girl named Harriet Kettle who was a pauper inmate of this union workhouse for several years was so frequently guilty of violent and insubordinate conduct as to render her frequent punishment necessary, both in the workhouse and commitment to prison.' The clerk went on to summarise the events of the previous five years, concluding that Harriet, 'is supposed to be now of sound mind, but as she requires parochial relief and wishes to reside with her friends in Norwich, the board of guardians are desirous of complying with her request in order to avoid re-currence of any exciting cause for further violence or mental disease, and they therefore request your sanction to such a deviation from the terms of the general prohibitory order'.[65] The sanction was given, although the Poor Law Board added the qualification that they presumed that, 'the guardians have satisfied themselves, by enquiries, that the pauper will be properly taken care of if she goes to reside with her friends at Norwich'. The arrangement seems to have been successful for all parties.

What Harriet did in Norwich is not known. She may have returned to sex work, or she may have been content to live on her outdoor relief from Mitford and Launditch Union. Did she continue to live with her sister Matilda, and did she attend Matilda's wedding in January 1862? Those remain open questions, but she was not recorded as a witness on Matilda and William's marriage certificate. Matilda was again recorded as Harriet's nearest relative in 1863 but there is no other evidence of a continuing relationship between the sisters after 1861.

Harriet only remained in Norwich for no more than fourteen months. At the beginning of January 1863, she was back at Gressenhall workhouse. She was pregnant.

Notes

1   25th Report of the Inspectors of Prisons, Midland District, PP XXXV, 1860.
2   Background on Wymondham house of correction is drawn from J Hawkins (1987), N J Jenson (2000) and wymondhamheritagemuseum.co.uk, along with the evidence from inspectors' reports and local newspapers.
3   L Zedner in N Morris and D J Rothman (1995).
4   NM, 20 October 1848, 21 March 1849 and 12 January 1850.
5   NM, 8 January 1845.
6   NC, 6 December 1851.
7   L Zedner in N Morris and D J Rothman (1995).
8   NM, 12 April 1854.
9   18th Report of Inspectors of Prisons, Northern and Eastern District, PP XXXIII, 1856.
10 23rd Report of Inspectors of Prisons, Midland District, PP XL, 1859.
11 26th Report of Inspectors of Prisons, Midland District, PP XXIX, 1861.
12 23rd Report of Inspectors of Prisons, Midland District, PP XL, 1859.
13 Report on prisons in Norfolk, 19 October 1836, in *Accounts and papers relating to crime; gaols; criminals*, PP XLV, 1837, available via books.google.co.uk.
14 Their minute book for 1832-64; NRO, C/S5/15 survives, but regrettably is extremely fragile, with disintegrating pages, and (as advised by a searchroom assistant on 18

September 2020) cannot be handled.

15 NC, 16 April 1853.

16 BNP, 18 March 1846.

17 NC, 9 September 1854.

18 NC, 28 October 1854.

19 NC, 23 October 1875.

20 NN, 4 January 1862.

21 NM, 28 October 1857.

22 NC, 11 March 1848.

23 J Hawkins (1987).

24 26th Report of Inspectors of Prisons, Midland District, PP XXIX, 1861.

25 NM, 20 October 1860.

26 Thanks to Adrian Hoare and Wymondham Heritage Museum for this information.

27 NC, 27 April 1833.

28 NM, 11 January 1851.

29 23rd Report of Inspectors of Prisons, Midland District; PP XI, 1859 (session 1).

30 TNA: HO13/106 p.116.

31 CLA, reception orders 1857-60 and 1860-63; NRO, SAH 168/3.

32 MLU minutes, 12 August 1861; NRO, C/GP14/16; Office for National Statistics composite price index, accessed 16/06/2020.

33 CLA, admission register 1845-61; NRO, SAH 175.

34 CLA, case book 1853-61 (females); NRO, SAH 262.

35 MLU minutes, 21 May 1860; NRO, C/GP14/15.

36 TNA: HO13/106 p. 132.

37 CLA, clerk's letter book 1853-75; NRO, SAH 38.

38 MLU minutes, 13 August 1860; NRO, C/GP14/15.

39 TNA: HO13/106 p.153.

40 Quarter sessions minutes, Midsummer 1860; NRO, C/S4/12; NC, 7 July 1860.

41 NM, 7 July 1860.

42 Quarter sessions minutes, Michaelmas 1860; NRO, C/S4/12.

43 NC, 13 April 1878.

44 Wymondham burial register, accessed via freereg.org; census records accessed via findmypast.com.

45 MLU minutes, 10 September 1860; NRO, C/GP14/15; TNA: HO13/106 p.159.

46 MLU minutes, 1 October 1860; NRO, C/GP14/15; TNA: HO13/106 p.161.

47 Quarter sessions minutes, Epiphany 1861; NRO, C/S4/12.

48 26th Report of Inspectors of Prisons, Midland District, PP XXIX, 1861.

49 Dr William Harcourt Ranking was visiting physican to the Heigham Hall private asylum, Norwich; Mr Charles M Gibson was the resident surgeon of the Bethel hospital, Norwich (Harrod's Directory of Norfolk, 1863).

50 Quarter sessions minutes, Easter 1861; NRO, C/S4/12.

51 Catharine Arnold, *Bedlam* (2008).

52 Illustrated London News, 24 and 31 March 1860.

53 Quarterly Review, vol 101, p.356-365, 1857.

54 P H Allderidge (1974); Patricia H Allderidge, *The Bethlem Hospital Historical Museum*

Catalogue (1976).

55 C Arnold (2008).

56 Case notes, criminal patients; BM, CBC/3.

57 Quarterly report, 24 June 1861, in Resolutions, Correspondence and Returns concerning the State Criminal Lunatic Asylum, 1853-186; BM CSA-04.

58 Case notes, criminal patients; BM, CBC/3.

59 L Appignanesi (2008).

60 Michael Davitt, *Leaves from a Prison Diary* (1885), quoted by P Priestley (1999).

61 TNA: HO13/106 p. 277.

62 Marriage certificate of Matilda Kettle and William Pank.

63 The Norwich city asylum had been built in 1828 and moved to new premises in Hellesdon in 1880, after which it was known as Hellesdon hospital.

64 MLU minutes, 28 October 1861; NRO, C/GP14/16.

65 TNA: MH12 8481.

In Gressenhall Workhouse and the county lunatic asylum again

HARRIET Kettle was back at Gressenhall workhouse but the guardians were keen to avoid any trouble during the period up to the expected birth of her child. According to the minutes of their meeting on 5 January 1863:

'It having been reported to the board that Harriet Kettle had been again admitted into the workhouse under circumstances rendering her position therein somewhat different from those of an ordinary in-door pauper, the master is permitted to provide her with such little indulgencies as under the peculiar circumstances of her case he might in his discretion deem advisable so as not to interfere with the order and discipline of the workhouse until after the period of her approaching confinement.'[1]

This strategy (was it suggested by the chairman, Revd Philip Gurdon?) did not work. Harriet soon clashed with her old adversary, the assistant matron, Mary Ann Butcher. On 2 February, the guardians' visiting committee drew the board's attention to: '…the position in which Mrs Butcher the assistant matron was placed by the conduct and threats of Harriet Kettle…and the difficulty occurring thereby to Mrs Butcher in the exercise of her duties. The board having again considered the method of treatment to be adopted towards Harriet Kettle under the peculiar circumstances of her case, the master and matron are particularly directed to make such arrangements as may be necessary to avoid any intercourse between Kettle and Mrs Butcher until after Kettle's expected confinement and with that view to allow the porter Thomas Butcher to accompany his wife when proceeding to lock up for the night in the manner suggested by the master to protect her from any improper interference on the part of the said Harriet Kettle.'

This did not work either. A week later, 'on the report of the visiting committee, Harriet Kettle is directed to be taken before a magistrate on a charge of misbehaviour in the workhouse and with violently threatening the life of Mrs Butcher the assistant matron'. The punishment on this occasion, and the implications for Harriet's pregnancy, are unknown. It might have been a source of some satisfaction to Harriet that shortly afterwards, on 2 March, Thomas Butcher was dismissed from his post, having been 'inattentive to and neglectful of the duties of his office', and that meant that Mrs Butcher had to go as well.

Harriet lost her child. What exactly happened is not known, but there is no reference to a birth in the civil registration records, nor any reference to a baptism or burial in the Gressenhall chaplain's book, in which all the baptisms of children born in the workhouse, and burials of inmates, were recorded in this period. It seems most likely that Harriet miscarried, or aborted the foetus, or that the child was stillborn.

At the beginning of April 1863 Harriet was again 'allowed out-relief on the certificate of Dr Vincent that her bodily health required a residence out of the workhouse'. This suggests that however her pregnancy had ended, it had ended in March, which is consistent with a reference in July by Charles White, medical officer at the county lunatic asylum, to her confinement having been four months previously. In accordance with the decision to give Harriet outdoor relief, the guardians' minutes recorded that, 'the master is directed to provide her with proper and sufficient clothing to supply the place of those which were lost on her leaving the workhouse in 1858'. Harriet's clothes had actually been lost before 1858 (when her departure was to Wymondham house of correction prior to her trial for arson), as previous references make clear. It is also unclear why the clothes she was wearing when re-admitted in January 1863 were not returned to her. Perhaps those clothes were not regarded as 'proper and sufficient'.

Harriet was now living in East Dereham. A few months later, on 10 July 1863, she was admitted to the county lunatic asylum for the fifth time, having taken laudanum in an apparent attempt at suicide. Following the issue of an order by a magistrate, stating that he and a surgeon had examined Harriet and found her to be of unsound mind, she was removed to Thorpe by the former porter at Gressenhall and now relieving officer, John Cary, who was paid the considerable sum of £2 19s 0d (£2.95) for his expenses in doing so. Cary completed a form setting out various particulars about Harriet. He gave her age as 26 and her previous place of abode as Gressenhall union workhouse, which suggests that Harriet had been admitted and placed in the female sick ward there (and perhaps made a disturbance), before being sent on to the asylum. Cary stated that Harriet was unemployed, that her religious persuasion was Church of England, that she was suicidal but (perhaps surprisingly) not dangerous to others. He provided the details of her nearest known relative as: 'Matilda the wife of William Pank of Minns Building, Sussex Street, Norwich, the sister of the patient'.[2] Matilda and William were still living in Sussex Street eight years later, when the 1871 census was taken.[3]

The precise circumstances in which Harriet took laudanum, or tincture of opium, are not recorded. Attempted suicide was a crime until the passage of the Suicide Act of 1961 but there is no evidence that Harriet, unlike many others who tried to take their own lives, was prosecuted. Apart from the involvement of the police and the appearance in the police court, the sequence of events in Harriet's case may have been similar to those involving another woman in September of the following year. Jane Marshall, of Norwich, was taken to a police station in the city, 'whilst labouring under the effects of a dose of laudanum which she had taken, and was conveyed thence to the hospital, where she received medical treatment.' After recovering, she was taken before the police court, where she, 'said that she had taken the laudanum because she was troubled with lowness of spirits. She purchased it at Mr Grant's, chemist, Ber-street. The bottle was not labelled but she knew the nature of what she was taking'. She was cautioned and discharged.[4] Reports of such cases, and other occasions when the suicide attempt was successful, appeared regularly in the local newspapers.

Laudanum was freely available in mid-19th century England. Famous users included the poet Samuel Taylor Coleridge and the Liberal Prime Minister, William Ewart Gladstone, who took laudanum in a cup of coffee before delivering speeches in the House of Commons.[5] Laudanum was manufactured by dissolving opium in alcohol. Most of the opium used in England was imported from Turkey although a little was derived from the cultivation of poppies in the Fens and West Norfolk, which were also significant centres of opium consumption.[6] Opium was widely used by medical practitioners to alleviate the symptoms of tuberculosis and as a treatment for 'female complaints' and nervous disorders. Laudanum was also on general sale, not only by pharmacists and apothecaries but also by grocers and local shops. For poorer people, laudanum, purchased over the counter, was an inexpensive and widely consumed narcotic. Many kept a bottle in their homes.

Opium was also an ingredient of various patent medicines, such as Dr J Collis Browne's Chlorodyne and Godfrey's Cordial, the latter being a mixture of opium, treacle and an infusion of the root bark of the sassafras tree. Godfrey's Cordial was widely given to children to keep them quiet; or, as L Marion Springhall put it, 'the usual comfort administered to a squalling baby when its mother was too busy working in the fields to feed it'.[7] In October 1861, the Norfolk Chronicle reported in patronising terms about the dangerous mistakes that could occur when, 'laudanum…is purchased at small hucksters' shops, where, we regret to say, the most deadly poisons are sold, and kept on shelves in bottles side by side with hair oil, sal volatile, tincture of rhubarb, senna and Godfrey's cordial…with hundreds of chemists' shops in the city, it is the height of stupidity if the poor will go to the small general shopkeepers for drugs'.[8]

From the 1830s onwards, concerns had been expressed about the dangers of opium in its various forms, and particularly about self-medication and the administration of the drug to children by working class people. A campaign to regulate the sale of laudanum and other opium-based products developed in the 1860s. Statistics published in the annual reports of the Registrar General provided supporting evidence of the dangers; between 1863 and 1867, 235 infants under one year old and 56 children aged one to five, along with 235 adults, died as a result of opium poisoning. A Pharmacy Bill was introduced in 1868 but met strong opposition from 'chemists residing principally in Cambridgeshire, Lincolnshire and Norfolk, against interfering with their business—opium, as they stated, being one of their chief articles of trade'.[9] As a result of their representations, opium was not listed as a 'controlled poison' and instead was made subject to weaker requirements relating to the labelling as 'poison' of the bottles in which laudanum was sold. This requirement did not apply to patent medicines and a campaign to regulate them continued. Nevertheless, the Pharmacy Act of 1868 did result in an immediate and significant fall in the number of deaths, including the deaths of children, attributable to laudanum.

Ironically, but unsurprisingly given that it was sometimes (though decreasingly) used as a treatment for mania, Harriet Kettle may have been introduced to laudanum during her previous stay in the county lunatic asylum, when it had been prescribed for her by Edward Casson. It may have been then that she acquired a taste for it, although it was such a universal feature of the life of the poor that it seems more likely that she had encountered it already, while living in Norwich. During her stay in the asylum in 1863-64, Harriet was prescribed a stronger opium-based medication: morphine.

There had been changes at the asylum since Harriet's previous sojourn there in 1860. On their visit in 1859, the commissioners in lunacy had commented that Edward Casson's remuneration was 'much too small' and below that of any other resident medical officer in the country.[10] His salary was accordingly raised from £125 to £150 per year in 1860 and in 1861, at the age of 33, following the retirement of the previous (non-medical) superintendent, Ebenezer Owen, Casson was appointed as medical superintendent at an annual salary of £400 minus £150 for board and lodging, a substantial increase in his income. Norfolk's was the last county lunatic asylum to appoint a medical superintendent, completing the process of putting doctors in charge of the care of the mentally ill.

However, on 27 July 1861, only a few weeks after his appointment, Casson was asked to resign from his new position, 'having shown himself unfit to fulfill the duties of the office'. He duly did so three days later. A week afterwards, Edward Casson committed suicide by taking prussic acid (hydrogen cyanide).

According to the Norfolk Chronicle's report on the inquest, 'he was found dead in one of the lower rooms of the establishment on Sunday morning [4 August]'. His body was discovered by his mother, who was staying with him and his wife at the asylum, lying face down on the carpet, with an empty mug on a table above him. She fetched the matron, Mrs Owen (Casson's sister-in-law, who had not yet retired) and they tried to revive her son, but he was dead. Casson's colleague, GW Firth said that he had found two almost empty bottles of prussic acid in the room. The chairman of the visiting justices stated that, before his death, they had called Mr Casson to appear before them and had read the charges to him. Witnesses were then questioned and Casson was recommended to resign, which, 'he was very unwilling' to do but eventually did. The chairman stated that Casson had, 'admitted the bulk of the graver of the charges brought against him' (which were never disclosed publicly). The newspaper report concluded, 'The jury…found Mr Casson came by his death by taking prussic acid while labouring under extreme depression of spirits or in other words, "temporary insanity."'[11] It was a sad and ironic end for the man who bequeathed to posterity his analysis and recording of Harriet Kettle's alleged insanity.

Edward Casson's successor, William C Hills, took up his post as medical superintendent on 17 October 1861 and remained at Thorpe until his retirement in 1887. Under him worked an assistant resident medical officer. The first person to hold that position, George MacKenzie Bacon, had to resign in July 1863 having been discovered with a nurse in her room. The nurse had to resign too.[12] Bacon was succeeded by Charles White, 'of Guy's hospital', whose appointment by William Hills at the salary of £80 per year was confirmed by the visiting magistrates on 28 July 1863.[13] He only stayed at Thorpe for one year.

Harriet's admission to the asylum pre-dated the confirmation of Charles White's appointment by over a fortnight but she came under his care. The case book includes a detailed account by White of Harriet's life, sections of which have been quoted already. A few of the details were inaccurate, and the tone was patronising, but Charles White showed a degree of insight and even, up to a point, sympathy, greater than that evident in most of Harriet's previous contacts with the various institutions in which she had resided. He took account of her family background and took her own statements seriously, thereby, to a greater extent than his predecessor, giving her a voice. This was the full text of White's initial note in the asylum's case book:

'Kettle, Harriet, aet [aged] 26, single, of no definite occupation, professing the established religion of this country, was admitted July 10th 1863. The life of this patient has for many years been one of vicious indulgence, and she has been endowed by nature with a most violent temper. Her mother died insane, her father did but little for her, and she was brought up in Gressenhall workhouse. She left this abode to seek her own living when quite a girl, being tired of the irksome monotony and confinement of the union. From this point her evil courses date. Inheriting a bad disposition and violent passions, having been deprived of a mother's care, or the gentler influences which might have guided so uncertain a nature, and being surrounded by the moral effluvia of a workhouse, a place always and necessarily unfavourable to any advance in rectitude, it is not wonderful that when set free in the world young and ignorant she yielded to her inclinations and got into trouble. It appears from the evidence available that, after a course of prostitution, she was sent to Walsingham gaol for assaulting the master of a workhouse and was sent from gaol to this asylum by order of Secretary of State. It is stated that she had a strong suicidal tendency then, and that she suffered from piles. She left in March '57. In February '59 she was sent here from Wymondham gaol, to which she was committed for theft[14] and left on July 28 for trial at the assizes, but when she found she was to be imprisoned, she made a great row, and was returned on August 6 to the asylum. She left again the following March ('60) and when she was sentenced to 18 months' imprisonment at her trial, she repeated the former scenes of disturbance and was sent back as insane, being again discharged in August as cured. She subsequently went to Bethlehem and while there was fed by the stomach pump. The accounts given of her behaviour in this asylum show but little evidence of true insanity, but make it very plain that she gave way to her feelings without any effort at control, and was extemely violent and troublesome, making it her habit to break windows, tear clothes, scream, attack other patients or nurses, when her wishes were not gratified. She was alternately treated with severity and indulgence, but managed to do pretty well as she liked, her outbreaks creating a terror throughout the establishment. She never showed any incoherence apparently, and if she was gratified on all occasions would keep quiet. Her language is described as "filthy and blasphemous" in the extreme. After a life of unbridled license, control or confinement seems to have been insupportable to her, and she displayed the real depravity of her nature and virulence of her passions in the variety of outbreaks of which she was so constantly guilty here. She honestly showed the meaning of her conduct when removed to gaol, saying she preferred this place to prison. She has had several children, and was confined only 4 months ago in Gressenhall workhouse. Since then she has had a liberal allowance from the parish and been living in East Dereham. A fortnight ago she took 2 drachms of laudanum and was considerably narcotized by it, afterwards she was restless, tore her clothes, refused food and was much depressed. No cause is assigned for this phase of her mental condition. The medical certificate states that "she threatens suicide, and has attempted it by taking laudanum, is incoherent, and at times violent, tearing her clothes and pulling her hair." On admission she was quiet, said she had a cough, to ease which she had taken the opium, and not with the idea of suicide, and that she felt weak and nervous. She is very short, and small, neat and tidy in her person, quick and intelligent, and with a great deal of self possession. Her features are somewhat coarse, the lips thick, and her face has a repulsive look, showing cunning, low breeding, the sort of defiance resulting from her long continued and well known wickedness. She talks without reserve as to her doings, says she will be glad to leave this world, without though desiring suicide, and that she was provoked to many acts of violence, by bad treatment she received here and elsewhere as she considers and by the tedious irksomeness of her confinement. She blames the world for some of her follies, and says she could not earn a living honestly, not being strong enough for service. She has had a cough a long time, is thin and supposed to be phthisical. There are no definite signs of phthisis [an old term for tuberculosis], but the respiration at the l. apex is doubtful, and she frequently spits blood.'[15]

For the first month of her stay at Thorpe, Harriet was very unsettled. She was given morphia and seemed 'quieter for it', while remaining 'very discontented and untruthful'. On 4 August 1863, 'in consequence of being denied the washing of her own clothes, she, after using the most filthy and blasphemous language, swore she would destroy herself and went on in such a violent manner that she was removed to a strong room, where she continued for a greater part of the night, making night hideous with her hideous screams and obscene songs'. The strong room may have been in one of the detached buildings erected in 1862 as isolation wards for patients with infectious diseases but which, William Hills noted, would also 'prove extremely useful as a means of isolating our more noisy and refractory patients'.[16] Perhaps Harriet had been worried about the possibility of losing her clothes, as had happened at Gressenhall. The following day, she continued 'in this violent mood. Pulled her bed on to the floor. Uses desperate language, says she is the worst tempered woman in the world and as she inherited it from her parents, there is no cure for it. At all events, she won't try to command herself. Would not take anything until after some coaxing. When wishing for some beer, ½ gr of morphia was added, and then quieted down.' Harriet's comment about her parents is noteworthy; perhaps she did have some vague memory of them, possibly reinforced by the recollections of her elder sister Matilda.

On 22 August, it was noted that: 'having improved lately, she began yesterday to do a little work and while lifting a pail of water after cleaning her room, she had prolapsus uteri, from which it now appears she had previously suffered'. The following day, Harriet was 'complaining of severe pain in the region of the left ovary with great tenderness on pressure. She was removed to the infirmary, had leeches applied' and was given medication, which was stopped the following day when she was 'much relieved'. Because of the prolapse of the womb, she remained in bed. On 6 September, she was 'better in every sense…though at times she breaks out [that phrase again] in an excited state. She wets badly…'

Two months later, on 6 November, 'after dancing at the bi-monthly ball of last Wednesday, and behaving herself very well, she on the following morning broke 6 panes of glass and again went through her choice vocabulary of elegant expressions. She says she is determined to outdo all that has been done by other patients in this asylum with regard to mischief and noise. She is in a strong room in ticking as she destroyed the sheets.' The following day she was calmer but: 'won't eat, the stomach pump hinted at to her. Threatens a great deal but it is all smoke for when she had the arm of Mr John medical officer between her teeth she never attempted to bite'.

Until February 1864, although Charles White noted improvement, there continued to be periods when Harriet was unsettled. In December, she seemed to be able to 'control herself much more than heretofore', but at the end of January she was 'confined in a single room in consequence of her excitement returning' and was still there on 15 February, having been force-fed 'as she refused all food'. She was 'at times noisy' and 'threatens all sorts of things'; three days later she was 'behaving well, though full of complaints'. Two days after that, it was reported that: 'In order to attract attention last night, she cried out that she had "cut her throat". On examination it was found she had scratched her neck, the wound being just visible to the naked eye. She became very violent, was placed in a strong room and [given medication]. She vomited and was soon quiet.' This appears to have been the last crisis. On March 18, it was noted that she had 'lately been quieter'. She had been menstruating (previously, presumably, her periods had been interrupted, as had happened before) and had, 'passed her last catamenial period, without any of the violent pain to head which usually accompannies [sic] it'. Harriet was also 'of great assistance in ward'.

On April 6, after Harriet had been in the county lunatic asylum for almost nine months, Charles White wrote that: 'The great change which has taken place in this patient, has given rise to the hope that she will be able to go out next committee. She is now very quiet and very useful and from the tidy manner in which [she] always appears, ornamental also. Should she leave on trial at the end of the month. "a consummation most devoutly to be wished", it is probable she will be missed by "everybody", regretted by "none".'[17] There is a curious ambivalence here: Harriet was quiet, useful and 'ornamental' but there would be no regrets about her departure. Perhaps she retained the capacity to be 'obnoxious', or the potential for a further outbreak remained evident or suspected.

The clerk of the asylum wrote to the board of guardians to inform them that Harriet would be discharged on probation on 26 April, a process permitted by legislation of 1853 and adopted at the county lunatic asylum. The Clerk informed the board, 'that it would be necessary that some person should meet her at the asylum on the occasion prepared with a proper change of underclothing for her use'. The board agreed to send the relieving officer, John Cary (who had taken her to the asylum on her admission), to meet her, 'and that out-relief be provided for her at such place as Mr Cary may find most suitable under the peculiar circumstances of her case'. Having appeared before the committee of visiting justices, Harriet was duly discharged on a month's probation on 26 April, Charles White commenting that, 'the parish have consented to giving their former liberal allowances, in the hopes of quieting her. Should she remain steady there is no reason why she should not stay out of the asylum, as far as her mental symptoms are concerned'. He added, however, that on leaving the asylum, Harriet, 'gave a very good proof of the intractability of her temper…in a noisy argument with the overseer who came for her'. Perhaps they were arguing about where Harriet should receive the out-relief. Despite this episode, Harriet's period of probation appears to have been completed successfully: on 31 May 1864, she was 'discharged cured' and the board of guardians was duly informed in a letter sent the following day.

Four days before Harriet's discharge on probation, the asylum had been visited by the commissioners in lunacy, who found everything, 'highly satisfactory'. They once again praised the food served at dinner-time, and noted that horsehair had been obtained to replace the straw in the mattresses, that the attendants and nurses, 'appear to be kind and judicious in their treatment of the patients' and that: 'Every care seems to be taken to provide occupations and amusements for the patients.' The patients, they reported, 'were without exception free from excitement'.[18]

Notes

1   MLU minutes; NRO, C/GP14/17. The first part of this chapter is drawn largely from this source.
2   CLA, reception orders 1857-60 and 1860-63; NRO, SAH 168/3.
3   In 1871, Matilda was recorded as aged 33, born Cranworth, and William as aged 40, labourer, born Norwich. They had a 78-year-old parish clerk as lodger. In 1881, they had moved to Waddington Street and William Pank, now 50, was recorded as a hospital servant, 'attendant of lunatics'; Matilda was 44 and they had a boarder, Philip Hastings, aged 10, who was at school. William Pank died in the fourth quarter of 1883 and the 1891 census found his widow Matilda, aged 54, working as a needlewoman and residing with a tailoress over 20 years her senior in Neal Square, St Benedict, Norwich. In 1901, Matilda, aged 65, had moved to Bailey's Yard, off Duck Lane, still in the parish of St Benedict, where she was to live for the rest of her life. She was working at home as a needlewoman. In 1911, aged 75, she was a patient in the Norwich workhouse in Bowthorpe Road but she must have recovered and returned home, as the address given on her death certificate was Bailey's Yard. Matilda actually died at The Lodge, Bowthorpe Road, on 17 January 1926, aged 89, the cause of her death being bronchitis, for which she had presumably been hospitalised. Information from census returns accessed via ukcensusonline.com, findmypast.com and ancestry.co.uk.
4   NN, 24 September 1864.
5   V Berridge and G Edwards (1987). Much of this and the next paragraph is based on information from this source.

6   Francis Pryor, in *The Fens* (2019), recalls that his father (he thinks), in the 1930s, saw an elderly man in a chemist's shop ask for 'a penny-worth of comfort', and receive a twist of brown paper containing laudanum, commenting that laudanum gave relief from the pains that persisted after an attack of 'fen ague' (malaria).

7   L M Springhall (1936).

8   NC, 12 October 1861.

9   'Report of the Pharmacy Bill Committee to the General Medical Council', *British Medical Journal*, 2 (1868), quoted in Berridge and Edwards (1987).

10   CLA, reports of the commissioners in lunacy 1844-1925; NRO, SAH 141.

11   NC, 10 August 1861.

12   S Cherry (2003).

13   CLA, minutes of the visiting justices, 1862-68; NRO, SAH 9.

14   Clearly an error on Charles White's part.

15   CLA, case book.1861-65; NRO, SAH 263.

16   CLA annual report 1862; NRO, SAH 28.

17   CLA, case book 1861-65; NRO, SAH 262.

18   CLA, reports of the commissioners in lunacy 1844-1925; NRO, SAH 141.

Wife and mother

ON 20 June 1865, a year after her discharge from the county lunatic asylum, Harriet got married. Her husband was William Head, an agricultural labourer, and the ceremony took place, after banns, at the parish church of St Nicholas in East Dereham. Both Harriet and William signed their names in the register.[1] William Head lived at Shipdham Road in Toftwood Common, a suburb on the south side of East Dereham.

Despite her marriage, the involvement of the board of guardians of Mitford and Launditch Union in Harriet's life did not end just yet. Following her discharge from Thorpe, the guardians had paid her outdoor relief but on 10 July 1865 they directed the clerk to write again to the Poor Law Board 'to ascertain their opinion whether under the special circumstances attending her position the guardians are justified in giving her out-door relief'. The letter was sent on 17 July 1865.[2]

The clerk provided a summary of the punishments received by Harriet from 1852 onwards, her periods of confinement in Walsingham house of correction, Wymondham house of correction and the county lunatic asylum, and her trial and sentence for arson. He noted that she had been discharged from St George's in the Fields [sic] on 18 October 1861 and continued: 'Since her return she has from time to time been allowed outdoor relief (as sanctioned by your letter of 14th of November 1861) and having previously exhibited symptoms of phthisis, a small allowance has been continued to her during her residence as a single woman in the parish of East Dereham, the cost of such relief being then, under the provisions of the late statutes, charged to the common fund of the union.[3] Within the last month or thereabouts Harriet Kettle has been married to one [blank] Head an agricultural labourer belonging to the parish of East Dereham, but as he is for the remainder of the current year, up to Old Michaelmas next under contract of service as team-man to his master, with whom he resides, and as he has no weekly wages nor other means to maintain his wife or to provide her with a home, the guardians, having regard to her antecedents, and to her present state of mental and bodily health, deem it advisable to continue her outdoor relief until her husband is in a position to contribute to her maintenance. The guardians and parish officers of East Dereham to which she is now chargeable are dissatisfied with this arrangement, and I am, therefore, directed to bring the matter again under your notice and to enquire whether the guardians are justified in the course they have adopted.'

The clerk enclosed the last certificate of the medical officer for the district, Horace Crofts Hastings, dated 15 July 1865. Hastings wrote: 'Harriet Head age 26 of East Dereham has for some time past suffered from symptoms of phthisis, and she is never free from cough and frequently has attacks of haemophysis (a spitting of blood). It is true that the lung disorganisation progresses slowly but consumption is frequently a malady of very slow progress.[4] Her general health, I think, is somewhat improved since she left the lunatic asylum at Thorpe but I do not consider her state of mind at all improved, and altho' she is hardly a fit subject for confinement in an asylum, yet, she may be said to suffer from what I sh[oul]d call <u>moral insanity</u> a term according to Forbes Winslow[5] used to designate a form of disease in which the sentiments, affections, habits and the moral feeling of the mind rather than the intellectual faculties are in an unsound and disordered state. I am of opinion that her removal to the union workhouse would prove injurious in a medical point of view: at all events, aggravate or be likely to aggravate, the form of mental disease for the treatment of which she has already been twice sent to asylums.'[6]

The term, 'moral insanity' was coined by JC Prichard in 1835 to describe individuals who displayed, 'an unusual prevalence of angry and malicious feelings, which arise without provocation or any of the ordinary incitements'.[7] Forbes Winslow used the concept in support of pleas of insanity by the defendants in some celebrated criminal court cases; now it served to spare Harriet another spell in Gressenhall workhouse. Payment of outdoor relief was duly sanctioned by the Poor Law Board.

James Cowles Prichard.

William Head, Harriet's husband, came from one of several families named Head in East Dereham. He was the son of Robert Head, an agricultural labourer,[8] and his wife Charlotte, who lived at Toftwood Common. Robert and Charlotte had nine children. William, born on 31 August 1842 and baptised in the parish church of East Dereham on 11 September,[9] was number two, and the eldest son. After William had completed his contract with the farmer for whom he worked, William and Harriet Head set up house in Toftwood Common.

And then Harriet became a mother. William and Harriet's first child, Matilda, named perhaps for Harriet's sister, was baptised 'privately' by the curate of East Dereham, FH Atkinson, on 24 November 1865. Harriet had, therefore, already been pregnant when she married William.[10] A second child, Ernest William, followed two years later. He was baptised by the long-serving vicar of East Dereham, Benjamin Armstrong, on 19 November 1867.[11] The records of both baptisms refer to William Head as a labourer. By the time of the census in 1871, the family comprised William Head, aged 29, agricultural labourer; Harriet Head, 29, agricultural labourer's wife; Matilda Head, 5; and Earnest [sic] W Head, 3. The age given for Harriet was inconsistent with that recorded for her in 1851,[12] as it was also to be in 1881, 1891 and 1901, but it seems that Harriet simply did not know how old she was. Normally, parents would have provided the reminders and evidence of a person's age, but confirmation of that kind was not available to Harriet.[13]

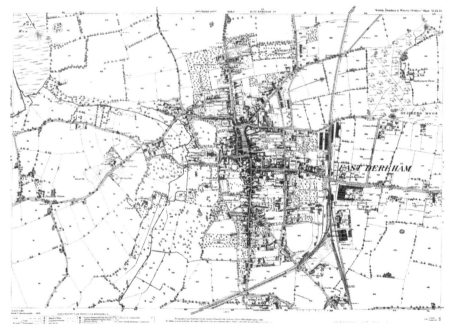

OS map XLIX 13 East Dereham, 1884.

In 1871, East Dereham's population was 5,107. By 1901, it had grown to 5,545: the town was expanding, in contrast with the villages of Cranworth and Letton whose populations were declining. Dereham (as it is usually known) was described in White's Directory of 1883 as 'the most central and one of the handsomest market towns in Norfolk', and 'one of the most improving towns in the county'. A railway line from Dereham to Wymondham and thence to Norwich, was completed in 1846 and passenger trains began to run on 15 February 1847.

A line to King's Lynn was completed in 1848 and the line from Wymondham was extended to Fakenham in 1849.[14] Brewing was already an important industry in Dereham, but after the arrival of the railway large maltings and granaries were built near the station, iron-founding expanded and agricultural engineering firms, the Elvin coachworks (suppliers of two of the Revd Philip Gurdon's vehicles), leather, boot and shoe factories and sawmills developed.

Though it was quite a thriving place, Dereham, like other towns and cities at the time, faced challenges in safeguarding and improving the health of its inhabitants. A Local Board was established in 1877 and took responsibility for water supply, sewerage, waste disposal and paving the streets. Although any proposed developments aroused controversy because of their expense, progress was made in the 1880s. Streets were paved, and a new sewerage system and water mains, supplied by a tall brick water tower, were constructed.[15]

Toftwood, where William and Harriet Head spent most of their married lives, lay a mile and a half south of the centre of Dereham. The original Toftwood was an extensive area of ancient woodland owned by the Crown, which was eventually cleared for agriculture. A large open area of common land, Toftwood Common, remained until 1813, when it was divided into small plots following the Dereham Enclosure Act and the road from Dereham to Shipdham and Watton was laid out across it.[16] The only buildings at this time were a windmill and miller's house. In 1848, this was the mill to which the Revd Philip Gurdon sent his corn to be ground, the wagon that delivered the corn then loading up with coal to take from Dereham back to Cranworth on its return journey.[17] As the 19th century progressed, increasing numbers of cottages, singly, in semi-detached pairs and in short rows were built facing the main road and along a side road leading to Scarning Fen, although when the Ordnance Survey six-inch map was published in 1905 there were still many gaps between the built-up plots. In May 1869 'three newly erected brick and tile freehold cottages' with 'garden and convenient outbuildings to each cottage' fronting the Shipdham Road were offered for sale by auction,[18] and there were several similar advertisements in subsequent years; in March 1898, for example, 'new houses' in Toftwood were offered for sale.[19] The rents of these cottages were low and they provided accommodation for some of the less wealthy inhabitants of Dereham.

The census returns of 1871 recorded two large farms in Toftwood; perhaps William Head, who would no longer have 'lived in' with the farmer for whom he previously worked, worked on one of these farms until the family moved to Shipdham at some point in the next two years. There were also four smallholdings of six, seven and eight acres. Three public houses provided refreshment for the inhabitants and those passing through along the road: the Tuns, the Millwright's Arms and the Rambler's Rest.[20] Many of the adult residents of Toftwood had

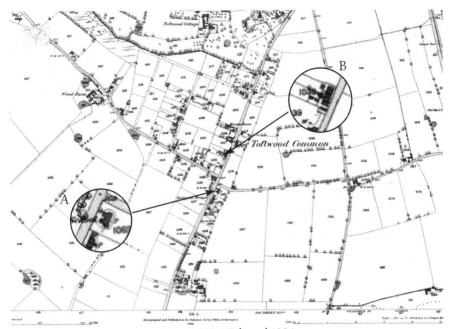

OS map LXI 1 Toftwood,1884
(the position of the school 'A' and the Millwright's Arms 'B' are magnified).

jobs connected with farming, working on their own land or on local farms as agricultural labourers or, in three cases, as shepherds. Others had occupations indirectly connected with agriculture: millers, a corn merchant, a potato merchant and carter, a corn porter and a pig dealer. The continuing importance of horses in the local economy was reflected in the presence of a horse dealer, two grooms, a harness maker and a stable boy, but the impact of the railway was also evident, three men being employed directly on it as engineer, platelayer and labourer, and two more carting coal from the station. Others worked in the breweries and sawmills; as blacksmiths and in other crafts such as tailoring; as dealers; and in providing services such as vermin killing. Ten women worked as laundresses. Toftwood was a mixed, but mainly working-class suburb.

William and Harriet's house was near to that occupied by William Head's parents, Robert and Charlotte Head, and three of their younger children, and both households were a few doors in the Shipdham direction from the Millwright's Arms public house. William and Harriet's immediate neighbours were blacksmiths, agricultural labourers and a mole killer.

A few months after the census, on 23 August 1871, William and Harriet's third child, Alice, was baptised by the Revd Benjamin Armstrong in Dereham. And then, at some point over the next two years, the family moved from Toftwood to Shipdham, a mile or two away on the road leading to Watton. They probably lived in a cottage belonging to East End Farm, near the parish boundary

Postcard showing Shipdham Road, Toftwood, 1888. (Courtesy Robena Brown)

between Shipdham and Dereham, which was owned by Robert Potter, son of one of the large farmers in Cranworth and proprietor of granaries at Dereham railway station.[21] William and Harriet's fourth child, Laura, was born there on 26 November 1873. William Head, described as a farm labourer, registered the birth and signed with a mark, having apparently lost the ability to sign his name that he had demonstrated on his marriage to Harriet in 1865.[22] There is no record of Laura's baptism; perhaps the Church of England was not proactive in Shipdham, unlike in Dereham where the vicar, Benjamin Armstrong, sought to engage with all sections of the community.

The growth of Toftwood prompted the introduction of regular Church of England services there. Previously, there had been 'missions' at certain times of the year. On 18 October 1871, Benjamin Armstrong noted in his diary: 'Went to my mission at Toftwood. Baptised two children there & have been looking the people up in order to induce them to come.'[23] Perhaps the Head household was one of those at which he called; it was barely two months earlier that he had baptised Alice. By 1873, with a second curate having been appointed for the parish church of St Nicholas in the centre of the town, it was possible to provide services in the 'mission room' every Sunday, and to organise a choir. It is not known whether Harriet attended the services, but her religious affiliation had always been recorded as Church of England (as was that of her son, Ernest William, when admitted to the Norwich city asylum in 1899), and so she may have resisted the rival attraction in Toftwood, the Primitive Methodist chapel. The Primitive Methodists had a strong presence in Dereham, Shipdham and elsewhere in the area (including, as has been seen, in Cranworth), particularly among the agricultural labourers, and were associated with the development of agricultural trade unionism. From 1872 until the 1890s, Dereham had an active branch of the National Agricultural Labourers' Union,[24] but it is not known whether William Head was a member.

A significant development for Dereham, and specifically for Toftwood, was the formation of a school board for the town in 1873, and the opening of a board school in Toftwood two years later. Under the provisions of Forster's Education Act of 1870, school boards were to be constituted in places where the number of school places provided by the voluntary bodies supported financially by the government—the Anglican National Society and the non-denominational British and Foreign School Society—was insufficient to meet the needs of the local population. The Committee of Council on Education, the government's education department, found that such was the case in Dereham. Although there were 'National' and 'British' schools in the town, there was little provision in Toftwood other than rudimentary 'dame schools' conducted in private houses. In 1877, despite the establishment of the school board, it was claimed that about 200 pupils in Dereham still attended dame schools,[25] at fees of under ninepence a week and, 'in some instances, crowded together in small rooms wholly unsuitable for the purpose, and detrimental to the health of the children'.[26] No doubt some of these 'uncertified' establishments were in Toftwood. They disappeared once Lord Sandon's Act of 1876, which made elementary education in 'efficient' (government-supported) schools compulsory to the age of ten, had been fully implemented.

The Committee of Council on Education determined that eighty school places were needed in Toftwood, including some (initially 30, later revised down to 12) that would be taken by children from the Dereham end of Shipdham. There was also a need for greater provision in the town centre and in Etling Green, a district to the east of the town. A meeting of Dereham ratepayers was called on 19 February 1873 to discuss the formation of a school board. The Revd Armstrong attended and, while expressing his unhappiness with the development, because it might weaken the link between (Anglican) religion and education, he acknowledged its inevitably.[27]

The Dereham School Board was duly set up in May 1873. Initially, it had seven members; four (including Robert Potter) were businessmen or shopkeepers in the town; the chairman, George Halcott Cooper, was a solicitor; the treasurer was the manager of the Dereham branch of Gurney's Bank (from which the board arranged loans on more than one occasion); and the remaining member was a farmer in Etling Green. Three years later, one of the businessmen dropped out to be replaced by the Revd William Freeman, a Baptist minister, and the board was joined by two members from Shipdham, the rector and a farmer. In 1877, the chairman was replaced by Charles Norton Elvin, the coach-builder whose company had manufactured Philip Gurdon's 'easy-running brougham'. As their clerk, the board elected Mr Charles BL Norgate, solicitor and business partner of the chairman, who served in that role throughout the board's existence. It was all rather cosy, but the board faced challenges in extending universal elementary education across its district, including the resistance of some parents and the difficulty of obtaining and retaining suitable teachers.[28]

In 1874, work began on erecting a board school for Toftwood, and by the spring of 1875, the new building was ready. At its opening, at 9 am on Monday 5 April 1875, the chairman of the board, GH Cooper, sought to assuage the anxieties of the Revd Armstrong and those of similar mind. A local newspaper reported: 'The chairman opened the school with a short address, referring to the report current in the town and district that the children received no religious education in the board schools. This he said was false, as the first half-hour in each day was spent in the singing of a hymn, the reading of a portion of scripture, and the Lord's Prayer, audibly repeated by the children. The punctual and regular attendance of the children was also pressed upon the parents, several of whom were present.'[29] Perhaps Harriet was one of them. Although the Head family now lived in Shipdham, their cottage was probably not far from the boundary with Dereham and William and Harriet sent their children to school in Toftwood. Their first two children (Matilda, aged nine and Ernest, aged seven) could have been among those admitted to the school on its opening day.

The newspaper report continued: '"God save the Queen" was then sung, a portion of scripture read and prayer offered. The chairman then declared the school opened. Other members of the board made several remarks, and then left the schools ['schools' in the plural because the infants' class was treated as separate from the main establishment] at ten o'clock. The certificated mistress is a Miss Marion Don, from Scotland.[30] There were 49 children present and enrolled at the commencement of the school, which was considered a good start. Many of the parents expressed to the board their great pleasure at the opening of this school.'[31] A month later, there were over 70 pupils on the books and the board agreed to appoint Miss Leah Parfitt (or Perfitt) as an assistant teacher to relieve the pressure on Miss Don.[32] Four members of the school board, including Robert Potter, were appointed as the school's managers.

Miss Don seems to have struggled as the numbers in the school rose further.[33] In September, she took sick leave and offered to resign. When the school board expressed its reluctance to accept her resignation, she gave another reason: 'the salary [£65 per year] was not as much as she required'. And so, after little more than six months in post, Marion Don left the school. The new headteacher

₄½ⁿ 6140   The School, Toftwood.

Toftwood school with pupils and staff, 1888. (Courtesy Robena Brown)

was Miss Emily Eliza Goodall, aged 30, born in Somerset, the daughter of a schoolmaster. She was the only suitable applicant and commenced her duties on 10 November 1875. Miss Goodall found the children, 'dreadfully backward and very noisy, approaching to complete anarchy,' and the registers 'in a confused condition'.[34] Leah Parfitt had been absent; when she returned to school, according to Miss Goodall, 'she spoke very rudely to me…saying that when Miss Don was here, she stayed away without asking leave'.[35] Miss Goodall reported Miss Parfitt to the board, with the result that the latter left the school in January 1876. Until 11 Sepember, when a new assistant teacher, Louisa Jane Bowler joined the staff at a salary of £25 per year, the only support for Miss Goodall came from two monitors (pupils who took on supervisory roles under the direction of the teacher), Anna Fairweather and Harriett Brett.

Miss Goodall appears to have been both efficient and strict but she may also have been strident and unbending. She worked hard to organise the registers and to deliver the required curriculum. After the initial half hour of religious instruction, the school day was dominated by reading, writing and arithmetic, with occasional singing and, for the girls, regular needlework. The monitors were instructed not to punish or speak 'improperly' to the children. Miss Goodall herself punished pupils who threw stones at the building, arrived late because they, 'loitered on their way to school playing marbles', left the playground during play-times or misbehaved in other ways. She made some headway. The school was inspected by HMI for the first time in early May 1876 and the summary of the report was moderately supportive, stating: 'The school has passed through a difficult year owing to change of teachers and irregular attendance. The order is fair[36] and the children are being taught but their attainments are as yet very low. The teacher needs more efficient help so as to bring forward the old and backward children satisfactorily.'

In July 1873, the school board had adopted bye-laws making elementary education compulsory in Dereham, and in June 1875, with Toftwood school and another new school at Etling Green now open, an inspector, Samuel Parker, was appointed to enforce them. He checked the registers, investigated cases of irregular attendance, visited the pupils' homes and served notices on their parents. In January 1876, four parents of irregular attenders were summoned to appear before the magistrates, the first of a succession of such cases, although none of those recorded related to William and Harriet Head. Despite being intended to reduce the exploitation of children as low-paid or unpaid labour, the activities of the inspector were probably viewed by some parents as oppressively intrusive, as they prevented children from contributing to the family income and disrupted traditional patterns of working-class family life in which children, especially girls, helped with the housework and looking after younger siblings.[37] Emily Eliza Goodall tried hard to improve the pupils' attendance and marked them absent if, as happened not infrequently, they were sent for by their parents before completing two hours of 'secular instruction' in a morning or afternoon, the minimum required to earn the government grant received by the school.[38] Being marked absent would bring them to the attention of the attendance officer.

Another source of grievance was that elementary education in Dereham was not yet free. William and Harriet Head would have had to pay one penny per week for each child.[39] The log book records occasions when parents failed to send the 'school pence', and others when the money was spent by the pupils on their way to school. The issue was clearly causing friction in Toftwood and it seems likely that there was also resentment of Emily Eliza Goodall personally. On 9 November 1876, the school board discussed the possibility of Miss Goodall and the mistress of Etling Green board school swapping posts but the latter would have none of it. At the same meeting, one of the managers, the Revd Freeman, said that he would attend at Toftwood board school 'every Monday for a few weeks at the time that the fees were paid'. On 20 November 1876 Emily Eliza Goodall noted: 'Several children coming to school without their school fees were in accordance with directions from the board directed to return home for the money.[40] The mother of three of the children came into the school abusing and using threats towards me in the presence of the children.' The mother was not named but might have been Harriet Head, as three of her children (Matilda, Ernest and Alice) would by now have been attending the school. Miss Goodall added: 'I was also annoyed in the street by another woman on my way home, regarding another girl sent home for school money.' Feelings were evidently running high.

Two days later there was another, more serious incident, and this time there can be no doubt about Harriet's involvement. Miss Goodall wrote: 'Having punished a boy in the morning for open disobedience and defiance towards myself, his mother came into the school in the afternoon, threatening me with personal violence; and on my refusing to allow him to leave, until the two hours were expired, attacked me in a ferocious manner by grasping my throat, pulling my hair, and pushing me across the room, at the same time ordering the boy also to assault me. Miss Bowler, on coming to my assistance, was also attacked by Mrs Head.' Ernest Head, who had just had his ninth birthday, had clearly inherited his mother's rebelliousness and Harriet herself, over a decade after her marriage, still had a short fuse and was ready to confront violently those in authority. Two days later, on 24 November, Miss Goodall recorded the sequel in the log book: 'School closed in the afternoon, myself and teachers having to appear before the magistrates in consequence of Mrs Head being summoned for assaulting me.' Harriet was convicted and had to find two sureties for £5 each to keep the peace for six months.[41] She and William, still resident in Shipdham, removed their children from the school but then sent them back again on 11 December.

Harriet's feud with Emily Eliza Goodall continued. On 10 March 1877, the Norfolk Chronicle reported that William Head of Shipdham, labourer, had charged Miss Goodall with assaulting his child Matilda Head, now aged 11, at the school.[42] The case came before the petty sessions and, according to the newspaper report: 'It transpired that the act complained of took place during the dinner hour, when a quarrel having arisen between some of the young ones, the defendant had to interpose, and her authority being set at defiance she administered a little correction which formed the ground for these proceedings, After a lengthy investigation, the bench dismissed the case.'[43] Doubtless Harriet was behind this, using, for the first time, to defend her family and to gain revenge on Emily Goodall, the legal tools that she had seen used against herself, both in her youth and in the more recent past. She clearly acquired a taste for legal action, as in October of the following year, in her own name, she successfully summoned Mary Stimpson, of Baxter Row in the centre of Dereham, for assaulting her.[44]

The inspector's report on Toftwood board school for the year ending 30 April 1877 illustrated the progress made over the year and provided a positive commentary on Emily Eliza Goodall's work: 'The order is good and the children, though not as yet far advanced, are well taught.' Miss Goodall, the inspector stated, would receive her certificate. However, she did not command the confidence of the school board. The previous September, they had turned down her request for an increase in her salary, and in March 1877, despite a protest from the Revd Freeman, they decided to ask her to resign. Emily Eliza Goodall left the school on 22 June 1877, having led it for under two years. She asked for a testimonial and the Revd Freeman persuaded the board to provide one, reminding them of the, 'annoyances to which Miss Goodall had been subjected by the interference of some of the parents' and the 'satisfactory nature' of the inspection report. Miss Goodall had moved to Cumberland by 1881, where she was recorded working as a schoolmistress near Whitehaven, while in 1901 she had moved back to East Anglia and was the mistress of a board school in Suffolk. In 1911 she was still living on her own in Suffolk, aged 65 and retired. Her career as a single female schoolteacher had spanned the country.[45]

Three days after Miss Goodall's departure, a new principal teacher, Marion Sophia Wadeson, aged 22, previously an assistant teacher at the London Road board school, started work in Toftwood, at the higher salary of £75 per year. She was assisted only by Harriett Brett, now a third year pupil teacher, as Louisa Jane Bowler had left a month before Miss Goodall. Miss Bowler's services were no longer required, probably because of the decline in pupil numbers (which may have contributed to the board's lack of confidence in Miss Goodall). When Marion Wadeson arrived, there were only 57 children on roll. The attendance on her first day was 45 in the morning and 50 in the afternoon, figures would have been regarded as quite good at the time.

It was still an uphill battle for the teachers and the attendance officer to persuade all the pupils, and not just the irregular attenders against whose parents proceedings were taken, to attend regularly, and some of the reasons for absence which they accepted would not pass muster in the 21st century. There were many days, for example, when a substantial proportion of the pupils did not turn up, owing to: inclement weather; traditional activities such as taking lunch to their parents during the harvest, gleaning in the fields after harvest, and collecting acorns; and rival attractions such as market day on Friday, Dereham Fair in July, or a circus visiting the town. Children who had to walk some distance to the school, like the Head children when they lived in Shipdham, would tend not to come when there was heavy rain, or when it snowed during the winter (as it seems to have done, heavily, every winter in those days). There were even occasions when children who had made the effort to attend on wet days were sent home because they were judged too cold and wet to learn.

There was also much absence owing to illnesses such as measles, mumps and various fevers, their impact exacerbated by poverty and poor nutritional standards.[46] In the winter of 1877-78, an outbreak of scarlet fever, also known as scarlatina, an infectious disease causing a high fever and red rash, occurred in Toftwood. The local medical officer, Dr Hastings (who had written Harriet's medical certificate in July 1865) called at the school on 13 November 1877 to inform Miss Wadeson that, 'scarlet fever was in a house close by'. Three of the school's pupils lived there and they were not to be re-admitted until the doctor gave permission. More pupils went down with the disease in the first three months of 1878.

The Head family was affected. Dr F Bateman, the medical officer of health for Mitford and Launditch and two other poor law unions, reported on 1 March:

'...I went to Shipdham, as Mr Clarke [the public health inspector for the district] informed me of some cases of scarlatina in that parish. I visited the cottage of William Head, where I found one child recovering from scarlatina, and two others still affected with that disease. I gave all necessary directions to keep the disorder confined to this cottage.' Following a procedure familiar from the recent Covid-19 pandemic, Bateman continued: 'It is always most desirable to trace the source of infection in these cases, and I ascertained that two of the children [these would have been Ernest and Alice, as Matilda would almost certainly have left school by now] go to Toftwood Common school, where it is known to have been prevalent.' Dr Bateman alleged that Dereham had been, '...a focus of infection...for many months past, owing in a great measure to the grossly defective arrangements as to drainage etc which prevail in every part of the town...' He said that there was little he could do about the situation as Dereham was no longer part of the Mitford and Launditch Union, the local government of the town was in an 'unsettled state' and the 'whole re-organisation of the sanitary arrangements of the town was under consideration'. Dr Bateman's report, read out at a meeting of the Dereham Local Board, provoked a furious response from its medical officer, HB Vincent, who denied that conditions in Dereham were as bad as painted by Dr Bateman. Vincent was supported by the board's chairman, who 'indignantly' rejected Dr Bateman's 'libel'.[47] Despite their protestations, there were grounds for Dr Bateman's allegations. As late as 1897, the managers of Toftwood board school found that the ditch at the back of the playground, 'was used as a common sewer' by the tenants of the neighbouring houses and constituted, 'a serious and dangerous nuisance to the school.'[48]

Marion Wadeson had several occasions to mention members of the Head family in the Toftwood board school log book in 1878 and 1879. On 15 October 1878 she, 'cautioned Ernest Head against using bad words on playground,' and on 24 October, 'spoke to William Head a labourer for using disgraceful language to my children during dinner hour on the playground,' a rare reference to Harriet's husband if this was indeed he, but it may have been another William Head, who was charged with assaulting Harriet in 1887, as will be related in the next chapter. At the end of July 1879, Miss Wadeson spoke to one of the managers, 'concerning Mrs H Head who came in school, who had put herself out about her little one [Alice] and another quarrelling in school. Her lad [Ernest] was very saucey [sic] to Miss Brett in the afternoon,' and so the manager was asked to speak to him.[49]

The school seems to have done very well under Marion Wadeson's leadership. In June 1879, HMI reported: 'This is a nicely conducted school, the children are bright, clean and orderly and the examination has been fairly passed. Care should be taken to obtain more intelligent reading. The needlework and singing are good…' Having led the school to this level, Miss Wadeson left on 20 August 1880. She got married in Great Yarmouth, her family home, on 9 September, moved to Camberwell in South London with her husband, and died the following year.[50]

Marion Wadeson's successor, Margaret Starling, was appointed, aged 23, at the lower salary of £65 per year and took up her post on 20 September.[51] Harriett Brett had completed her apprenticeship and left the school; Miss Starling was assisted only by Louisa Jane Bullard, a pupil teacher who had been appointed aged 14 in 1878 and (with a break from 1883 to 1888) was to serve the school until her marriage in 1906.[52] Initially, the effectiveness of the school suffered, HMI reporting in 1882 that: 'Order is fair but instruction is capable of considerable improvement'. However, Miss Starling worked conscientiously with the staff and pupils and by 1886 the inspector was able to note that: 'The school is well conducted and I am glad to be able to report an improvement in the character of all the elementary work, in which the children have passed a very fair examination.'

In December 1879, while still living in Shipdham, William and Harriet Head had become involved in a dispute with Robert Potter - businessman, school board member, one of the managers of Toftwood school and the owner of the farm in Shipdham on which William Head had probaby worked from 1873 or earlier. Potter was listed in the entry for Dereham in White's Directory of 1883 as a 'corn, seed, cake, wood & gen[era]l mer[chan]t' with granaries and offices at the Great Eastern Railway station. His premises were immediately adjacent to the station, where he had a siding with capacity for 22 corn trucks for his use.[53] He was wealthy enough to employ three servants, who were listed in the 1881 census returns as living in his house in Commercial Road, Dereham. Potter took William, described again as William Head of Shipdham, labourer, to the county court for payment of a debt which he was said to owe. A report of the case stated that: 'The claim was for 18s 6d for coals and flour supplied; and Mrs Head, who appeared for her husband, emphatically denied the debt. Mr Potter said the goods had been delivered, but he did not know that of his own knowledge.—Mrs Head: That's a lie. (laughter)—His Honor [sic] adjourned the case till the next court in order that evidence as to the delivery of the goods might be adduced.—

Mrs Head said she had been brought here and she estimated her loss at half a crown, which His Honor allowed, the lady retiring from the court with the remark—"That the Almighty was always above the Devil'"[54]. Harriet was here using words and legal process, rather than violence, to get her way, and seems to have been doing so quite effectively. There is also just a hint of a religious sensibility—and half a crown (12.5p) must have been good compensation for a day in court.

Harriet's battle with Robert Potter continued. In February 1880, William Head, on her behalf, brought a claim of his own for the same sum, 18s 6d, against Robert Potter in the county court. Although the claim was in William's name, it had clearly been brought on behalf of Harriet, who played an active part in the proceedings. According to the press report: 'It appeared from the evidence of the plaintiff's wife that Mr Potter supplied her with a quantity of flour in the year 1876, which turned out to be bad from the depredations made in it by rats and mice.' There was a striking echo here of the actions that the Mitford and Launditch board of guardians had sometimes taken against contractors who supplied sub-standard goods to Gressenhall workhouse; now, Harriet was making similar allegations herself. The report continued: 'Mrs Head called the attention of the defendant to the state of the flour and he replied, "what stupid asses and fools to send such as this," and then promised to deduct 18s 6d from the amount. This he had not done and the present action was brought.—A witness named Lee stated that the flour was bad. The defendant stated that he did not know anything of the transaction. The plaintiff's daughter, [Matilda] who at the time of the transaction was only eleven years of age, deposed that the defendant refused to take the flour back; he would allow her mother 18s 6d. Defendant said that had the flour been bad, he would have gladly taken it back, but this was the first he had heard of its badness. His Honour said that the defendant had been outsworn and he was compelled to give a verdict for the plaintiff, although at the same time it was rather strange that four years should elapse before any complaint was made of the condition of the flour or any action brought for the recovery of the amount.' It was, no doubt, not coincidental that William Head's claim was for exactly the same sum as that claimed by Potter against him the previous year. The report concluded: 'The plaintiff's wife [Harriet], who caused much amusement in court by her excitable behaviour, applied for costs, which, however, were not allowed.'[55]

Robert Potter did not allow matters to rest there. Through his attorney, he successfully applied for a new trial, and also renewed his action against William Head for the alleged debt of 18s 6d, which William was ordered to pay by monthly instalments. These cases did not make the columns of the newspapers. Harriet, meanwhile, claimed that Potter had promised to deduct the 18s 6d from the account for the flour, 'but when Mrs Head left the defendant's cottage, he said he should not do so', which indicates that Potter was the landlord of the house in Shipdham in which the Head family had been living. The case came to the county court again in April 1880, at which point William Head had paid six shillings of the amount he had been ordered to pay Potter, and Harriet was refusing to pay the remaining 12s 6d.

According to the newspaper report: 'The case again occupied the attention of the court for some considerable time, Mrs Head advocating her husband's cause with considerable skill, her warm and pertinent answers, when under the examination of Mr Vores [a solicitor acting for Potter], creating a great deal of hearty laughter. A daughter of Mrs Head [Matilda again] was called, and though she at the time was only eleven years of age, she said she remembered Mr Potter's remarking when his attention was called to the quality of the flour that his men were stupid fools for sending it out. Mr Vores attempted to throw discredit upon this evidence by insinuating that the girl had been tutored by her mother. Mr Potter, for the defence, distinctly denied that he had ever served the plaintiff with bad flour, that any complaint had ever been made by Mrs Head regarding its quality, and that he had ever promised to deduct anything from the account, and that no complaint was ever made till he brought an action to recover an amount due to him. Other evidence was given for Mr Potter, and one of the defendant's witnesses then lodging with Mrs Head, having confirmed that lady with regard to the flour, His Honour gave a judgement for the amount claimed, to be set off against the sum for which judgement had been obtained in the case Potter v Head. No costs were allowed.'[56]

So Potter would have had to pay the Heads six shillings, reimbursing them for the payments they had already made to him. Whatever the rights and wrongs of the case, Harriet had won, a significant achievement for a poor cottage-dweller in combat with a wealthy farmer and merchant. The reference to the 'considerable skill' shown in court by Harriet, now a mature woman of 41 or 42, is testimony to both her intelligence and her determination. Not only that, but her daughter Matilda had held her nerve in court and had learned skills that she, in turn, was to deploy in January 1882 when she successfully charged four men with stealing from her at the Duke of Wellington public house in the Market Place of Dereham, where she was employed.[57]

Meanwhile, the Head family had moved from Shipdham into the centre of Dereham. The 1881 census enumerator recorded them at Cowper Cottages, George Yard, Cowper Road, a close-packed group of houses where the conditions may have been as insanitary as those in the yards of Norwich. The household now comprised: William Head, 38, general labourer; Harriet Head, 35;[58] Matilda Head, 15; Ernest W Head, 13, errand boy; Alice Head, 9, scholar; and Laura

Cottages in Toftwood in 2020 looking towards Dereham. The Millwright's Arms is in the background.

Head, 7, scholar. The family's moves, from Toftwood to Shipdham to the town centre, reflected a national pattern. As one authority has written of the working class in London: 'Many children did not spend their whole childhood in one place. Moves were very common and 'nomadic' and 'migratory' were terms often applied to the poor'.[59] The same seems to have been true in Dereham, the moves possibly being occasioned by factors such as changes in the employment of the husband, the birth of children and difficulties with landlords. It is not known how long the Head family lived in the town centre, but by 1887 they were back in Toftwood. As far as is known, that is where William and Harriet lived for the rest of their lives, while their children and grandchildren gradually moved away or died.

Notes

1   Marriage certificate of William Head and Harriet Kettle, 20 June 1865.
2   TNA: MH12 8482. A transcript of the full text of this letter is in A Reid (1994), p68-9.
3   As noted in Chapter 3, sickness was often used as a justification for providing outdoor relief.
4   This diagnosis seems unlikely to have been correct, given how long Harriet survived subsequently.
5   Forbes Benignus Winslow (1810-1874) was a well known British psychiatrist, who helped to establish the use of pleas of insanity in judicial proceedings (Wikipedia).

6   TNA: MH12 8482.

7   JC Prichard, *Treatise on Insanity* (1835), quoted in L Appignanesi (2008).

8   He is described as brickmaker on William and Harriet's marriage certificate, but is referred to as an agricultural labourer in the census returns.

9   Dereham baptism register 1837-1861; NRO, PD86/4.

10   Dereham baptism register, 1861-1881; NRO, PD 86/5.

11   Ibid.

12   In 1861, she was at the Bethlem hospital.

13   This was not as unusual as might have been thought. Some of the parents of pupils at Toftwood board school in the 1870s did not know the precise age of their children, as is evident from entries in the first log book of Toftwood board school; NRO, C/ED167/1.

14   NC, 20 February 1847; J Adams et al (1989).

15   J Adams et al (1989).

16   C Barringer (2011).

17   Known because there was once a fatal accident involving this wagon in Shipdham, NN, 25 March 1848.

18   NC, 22 May 1869.

19   NC, 5 March 1898.

20   In 1906, the three pubs of 1871 were still there and two more had opened: the Horseshoes and the Golden Ball; NC, 17 February 1906. Only the Millwright's Arms survives as a pub in 2020.

21   Electoral roll for Shipdham, 1872, accessed via findmypast.com.

22   Birth certificate of Laura Head, 7 January 1784.

23   C Armstrong (2012).

24   A Howkins (1985).

25   The Revd Benjamin Armstrong referred to 'two "dames" who keep schools,' in Toftwood in his diary in 1854; C Armstrong (2012).

26   NN, 7 July 1877. Under Forster's Act, schools charging fees over ninepence a week were not classed as elementary schools and therefore fell outside the scope of the Act.

27   NC, 22 February 1873. See also Adam Longcroft and Susanna Wade Martins (eds), *Building an Education: an Historical and Architectural Study of Rural Schools and Schooling in Norfolk c1800-1944* (2013).

28   Minutes of the East Dereham School Board May 1873—January 1879; NRO, C/ED3/61.

29   NN, 10 April 1875.

30   Another teacher from Scotland, Miss Anna Gordon, was appointed as mistress of the new Etling Green board school, which opened on 24 May 1875. Later, she became head mistress at the former British School, which had been transferred to the board and became known as the London Road School. Miss Gordon worked there for three years and, having left to get married, successfully took a member of the school board to court for slandering her by questioning her morality and calling her 'no better than a common prostitute' and a 'disgrace'; EDP, 3 April 1878.

31   NN, 10 April 1875.

32   NC, 15 May 1875.

33   The number on roll rose to 94 in June, fell back by a third subsequently but then grew again, reading 100 in March 1878 and 126 ten years later.

34   These comments were recorded on the first page of the first school log book, which is now missing. The log book begins at page 3, but an undated newspaper cutting of a

letter written by a pupil, attached to the first page of the punishment book; NRO, C/ED167/3 includes quotations from the missing page. Miss Don appears not to have kept a log book, which was a requirement of the government's education department.

35 First log book of Toftwood board school; NRO, C/ED167/1. Unless where otherwise indicated, the next few paragraphs are based on this source and on the minutes of the East Dereham School Board, May 1873–January 1879; NRO, C/ED3/61.

36 For which read 'satisfactory'; the scale of excellent, good, fair, moderate, imperfect and failure was still in use.

37 A Davin (1996).

38 Revised Code, 1862, available on educationengland.org website. 200 morning or afternoon attendances were required if the government grant was to be paid in respect of a pupil.

39 Fees continued to be paid by the parents of children attending the board schools in Dereham until September 1891, although in July 1877 the school board decided to exercise discretion in cases of arrears, 'having respect to honest poverty on the one hand as opposed to negligence on the other'—Lynn Advertiser, 21 July 1877.

40 The directions were issued following a board meeting in June 1876.

41 Court register, Mitford Hundred; NRO, PS12/1/2.

42 The page of the logbook covering events between 19 February and 18 April 1877 is missing.

43 NC, 10 March 1877.

44 NC, 19 October 1878. Mary Stimpson was fined one shilling, with 11 shillings and sixpence costs.

45 Evidence from civil registration and the census returns of 1871, 1881, 1901 and 1911 (she was not found in 1891) accessed via findmypast.com. Miss Goodall died in 1931, in her native Somerset.

46 A Davin (1996). In January and February 1892, Toftwood board school had to be closed, first for one week and then for three weeks, because so many of the pupils had gone down with measles.

47 NN, 27 April 1878.

48 Minute book of the East Dereham School Board, June 1897–September 1903; NRO, C/ED3/63.

49 There are other possible references to Harriet, but as there were other Head families in the area they cannot be confirmed. A Mrs Head appears to have been the school's cleaner but as Harriet lived in Shipdham this may not have been her.

50 freereg.org; freebmd.org (accessed 21 November 2020).

51 EDP, 6 August 1880. Margaret Sarah Starling (1857-1939) was born in Lowestoft, the daughter of an engine driver. In 1881 she was lodging with a female boot machinist in London Road, Dereham, next door to the house of Mary Anne Dunn, a widow, who was the infant mistress at London Road board school in Dereham. At the time, Mrs Dunn had a lodger, Flora Steel, another teacher. By 1883, Margaret Starling had replaced Miss Steel as Mary Anne Dunn's lodger. Female teachers tended to stick together, as seen previously in the case of Eliza Underwood and Eliza Dunham in Gorleston. Later, Margaret Starling lived on her own in South Green, Dereham. She married Frederick Staines towards the end of 1904, and in 1911 was living with him in a nine-roomed farmhouse at Woodrising, the parish to the south of Cranworth. She died at Shipdham in 1939, aged 81. Information from civil registration, parish, probate and census records accessed via findmypast.com; NM 11 April 1883.

52 Louisa Jane Bullard (1863-1951) was the daughter of a painter who later became a printer in Dereham. In 1891 she was still living with her parents in Commercial Road, Dereham, but by 1901 she had moved to Toftwood, where she shared a house next door to the Methodist chapel with an aunt and a younger brother, Edgar, who was working as a pupil teacher (at London Road board school, Dereham). She married Edward Henry Hunter, a farmer ten years her senior, in 1906 and died in 1951, aged 88. Information from civil registration and census records, accessed via findmypast.com.

53 NM, 19 January 1870.

54 NN, 13 December 1879.

55 NC, 28 February 1880.

56 NC, 10 April 1880.

57 NC, 14 January 1882.

58 UK—unknown—was deleted; 35 must have been the enumerator's estimate.

59 A Davin (1996).

Grandmother

WILLIAM and Harriet Head became grandparents for the first time on 2 March 1887, when their eldest daughter Matilda, at the age of 21, came home and gave birth to a son. The father's name was not recorded. Matilda had been working as a domestic servant but no doubt lost her position as her pregnancy became evident. The child, Leonard John, was baptised on 15 April 1887 but died a year later.[1]

William and Harriet's second child, their son Ernest William, got married on 27 May 1888. Ernest was aged 20 and working as a bricklayer's labourer in Dereham and his bride was Sarah Fulcher, a domestic servant. Sarah, aged 24, was the third of seven children and, like Ernest, had been born in Dereham. She already had a child, Bertie Fulcher, who had been born on 22 September 1883. The witnesses to the ceremony at the register office in Dereham were Ernest's father William Head and his elder sister, Matilda Head.[2]

In 1889, although all William and Harriet's children had now left Toftwood board school, there was another incident involving a confrontation between members of the Head family and the school's headmistress. This was now Miss Ada E Chapman, who had taken over from Margaret Starling after the latter had left to become headmistress of the London Road girls' school in Dereham in March 1888. Just before Miss Starling's departure, Louisa Jane Bullard, who had been a pupil teacher at the school from 1878 onwards and assistant teacher in 1882—1883, returned to Toftwood, aged 25, as assistant teacher in charge of the infants' class. On Friday 25 January 1889, Miss Chapman wrote in the school log book: 'Laura Head [who was now aged 15 and would have left the school five years previously] was sent by Mrs Fitt with dinner for her two girls. L[ouisa] Bullard complained to me of the foul language she was using in the infant room. I told her to go out, which she refused to do using most obscene language. I put her out and called one of the teachers to lock the doors.'[3]

To Harriet, this treatment of her youngest daughter was a provocation. She walked to Ada Chapman's lodgings and attempted to confront her. Three days later, her mood darkened further when she received a letter from Mr Norgate, clerk to the school board, about which she remonstrated with Louisa Jane Bullard, a pupil teacher and monitor from the school also being present. On Thursday 31 January, Miss Chapman and Miss Bullard were called to a meeting of the school's managers, and on 1 February Miss Chapman received a notice from Mr Norgate, clerk to the school board, to close the school at 11.30 a.m. so that the teachers could attend the magistrates' petty sessions. There, Harriet was charged with using threatening language towards Ada Chapman.

The proceedings were reported almost verbatim in a local newspaper, the Dereham and Fakenham Times.[4] Miss Chapman, 'said she knew the defendant well by sight'. On 25 January, Harriet, she alleged, had come to her lodgings and asked for her, saying: "I'll make her remember 'black a top'.[5] I'll have my revenge if I wait for a year. I'd as least die on the gallows as anywhere else." Miss Chapman testified that she was afraid that Harriet would do her bodily harm, and that she was afraid to walk to the school. Harriet denied that she had ever spoken to Miss Chapman. The report continued: 'Louisa Jane Bullard, assistant schoolmistress, said she knew [Harriet], and heard her say on the 28th, in reference to [Ada Chapman], that she would pull her pluck[6] out. She did not care if she laid in Norwich Castle 12 months. She would do for her when she came out. If complainant came before the magistrates she would take a stick and hit her across the eyes.' Harriet's rage and the threats she made have echoes of her treatment of Mary Ann Butcher at Gressenhall workhouse.

Continuing her testimony, Louisa Bullard said that: 'The beginning of the whole affair was that [Harriet] asked [Louisa] what it meant by her having a letter from Mr Norgate…Two others were with [Louisa] and heard all that was said. [Harriet] got very much excited, and said it was all lies….She had been very much insulted by [the] letter.' Sarah Head, Ernest's wife and Harriet's daughter-in-law, was called and said that on 28 January she was with Harriet, 'when she met Miss Bullard with two others. [Harriet] said, "Well, Louisa, what's all this about? What have I got this letter for? Why don't you let me alone? If you and your other teachers don't let me and my children alone you'll get it hot, so you know what to prepare for."' Sarah Head denied that Harriet had made the other threats attributed to her by Louisa Bullard, but Edith Billing, one of the pupil teachers, said that she had been with Miss Bullard when they met Harriet, and that Harriet had threatened to, 'pluck [Miss Chapman's] b----- liver out and hang it round her neck. She would lay in Norwich Castle for it and do for her when she came out'. Mr Norgate's letter was produced in court and was found to be, 'simply a warning to defendant to keep off the school premises in consequence of her violent language'. When asked if she had any questions for Miss Billing, Harriet said that, 'she did not wish to talk to any such fools'. Edith Wells, a monitor in the school, also corroborated Louisa Bullard's evidence. When Edith was asked by the chairman (none other than Colonel Robert Thornhagh Gurdon of Letton Hall) if she had heard everything the defendant had said, Harriet interjected, "Oh, I dare say she did; anyone can hear me when I open my alarum."[7] Miss Chapman was recalled and said that Mr Norgate's letter had been written 'on account of defendant's outrageous behaviour and language'. Harriet then said that: 'If there is a rope put round my neck before I murder anyone it will stop me from doing it'.

Harriet maintained that she had heard, 'that there had been a litle "flare up" at the school with her daughter [Laura] and [Miss Chapman] and so she thought she would have a little "stir up" herself. She went to [Miss Chapman's] lodgings but was not permitted to see her. On the 28th ult [last] she laid in bed rather late, a custom she was rather good at, when that insulting letter came from Norgate. On the evening she was going to see Vores about it,[8] when she met with Bullard, to whom she said, "Well, Louisa, what's this hie up?" She was very polite…She was a 'genic' [genial?] woman, although a bit rough at times' ('rough', at the time, being the opposite of 'respectable').[9] Harriet again denied using threatening language, either outside Miss Chapman's lodgings on 25 January or to Louisa Bullard and her colleagues three days later. She wanted the case to be settled at the assizes rather than before the magistrates and said she would be happy to be detained in gaol in the meantime, 'but she would have her revenge if she waited for 20 years,' adding: 'I know a good deal about law, and have been before London and other magistrates.'[10] On the chairman expressing regret about that, Harriet replied: 'I ain't [sorry], it does me credit; and I learnt more law than ever the Toftwood teachers knew.' The chairman, addressing Harriet, responded that it was quite clear that she had lost her temper and used violent language towards [Miss Chapman], 'whom the magistrates would do all they could to protect.' Harriet would have to find two sureties to keep the peace. Harriet replied: 'My compliments to you, Sir, and I'll take it… I'll go to gaol. I won't be bound out.'

A member of the bench, Major Hyde, commented: 'Her husband [William] and son [Ernest] were sureties on a former occasion;[11] they will be bound again.' The report continued: 'The husband and son, however, were not inclined to be bail again, saying they had enough of it the last time. Defendant—Don't you be bound. I'll go [to] gaol, I tell you. I can get sureties if I like. There's Major Hyde there, he has known me for 10 years and knows I never told him a lie, he'll go bond for me, won't you Major? (loud laughter.) Major Hyde (laughing)—I should not care to undertake that. Defendant—Three cheers for the Major. I'm the best soldier he ever had. (More laughter.) I'll go to gaol. The chairman—You certainly will have to if you do not find sureties. Defendant—I'm really glad of that. I shall get a good doctor there. I have got a fool attending me here.[12] The chairman, calling the husband and son aside, prevailed on them to be bound, defendant continually interrupting. Defendant afterwards left the court smiling, and a large crowd assembled outside, but she went away very quietly.'

This was a remarkable performance. Harriet's evident confidence, the assertion of her knowledge and experience of the law, and her ability to use humour and play to the gallery, stand out, as do her flat denial of all the evidence against her and her refusal to be intimidated. She seems to have been daring the magistrates to send her to Norwich Castle and it is interesting that her (perhaps long-suffering) husband and son needed some persuasion to spare her that fate. The presence of a large crowd suggests that she was well known in the Dereham area, but whether the spectators were supporters or people who had been attracted to the scene by Harriet's notoriety is a matter for speculation.

Only a fortnight afterwards, in a development possibly not unconnected with these events, Miss Chapman received notice of her appointment to the post to which Margaret Starling had moved only a year earlier—headmistress of the girls school at London Road, Dereham. She left Toftwood board school on 29 March. Her successor, Miss Jones, was not impressed with the state of the school, writing in the log book that, 'she finds the children careless in their work, inattentive and exceedingly disorderly'.[13]

William and Harriet's youngest daughter, Laura, whose actions in January 1889 had resulted in her mother's appearance in court, gave birth to a son on 20 November 1890. She was days short of her 17th birthday. The infant, William and Harriet's second grandchild, was named Horace Reginald. Harriet was present at the birth. Laura's occupation, like Matilda's, was recorded as domestic servant. The column of the registration form headed 'name and surname of father' was left blank.[14]

Horace Reginald died before his first birthday but was still alive on 6 April 1891 when the decennial census took place. The Head family was still living in Shipdham Road, Toftwood and comprised: William Head, 48, farm labourer; Harriet Head, 45;[15] Alice Head, 19, 'domestic'; Laura Head, 17, 'domestic'; Horace R Head, grandson, 4 months; and Robert Head, [Harriet's] father in law, widower, 75, farm labourer.[16] With four generations now living under one roof, the house would have felt crowded. Matilda, however, was no longer at home and Ernest, as noted above, had married and moved away.

With Horace Reginald's death, William and Harriet had lost their first two grandchildren. Another tragedy struck the family in 1892. Harriet and William's eldest daughter, Matilda Head[17], had been working as a domestic servant but became pregnant and came to the parental home to give birth. The baby, Matilda's second child, was born on 21 January 1892 and named Arthur Fellows Head. Harriet was present at the birth of her third grandson. Arthur survived but by the time his birth was registered a fortnight later, Matilda was dead. According to her death certificate, it had been a 'very difficult' labour, with the baby's 'impacted head' necessitating forceps delivery. Two days after the birth, peritonitis set in and then, after another three days, pleurisy. Matilda died on

29 January 1892. There may have been joy at Arthur's birth but the death of their eldest daughter, aged only 26, must have been a heavy blow for Harriet and William.

The name of the child's father was not recorded,[18] but Arthur's second forename provides an indication. Arthur Fellows Head was probably the son of someone whose surname was Fellows. Several possible candidates were listed in the area in the 1891 census returns.[19] There is no subsequent indication that Arthur's father played any part in his life: he was brought up by Harriet and William.

Arthur Head seems to have been a frail child and may have had a congenital condition of some kind, as it appears that home visits by Davy Turner Belding, surgeon and physician, medical officer for the Dereham District of Mitford and Launditch Union, were required. As a result, Harriet's name appeared once again in the pages of the minute book of the board of guardians. On 12 March 1894, the clerk presented the board with a letter from Dr Belding, 'complaining of the conduct of Harriet Head'. What Harriet, now aged 56, actually did is not recorded. The clerk was instructed to, 'give notice to her in such terms as in his opinion will be most likely to prevent a recurrence of such conduct.'[20] Harriet, characteristically, hit back by making her own complaint. On 26 August 1895, the board received a letter from Dr Belding denying that he had refused to attend Arthur Head or that he had 'been lawfully required so to do by the relieving officer'. The board decided that Arthur Head should receive quarterly visits from the medical officer. Given her experience of the early death of her other grandchildren, Harriet may have been particularly anxious about and protective of Arthur. Belding wrote a second letter to the board about Harriet Head, but its contents, and those of the reply he received, are unknown.[21] It sounds as though, once again, Harriet had been holding people in authority to account in terms that they found unacceptably robust.

Arthur survived and in due course attended Toftwood board school. The school had grown; the accommodation had been expanded to provide for 120 pupils by 1897 and was to be extended again to hold 156 by 1903. The head mistress was once again Margaret Starling, who had returned to her former post at the beginning of 1892 and was to remain in it until 1904, after the school board had been wound up and responsibility for the school had been transferred to Norfolk County Council. She might have remembered teaching Arthur's aunts Alice and Laura, if not his mother Matilda and uncle Ernest. When Arthur started school, in 1896 or 1897, he would have gone into the infants' class, still taught by Louisa Jane Bullard. The staff of the school at the time also included three pupil teachers and a monitor. Their work was closely monitored by Miss Starling, who watched and criticised their lessons and herself gave lessons for them to watch. Although for the most part she taught the older pupils in the 'first class', comprising Standard IV, V and VI, Miss Starling also took the other classes from time to time when she felt that their learning needed a boost. This was not difficult to do as Standards III-VI sat at parallel desks in different parts of the same classroom, with Standards I and II next door and all the infants together in a single adjacent classroom.[22]

The school's curriculum had widened a little since the time when Harriet's own children had been pupils. Object lessons became more varied and evolved into a programme of science education. Singing sessions were now complemented by lessons in music theory. The older boys received lessons in scale and freehand drawing from 1891 onwards, while cookery classes were provided off site for the older girls from 1899. Under Miss Starling, the school generally received good reports from HMI. In 1896, for example, the report on the 'mixed school' stated: 'The discipline and instruction are very creditable', while that for the 'infants class' noted: 'The instruction is vigorous, and intelligently given…'[23]

However, although the school was well run, Arthur Head may have had a difficult time there, perhaps because of the un-named complaint from which he suffered. Harriet worried a lot about her grandson. On 14 November 1899, Margaret Starling wrote in the log book: 'The mistress has been greatly annoyed lately by the constant visits of Mrs Head who makes very unjust complaints about the way in which her grandson is treated.' On 12 December, she noted a letter sent to her by Mr Norgate, the clerk of the school board, 'stating that Mrs Head had been to the doctor and complained that her grandson Arthur Head had been unduly punished in school'. She continued: 'As this statement was utterly false, the mistress wrote a letter to the board to contradict it.' The letter was read to the board in Miss Starling's presence, and the clerk was instructed, not for the first time, 'to write to Mrs Head cautioning her not to go into Toftwood School'. He was also to inform Harriet, 'that unless Arthur Head behaved properly in school he would not be allowed to attend that school'.[24]

This was not the end of the matter. A year later, on 14 November 1900, Margaret Starling wrote that, while she had herself been indisposed and absent from the school, 'Mrs Head grandmother of Arthur Head came up to the school and made most offensive remarks to the teachers before the children assembled in the porch. At 11.10 she came again and ordered her grandson out of school. The teachers in order to avoid a disturbance did not oppose her, but allowed him to go.' Two days later, Harriet was back. She 'complained that Arthur had been unfairly treated by M Lovett'. Minnie Lovett had started work as a monitor at the age of 13 in June 1896 and the following October had been cautioned by Miss Starling, 'against administering corporal punishment, several complaints having been made by parents about her doing so'. Despite this, Miss Lovett subsequently became a pupil teacher, and clearly worked hard at the job.[25] Margaret Starling's confidence in her grew, and she now came to her defence, dismissing Harriet Head's accusation as, 'entirely false'. The entry in the log book continued that as Harriet, 'had so many complaints to make the mistress advised her to go to the managers', adding: 'During the month of December 1899 she received a letter from Mr Norgate warning her to keep off the premises and although she has been twice reminded of the fact she still persists in coming.'

There is no evidence that Harriet did take her complaint to the managers. All was quiet until 25 March 1901 when, again returning from a short absence from school owing to illness, Miss Starling was told by the teachers that: 'Arthur Head had created a great disturbance in school the day before, acting in a very violent manner towards the teachers.' One of the managers was called in but no further action was taken. On 2 August, before the school broke up for the harvest holiday (the timing of which, in those days, varied greatly from year to year, reflecting the state of the crops in the fields), Miss Starling confided to the log book: 'The mistress has experienced great annoyance during the week from Mrs Head, who is continually making complaints about the treatment her boy receives from other boys out of school. As he is always allowed to go home before the other scholars on purpose to avoid these quarrels, the mistress has told Mrs Head that she will not have anything to do with affairs outside the school concerning Arthur Head. As she threatened to take further proceedings and bacame abusive, the mistress refused to listen to her.' In the formidable Margaret Starling, it would seem, Harriet had met her match.

The following year, on Friday 11 April 1902, another incident was recorded in the log book: 'Arthur Head a scholar in the fourth standard (who ever since his admission to this school has done little else but give trouble) on Friday morning had all his sums wrong through carelessness, the mistress therefore told him he should lose all his lesson marks for the morning, he thereupon became very insolent and the mistress administered slight corporal punishment by slapping his face once. He immediately doubled his fist and struck her in the face. Being well acquainted with the violent disposition of the boy, mistress refrained from further punishment but quietly ordered him to leave the school and not to return till he received permission to do so. A few minutes after, his aunt [Alice Head] came to enquire what was the matter but mistress declined to discuss the affair beyond saying she did not intend to submit to such behaviour from a scholar and should bring the case before the managers.'[26]

Subsequent entries in the log book recorded what happened afterwards. On Monday morning, 14 April 1902, Harriet, 'brought A Head to school…but mistress refused to allow him to stay'. Harriet probably protested to the board as the following Monday she brought a letter from the clerk, Mr Norgate, stating that

Arthur was to be readmitted and, 'allowed to stay in school so long as he behaved properly and did his work'. Margaret Starling, however, must have made her own representations to the board as on Tuesday 29 April she attended a meeting of the managers, 'to determine what should be done in reference to Arthur Head. After due consideration it was decided that he should not be readmitted and the mistress received instructions to that effect. Mrs Head who was present also was informed that he must be removed.' On 3 June, the matter came before the full board and the decision was confirmed. According to the minutes: 'Miss Starling attended and was asked her opinion as to the desireability of readmitting the boy Head to Toftwood School and it was unanimously agreed that in consequence of the peculiar state of health of the boy and Dr Belding's report, the boy should not be readmitted and no further notice should be taken by the attendance officer.'[27] Again, the malady from which Arthur suffered was not named, although details were presumably given in the report by Dr Belding—the same doctor who had clashed with Harriet when required to visit Arthur in his infancy. Perhaps he felt that he owed Harriet and Arthur no favours.

Margaret Starling was unforgiving. When the school reopened after the harvest holiday, on Monday 15 September 1902, Harriet again brought Arthur and Miss Starling refused to admit him, saying she had not received any instructions to do so from the managers. Harriet must then have approached the managers because on the Thursday she was back with a letter from Mr Norgate, the clerk, which (as Margaret Starling noted tartly in the log book), 'she had opened although addressed to the mistress'. The letter stated that Arthur, 'could be admitted on the production of a certificate from the medical officer provided he behaved properly'. Miss Starling noted, however, that: 'As the medical certificate was not produced [perhaps Dr Belding had been reluctant to provide it], the mistress politely informed Mrs Head that she could not act contrary to the instructions of the managers and must again refuse to admit her grandson.' At this, Harriet, perhaps understandably, became angry. According to Margaret Starling, she 'became very abusive and after using some very threatening language left the premises'. She made one further attempt, bringing Arthur to the school on 22 September, but Miss Starling, 'ordered her to take him back again'. Arthur remained excluded for eighteen months, until he was quietly readmitted on 7 March 1904. He was now aged 12 which, from 1899, was the school leaving age. Either he or his grandmother, or both of them, wanted him to continue his education, and he may have derived considerable benefit from his lessons, particularly in scale drawing, as the census returns of 1911 recorded him, aged 19, still living with his grandparents William and Harriet, and working in 'agriculture—engineer'.

Despite his problems at school, Arthur made a success of his life. He married

Lily Stalham in the Freebridge Lynn district of West Norfolk in 1914 and their first daughter was born at King's Lynn in the same year. They had two more daughters: one born in Freebridge Lynn district in 1918 and the other in Willesden, London, in 1920.[28] The birthplace of the latter means that her father can be identified with the Arthur Head who, at the age of 27, became a member of the National Union of Railwaymen when working for the London and North Western Railway Company as a 'stableman' at Euston Station.[29] Later, the family moved to Ealing, where (minus the eldest daughter) their details were recorded in the 1939 Register.[30] Arthur's occupation was 'centre lathe turner, heavy and light, also tool turner and capstan setter'. Clearly, a skilled man, still working in engineering. Harriet would have been proud of her grandson. Arthur's second and third daughters were working as clerks, the third also being employed as a shorthand typist, reflecting employment opportunities for women that would not have been available to their great-grandmother. All three daughters married and, later, Arthur and Lily returned to Norfolk, probably on Arthur's retirement. Lily died in 1974 and Arthur in 1975, aged 83.[31]

Meanwhile, sometime after January 1889, William and Harriet's second child Ernest and his wife Sarah had moved to Norwich. At the time of the 1891 census they were living at 28 Stone Mason's Yard, on St George's Street,[32] an area demolished as part of a slum-clearance programme in 1937.[33] Ernest, now 23, was employed as a bricklayer's labourer while Sarah, aged 28, was a shoebinder. Her son, Bertie, was now aged 7. By October 1895, the family had moved to Brady's Yard, Redwell Street, in the city centre. A year later, Bertie left school, at the age of 13. He must have had both initiative and good self-presentational skills, as 1901 found him, aged 17, working as a footman at Hampton Court and living on the estate. Bertie Fulcher served as a private in the Norfolk Regiment in World War I, was decorated and was killed in action at Gallipoli on 13 September 1915.[34]

It was not until 1896 that Ernest and Sarah definitely had a child together, although it is possible that there had been an earlier birth of an infant who did not survive. Their daughter Alice Matilda Head was born on 4 July 1896 and was baptised three weeks later in the St Clement with St Edmund's church in Norwich. At this time, the family was living at 20 Colegate and Ernest was working as a labourer. A son, Herbert William Head, was born on 31 January 1899 and baptised at St Giles Church six weeks later. Ernest was now working as a carter and the family home was at 1, Wellington Lane. Wellington Lane ran parallel with, and just inside, the old city wall, which formed the back of the dwellings on the west side of the street. The houses here had been described half a century earlier as 'imperfectly ventilated and very badly supplied with privies', with tenants who were 'compelled by their poverty to live there'.[35] Herbert

Bertie Fulcher as a footman at Hampton Court.
(Courtesy Herbert and Philip Howes)

Bertie Fulcher in uniform.
(Courtesy Herbert and Philip Howes)

William died before reaching the age of one. As in the case of the Head family in Dereham, the 'migratory' pattern of a poor family moving house regularly can be seen.

In December 1899, Ernest William Head died, aged 32. Until he became ill, he had been working as a builder's carter and living in the parish of St George Colegate, Norwich. His death took place at the Norwich city asylum, the institution where his uncle William Pank had worked, and the cause was recorded as general paralysis of the insane, said to have been developing for some time—a year, according to the admission register of the asylum, or for three according to Ernest's death certificate. He had been admitted to the asylum only five days earlier, on 19 December, when he was described as a 'short, well-made male, having grey eyes and dark hair'. He appears to have taken after his mother, Harriet, who was also short and probably had dark hair. The asylum's medical officer noted that Harriet had been 'insane' at one time (had Harriet talked about her experiences at the county lunatic asylum with Ernest and his wife Sarah?) and that Ernest spoke 'in a jerky manner, he says he has lost his nerves, he cannot say 'N' or 'W' very distinctly'. Sarah, who was present when her husband died and had probably accompanied him to the asylum, was reported to have said that, 'he cannot keep at his work because he shakes so and makes faces. If anything goes wrong he gets very irritable. He walks about razors in his pocket. He has threatened to drown himself.' Ernest had been living at the Woolpack Inn in Colegate. Sarah, no doubt to earn money to support them both and their daughter (who was boarding with another woman), was working as a domestic servant at 137 Rosary Road, Thorpe Hamlet, Norwich. After his admission to the asylum, Ernest suffered from convulsions and lost strength rapidly, dying at 5 am on Christmas Eve. A very sad and distressing end. [36]

And so, Ernest was the second of their four children whom Harriet and William had lost. At the time of his death there was already another grandchild on the way. Sarah, now a widow, gave birth to Edith Sarah Head on 17 May 1900 and the infant was baptised in St Giles' Church on 3 June. To support herself and her family, Sarah continued to work as a domestic servant at 137 Rosary Road, Thorpe Hamlet. In 1869, it was said that, 'many handsome villas which are mostly surrounded by gardens' and the residences of 'many of the city gentry' were to be found in this district of Norwich.[37] Sarah was still living there when the 1901 census was taken, described as a 'cook (domestic)' to two sisters born in Calcutta, the elder of whom was the secretary of a local charity. Unusually, but perhaps because she was a 'respectable' widow, Sarah was allowed to keep her younger daughter Edith, now ten months old, with her in the house. Alice Matilda, her elder daughter, was probably boarding with a Mrs Gooch, of 10 Cross Sussex Street, north of where the Norwich Inner Ring Road now runs, who had been recorded as her parent when she started school in January 1900.[38]

The arrangement at 137 Rosary Road came to an end, however, probably because Sarah became pregnant—no longer, therefore, 'respectable'. By January 1902, she had moved to 9 Fisher's Buildings on Magdalen Street, and this may have been where her son, Herbert Henry Head, was born. He was not baptised and the identity of the father is unknown. Three years later, Sarah was living at 66 Pelham Road in New Catton, the suburb north of the city centre, where William Pank and Matilda Kettle had been living at the time of their marriage. In October 1906 Sarah and her family were at 94 Shadwell Street, one of three streets of fairly new but cheaply built and insanitary houses in Crook's Place, west of St Stephen's Road, just outside the city walls.[39] Now, after six frenetic years of moving between different lodgings, during which the children had attended different schools and Sarah must have struggled to make ends meet, there was a period of stability.

The family was still at 94 Shadwell Street when the 1911 census was taken. Sarah, now 48, was a charwoman, a poorly-paid occupation that involved cleaning and washing in private houses or commercial premises.[40] Alice Matilda, aged 14, had left school the previous year and was working as a 'nurse girl' (perhaps looking after the small children of neighbours); Edith Sarah, aged ten, and Herbert Henry, aged nine, were at school. The house had four rooms.[41]

Life was not all gloom. Sarah Head could enjoy herself, as a memory recorded by one of her grandsons makes clear: 'Sarah had a wonderful singing voice and was always going to the [Church of England] Mission Hall, being quite poor compared to the other people there. When the service had finished, she dressed up as a gypsy and sang "Raggle, Taggle Gypsy Oh", with a ribbon around her waist with small items attached (thimbles, spoons, cotton. etc), stopping repeatedly at different people and asking them to purchase an item.'[42]

Edith Sarah Head became a domestic servant, a kitchen maid, in the stately surroundings of Houghton Hall in Norfolk in 1914, and met her future husband, Ernest Philip Howes, while working there. [43] They married in Norwich in May 1922, with Edith's mother, Sarah, being one of the witnesses. They had three sons. Alice Matilda had already married in Norwich in 1915, and went on to have four children, two sons and two daughters. Ernest Head's widow Sarah died in 1936. Alice Matilda and Edith Sarah both lived to great ages, dying in 1994 and 1991 respectively.[44] William and Harriet Head knew that their son Ernest had died[45] but it is not known whether, after his death, they had any contact with Sarah and the two surviving grandchildren born to Ernest and Sarah in Norwich.

Edith Sarah Head as a kitchen maid at Houghton Hall with dog Pipa, aged 14. (Courtesy Herbert and Philip Howes)

William and Harriet's third child, Alice, was still living with them in Toftwood, aged 29, at the time of the 1901 census. Two years later, on 22 March 1903, she married Frederick Guyton, an ironmonger's carter, aged 35, at Dereham Register Office, William Head being one of the witnesses.[46] A daughter, Blanche Maud Guyton, was born on 26 July 1903, and so Alice must have been pregnant when she married Frederick. The birth was probably in Alice's parental home, as the place of birth was recorded as Toftwood,[47] but by the time of the 1911 census, Alice, Fredrick and Blanche lived in a four-roomed house at 1 Lynn Hill, Yaxham Road, Dereham. Frederick Guyton died in 1922, aged 53. Alice continued to live at 1, Yaxham Road, and in 1930 had been joined there

Alice Matilda Fisher (nee Head) and Edith Sarah Howes (nee Head) with Alice Matilda's children at Great Yarmouth. c1928. (Courtesy Herbert and Philip Howes)

by a Maud Guyton, who was 11 years younger than her and was presumably a relative of her deceased husband. Blanche Maud Guyton, William and Harriet Head's fourth surviving grandchild, married in 1931. Alice Guyton nee Head died in 1961, aged 90, and was buried in the cemetery in Dereham.[48]

Edith Sarah Howes (nee Head) with her mother Sarah Head and two of her sons, posing on a motorcycle at Great Yarmouth, c1928. (Courtesy Herbert and Philip Howes)

The fourth child of William and Harriet, Laura, had already had a child, Horace Reginald, who had died before reaching his first brithday. The year after his death, on 11 May 1892, Laura gave birth again. The child was named Leonard George Head and lived until three months short of his fifth birthday, dying at Toftwood on 12 February 1897, as a result of broncho-pneumonia. This must have been heartbreaking for Laura and the whole family. The death was certified by Dr Belding, and was registered the following day by Leonard's aunt, Alice Head, who was present when he died. Laura was at an advanced stage of her next pregnancy at the time and the birth took place less than three weeks later, on 1 March 1897. The child, a boy, was baptised on 23 March and named Clement Head. He died in infancy. By the summer of 1897, therefore, Laura had had three children, all of whom were dead. Infant mortality remained high in poor districts in the late 19th century,[49] and Laura's experience provides a poignant example.

By the time of the 1901 census, Laura had moved away from Dereham. Now aged 27, she was living at 11 Cornhill, Ipswich, in the household of John C Pipe, grocer, where she was a 'domestic general'. Perhaps, after the death of her three children, Laura had wanted to make a fresh start in a new place. On 28 April 1906, she married Leonard Ernest Frederick Martin, aged 20, whose occupation was given as 'assistant cook'.[50] Laura was now working as a domestic servant at 'Cranbourne' in Westerfield Road, Ipswich, a road of large recently-built villas. She gave her age as 28, either forgetting or, perhaps, wanting to conceal that in reality it was 32. The marriage took place in Ipswich. No subsequent trace of the couple has been found as yet.

Life continued for William and Harriet Head in Toftwood. Over the 20 years after she had first become a grandmother in 1887, Harriet had occasional run-ins with her neighbours which resulted in her bringing cases before the petty sessions. In July 1887, a William Head was charged with assaulting her; not her husband but a namesake, a member of one of the other Head households, of which there were several in Toftwood. According to the Norfolk Chronicle, 'this was an old quarrel renewed amongst neighbours, and the bench dismissed the case'.[51] The Norwich Mercury added that, 'The chairman…said that it was a most unseemly row, and as usual there was a good deal of false swearing, and it was difficult to mete out justice.'[52]

In August 1893, Mary Ann Fitt, a near neighbour of the Heads (perhaps the same person who had sent Laura Head to Toftwood School with her daughters' lunches in 1889), summoned William and Harriet's daughter Alice Head, who would have been almost 22 at the time, for assaulting her, and was herself summoned for assaulting Harriet. Both cases were dismissed.[53] Two years later, Alice (perhaps encouraged by Harriet) again brought a complaint of assault, the perpetrator this time being Marie Lacey, aged 43, another resident of Toftwood Common. According to the Norfolk News: 'Complainant, who was a single woman, stated that defendant was a neighbour, and on Wednesday between 9 and 10 am the defendant challenged her mother to go and have a fight with her. The defendant was on the road, and witness was in the garden. The defendant called witness names and went and deliberately struck her in the face (a black eye presented bearing testimony) and used threatening and abusive language. Harriet Head, the complainant's mother, gave evidence in corroboration. The defendant here stated that it was with the last witness [Harriet] with whom the bad feeling existed, and it was her she would have liked to have hit instead of her daughter.' Perhaps, as in Bethlem hospital, Harriet had 'made herself obnoxious' to some of her neighbours; or perhaps they had made themselves obnoxious to her; or perhaps it was a bit of both. The report continued: 'The chairman, in addressing the defendant, said the assault appeared to be an entirely unprovoked one, and it was most intolerable that people could not walk about their own gardens without being subject to assault, abusive and disgusting language.'[54] So, vindication for Alice and Harriet and pain for Marie Lacey, who was fined 13s 6d, including costs, in default of which she would be imprisoned for seven days with hard labour, and was bound over to keep the peace for six months.

A feud between Harriet and Emma Head, who lived next door to William and Harriet, resulted in cases before the petty sessions in 1904 and 1907. In March 1904, Harriet charged Emma and Sarah Head, who also lived nearby, with assaulting her. Emma and Sarah were aged 24 and 27 respectively and therefore more than a generation younger than Harriet who was now 65 or 66. Emma was also charged with assaulting Arthur Head, Harriet's grandson, by this time aged 12. There was a cross-summons by Emma Head against Harriet. According to the Norwich Mercury: 'The squabble arose about an alleged assault on the boy, Arthur Head.'[55] The magistrates bound over both Emma and Harriet to keep the peace towards each other for three months. Harriet was now in her sixties but she was still a fighter, especially when the defence of her family was involved.

In December 1907, Harriet again summoned Emma Head for assault, and Emma, again, reciprocated. When the cases came before petty sessions: 'Harriet Head, the first complainant, stated that on Monday the 25th ult. she was on her knees clearing some water out of a soft water tank at the back of her house. The tank had a partition in it, and half of the tank belonged to defendant. Whilst in this position some warm water was thrown over her head and back. Defendant was inside her door. Witness asked defendant what she was up to, and defendant then threw a pailful [sic] of water over her. Witness did not throw water over the defendant, but she did throw some over her window and door after the water had been thrown over her. William Head, the complainant's husband, said he saw nothing of the row, but his wife came to him "dreeping wet".[56] The story of the defendant was that she was the person aggrieved. She stated that complainant became annoyed because witness asked her not to interfere with the water in her side of the tank, and that she threw a handcupful of water at witness which went on her legs and feet. She also swore at witness, and called her foul names. Gertrude Isbill, a neighbour, said she saw water thrown by Harriet Head but none by Emma Head. The parties started a wordy warfare, but were promptly stopped by the court. The chairman advised the parties to let each other alone. Both were bound over to keep the peace for six months and Emma Head was ordered to pay 7s 6d costs.'[57] This is currently the last known occasion on which Harriet made the pages of the local papers.[58]

The size of William and Harriet's household had gradually diminished. Laura had left for Ipswich between 1897 and 1901; Alice had got married in 1903; by 1911 only their grandson, Arthur remained with them, and he was to marry and move away in 1914. When the 1911 census was taken, William and Harriet had been married for 46 years. The ages recorded for them, 69 and 72 respectively, were (for the first time, in Harriet's case) consistent with those recorded in 1851. William was still working as a 'labourer—farm' (ten years previously, his occupation had been recorded as 'horseman on farm') and Harriet was 'at home'. They were now living in a five-roomed house in Toftwood, a larger property than might have been expected. However, as a 'horseman' in charge of the horses on a farm, William was a skilled worker, paid more than other agricultural labourers, and Arthur, probably earning good money as an engineer in agriculture, would have contributed to the household income as well. The house might have been one of a pair of cottages facing the Shipdham Road described, when offered for sale in June 1875, as containing, 'sitting and keeping rooms, pantry and 2 bedrooms,' with 'brick and slated outbuildings and large and productive gardens well planted with fruit trees,' and 'a pump and a constant supply of excellent water'.[59]

Harriet and William Head would—or, at least, could—have celebrated their golden wedding in 1915. William went on to outlive Harriet, dying at the age of 85 on 25 August 1927. He died as a result of heart failure precipitated by bronchitis and emphysema, at Gressenhall workhouse, which since 1913 had been known officially as Gressenhall poor law institution. On his death certificate it was referred to as 'Beech Hill'.[60]

Harriet Head nee Kettle died on 8 May 1916. Her age according to her death certificate was 74, but if her age as given in the 1851 census return was accurate it was actually 77 or 78. An inquest was held two days after her death and it was found that she had died, 'from shock following a fracture of the leg caused by a fall when getting out of bed'. The place of her death was recorded as

Beach Hill House, East Dereham
GRESSENHALL

Postcard showing the east (infirmary) wing of Gressenhall poor law institution (workhouse), published between 1902 and 1906. It was here that both Harriet and her husband William Head died, in 1916 and 1927 respectively. (Courtesy Norfolk Museums Service)

Gressenhall.[61] Either she had been taken to the institution's infirmary after her mishap or, possibly, she may already have been there as a result of illness.

And so Harriet's life had come full circle, ending at the place where she had spent most of her childhood.

Notes

1 Birth certificate of Leonard John Head, 15 April 1887; East Dereham register of burials, accessed via freereg.org.

2 Marriage certificate of Ernest William Head, 27 May 1888; East Dereham register of baptisms, accessed via freereg.org.

3 First log book of Toftwood board school; NRO, C/ED167/1.

4 Dereham and Fakenham Times, 9 February 1889. The defendant was said to be 'Hannah Head' but there can be no doubt that it was Harriet who faced the charge, all the details given of the defendant's family situation matching Harriet's precisely. There was a Hannah Head, aged 61, living in the next house to Harriet's in 1891, but she did not have a daughter called Laura. Unfortunately the petty sessions records for this date are not to be found in the NRO.

5 Probably a reference to the colour of Harriet's hair, which would have helped to give her the 'gipsy-looking' appearance mentioned in 1859.

6 A term for the heart, liver and lungs of an animal—D Yaxley (2003).

7 'When I exclaim loudly'?

8 The solicitor who had represented Robert Potter in the county court. It is interesting, and perhaps a sign of Harriet's confidence in using the law, that she was intending to consult him.

9 A Davin (1996).

10 Harriet may have encountered London magistrates during her stay at Bethlem hospital.

11 Presumably a reference to the case of assault brought against Harriet by Miss Goodall in 1876 although, as Ernest was aged only nine at the time, he can hardly have been one of the sureties.

12 Perhaps Dr Davy Turner Belding, with whom Harriet was to clash in 1894-5.

13 First log book of Toftwood board school; NRO, C/ED167/1.

14 Birth certificate of Horace Reginald Head, 9 December 1890.

15 As in 1881, NK (not known) was deleted; Harriet was no more sure of her age now than she had been ten years previously.

16 Robert Head died in 1899; civil registration records, accessed via freebmd.org.

17 Matilda is not to be found in Toftwood (or anywhere else) in the 1891 census returns.

18 Birth certificate of Arthur Fellows Head, 5 February 1892.

19 They were: James Fellows, aged 35 and his brother John Fellows, aged 28, both single, who were railway labourers living in Garvestone, near Dereham; William Fellowes, aged 40 (probably their brother and, like them, a railway worker), who was a married man with four children living in Westfield Lane, Toftwood; and Edward, Harry, James and William Fellowes who were all single agricultural labourers aged between 20 and 30 living in Yaxham, another nearby village. Information from census records, accessed via findmypast.com.

20 MLU minutes, 12 March 1894; NRO, C/GP14/35. The clerk's letter does not survive.

21 MLU minutes, 26 August 1895; NRO, C/GP14/36.

22 Survey of Norfolk Schools, 1903; NRO, C/ED183/1.

23 Toftwood school log book, 1896-1905; NRO, C/ED167/2. The following six paragraphs draw largely on this source.

24 Minute book of the East Dereham School Board, June 1897—September 1903; NRO, C/ED3/63.

25 Minnie Lovett (1882-1954), daughter of a coach-builder (possibly at the Elvin works), continued to work at Toftwood School after its transfer to Norfolk County Council in 1903 and the departure of Margaret Starling in 1904. She gave up work to marry Francis G Tabraham, tobacconist, in 1911 and they lived over his shop in St Benedict's Street in Norwich, later moving out to Earlham Road; information from census records, accessed via findmypast.com. It is noteworthy that three key long-serving members of staff at Toftwood board school (Misses Starling, Bullard and Lovett) were all the daughters of skilled workers, putting them in a more aspirational social class than that from which many of their pupils came.

26 The slap on the face was recorded (with the reason, 'impudence to mistress') in the school's punishment book which, according to an entry in the log book, had been received on 20 September 1900. This is the only reference to Arthur Head to be found in the book; NRO, C/ED167/3.

27 Minute book of the East Dereham School Board, June 1897—September 1903; NRO, C/ED3/63.

28 Information from civil registration records accessed via freebmd.org.

29 General Register of Members, National Union of Railwaymen, accessed via findmypast.com.

30 Accessed via findmypast.com.

31 Information from civil registration records, accessed via freebmd.org.

32 Census records accessed via findmypast.com. William Fulcher, also born in Dereham and probably Sarah's elder brother, lived two doors away, and it was possibly through him that Ernest and Sarah had acquired their tenancy.

33 F and M Holmes (2015).

34 The narrative in this and the next six paragraphs is based on information from the records of civil registration, parish registers, census returns and school records, accessed via freebmd.org, freereg.org and findmypast.com. I am grateful to Philip Howes for photographs of Bertie as footman and soldier, and for alerting me to his death at Gallipoli.

35 F and M Holmes (2015), quoting William Lee's report of 1851.

36 Norwich City Asylum register of admissions, 1895-1902; NRO, HH 18/5; Norwich City Asylum case book, November 1899-November 1910; NRO, HH 32/7; death certificate of Ernest William Head, 25 December 1899.

37 R O'Donoghue (2014).

38 School registration record accessed via findmypast.com (accessed July 2020).

39 F and M Holmes (2015). The area was cleared in the late 1930s and Shadwell Street disappeared from the map.

40 C B Hawkins (1910).

41 Census returns, electoral registers and school records available via findmypast.com (accessed July 2020).

42 I am grateful to Helen Bainbridge for putting me in touch with Philip Howes, the youngest of Edith Sarah's three sons, and to Philip Howes himself for further information, including this memory of his grandmother. Many thanks to Philip and his elder brother Herbert Howes, for permission to reproduce the photographs of their grandmother Sarah Head, their mother Edith Sarah Howes and their aunt Alice Matilda Head, with their children, which are included in this book.

43 Thanks to Philip Howes for this information. He recalled this anecdote about Edith Sarah: when she was working at Houghton Hall, she was helping the cook and was asked to take a pheasant out of the oven. Seeing maggots in the juices, she started spooning them out (obviously it had been hung up to get 'high'). Passing through the kitchen was the lady of the house and on seeing Edith Sarah doing this said, 'what are you doing, you silly girl'. To which my mother said, 'removing these maggots, Miss'. Replying, the lady of the house said, 'leave them in, they are all part of the flavour'.

44 Information from civil registration and parish records, accessed via freebmd.org and freereg.org.

45 They provided the 1911 census enumerator with the information that two of their four children were dead.

46 Marriage certificate of Alice Head, 22 March 1903.

47 Birth certificate of Blanche Maud Guyton.

48 Information from civil registration records, accessed via freebmd.org; and from electorial registers, accessed via findmypast.com.

49 A Davin (1996).

50 He was the son of a (deceased) foreman goods porter with the Great Eastern Railway and lived at Stoke, a suburb of Ipswich.

51 NC, 16 July 1887.

52 NM, 13 July 1887.

53 NC, 5 August 1893.

54 NN, 3 August 1895.

55 NM, 16 March 1904.

56 As far as is known, these are the only words of William Head recorded for posterity.

57 EDP, 7 December 1907.

58 More may yet be discovered in the pages of the Dereham and Fakenham Times which, at the time of writing, was only available in digitised form for 1889 via britishnewspaperarchive.co.uk.

59 NC, 12 June 1875.

60 Death certificate of William Head. A postcard showing the infirmary wing of the workhouse building, in the collection of Gressenhall Farm and Workhouse: Museum of Norfolk Life, gives it the name, 'Beach Hill House'.

61 Death certificate of Harriet Head, 12 May 1916.

Harriet Kettle, survivor

WHAT to make of Harriet Kettle? Was she insane? Was she in control of her actions between 1851 and 1864? Was she suicidal? Where did her rage come from? Was she a victim, or a successful rebel against the norms of Victorian and Edwardian society? What kind of person was she and to what extent did she change as she grew older?

Though considered a 'lunatic' by the authorities responsible for Walsingham and Wymondham Houses of Correction, who struggled to manage her, it seems clear that Harriet was not insane, in the sense of being subject to irrational delusions. The medical officers of the county lunatic asylum, and of the Bethlem hospital, were consistent on this point. The delusion of being possessed of property, noted on Harriet's admission to Bethlem hospital but denied by Harriet herself while she was a patient there, does not appear to have featured at any other time, and may even have entered the record as a convenient but spurious justification for sending her to Bethlem. Both the board of guardians at Gressenhall and the judge at her trial for arson suggested that Harriet might feign insanity in order to secure better treatment in the county lunatic asylum than that which she received in a workhouse or prison. There may have been more than a grain of truth in this; Harriet herself was explicit that she preferred the asylum, as well she might, as she received kinder and more generous treatment there. She did not want to be removed from the asylum if there was a possibility of being sent somewhere worse. But Harriet's outbursts of anger, violence and vituperation cannot be explained away as cynical attempts to convince the authorities of her insanity. They were both less and more than that.

Harriet's condition was characterised initially as 'mania' by the medical officers at the county lunatic asylum. In 1865, the medical officer for Dereham district in the Mitford and Launditch Union described her complaint as 'moral insanity'. In more recent times, it might have been labelled, if seen as a suitable case for diagnosis at all, as a personality disorder. Everyone, including Harriet herself, agreed that she had a short fuse and could fly off the handle with little provocation—she had, in the view of Charles White, the medical officer at the asylum, a 'naturally bad temper'. In her younger years, in institutional environments, Harriet's rage was often intense, sustained and unconstrained. She screamed and shrieked, sometimes for long periods of time, as when she screamed for most of the night at the county lunatic asylum. She swore, uttering obscenities and blasphemies that shocked those who heard them. She tore clothing, damaged bedding and broke windows. She threatened extreme personal violence, notably towards Mrs Butcher, the assistant matron at Gressenhall workhouse. She fought physically those who tried to restrain her, as when she 'kicked and bit, and became so violent as to require seven nurses to overcome her', or when she abused one of the nurses at the county lunatic asylum and 'tore her hair from her head'. However, although it was regarded as egregious in the institutions in which she was confined, Harriet's response to the institutional regime had much in common with the observed behaviour of those other female inmates of prisons who 'broke out' from time to time in much the same way. In reacting to the prison and workhouse, and even to the lunatic asylum, as she did, Harriet was unusually extreme and reckless, but she was not exceptional.

It was sometimes said that Harriet could not or would not 'command herself', that she lacked the ability to control her rages. 'She has little or no control over her temper', as Charles Hood at the Bethlem hospital put it. Harriet herself claimed that she had inherited her quick temper from her parents and could do nothing about it. Occasionally, it seemed that her outbursts were random, as on the occasion in the county lunatic asylum in May 1859 when she 'broke out suddenly without seeming cause and became violent and abusive'—although anxious anticipation of her forthcoming trial for arson may have been a factor on that occasion. And once a 'paroxysm' had begun, Harriet may have found it difficult if not impossible to snap out of it. At other times, however, there was a degree of control. Harriet refrained from biting the medical officer at the county lunatic asylum, for example, when she could have done so. Harriet seems to have known how disruptive her rages were for the institutions she inhabited, and herself suggested that the intensity of her outbursts was deliberate: at Thorpe, she said that she was, 'determined to outdo all that has been done by other patients in this asylum with regard to mischief and noise'. This knowingness in itself implies a degree of control over her actions.

Was Harriet sometimes suicidal? The evidence is contradictory. She was regarded as suicidal when transferred from Walsingham house of correction to the county lunatic asylum in 1856 and at her trial she claimed to want to end her life. On other occasions she denied that she had any such intention. When she took laudanum, she was thought to have been attempting suicide but claimed later that she wanted to soothe a cough, not to end her life. When she had an opportunity for suicide, in the county lunatic asylum in February 1864, she did not take it: she did not cut her throat but only scratched her neck. Overall, it seems that Harriet may have had suicidal thoughts at moments of extreme stress or despair but that she had no settled intention to commit suicide.

Harriet's rages, and the emotional trauma they expressed, may have been, if not occasioned, at least intensified and exacerbated by physical issues. She clearly had gynaecological problems: the irregular periods, the prolapse of the womb and the pain in an ovary. She had piles. She coughed a lot, which led some doctors to suspect phthisis. She could not eat meat, although whether that was because of a physical intolerance or a distaste for it is not recorded. She may have had a more general eating disorder, causing her to refuse all food, as she did at both the Bethlem hospital and the county lunatic asylum; as a result, in both institutions, she was force-fed, undoubtedly a deeply unpleasant experience, as several suffragettes were to discover not many years later. And there may have been other, unacknowledged health issues arising from the conditions in which she had lived. All these factors may have been both sources and expressions of stress.

However, there was much more to Harriet's anger than that. Among the poor of 19th century England, she was far from exceptional in hating the workhouse in which she grew up; it was the intensity of her hatred and the extent of her defiance which made her visible—and audible—to history. As a spirited individual, the environment of a workhouse or a prison was clearly oppressive to Harriet. She resented, it was said of her, the monotony and confinement of the institutional regime. She may also have imbibed something of the culture of resistance which was sometimes evident among the labourers in her home village of Cranworth and the surrounding area. She claimed to have been badly treated, and may have had at least some grounds for the allegation. In 'losing' Harriet's clothes, for example, the workhouse authorities were clearly at fault, and Harriet's ire was justifiable. Those with whom Harriet clashed were sometimes ineffective—and perhaps officious—authority figures, like Thomas and Mary Ann Butcher or, much later in her life, Ada Chapman, mistress of Toftwood board school. By contrast, the medical officers at the county lunatic asylum and even Emily Greenfield, the matron at Wymondham house of correction were, at times, able to gain her compliance and perhaps even respect. The longest-serving school mistress at Toftwood, Margaret Starling, faced her down with quiet determination.

Harriet certainly defied the norms and expectations of her time. As she grew up, she could not or would not follow the officially approved pathways which, for some workhouse inmates, led them, if not to wealth and high status, at least to financial security and social respectability. Instead, by becoming a sex worker, she put herself on the receiving end of the prejudices against the 'apparently irreclaimable women of her class,' becoming a target for the moral outrage affected by the 'respectable' in an age when evangelical Christianity was on the rise and prostitution, when acknowledged at all, was viewed as 'the great social evil'. Harriet's lifestyle represented the antithesis of Victorian values.

When roused to a frenzy, she defied all the contemporary norms of acceptable behaviour. On the first occasion when she appeared at the assizes in Norwich, Harriet created a scene which, 'was perhaps never before witnessed in this court,' and when eventually tried and sentenced, there was, 'a great deal of bad language on her part'. Harriet was no respecter of convention and, for those who witnessed it, her behaviour was shocking, and completely at odds with the submissiveness expected of women at the time. At these moments, Harriet didn't care. Others considered her 'bad', to have 'pure badness in her'. If not revelling in the characterisation, she seems, without shame, to have acknowledged it, admitting herself to be, 'more rogue than fool' and 'a bit rough at times'.

Harriet was certainly not a fool. She never became a helpless or hopeless victim. She was described by Charles White, the medical officer at the county lunatic asylum, who perhaps understood her as well as anybody, as 'quick and intelligent, with a great deal of self-possession'. She acquired some education. She could read. She had skills, and could use them, in needlework, knitting and childcare. One of the most affecting passages in the evidence about her periods in institutions is the reference to her nursing of an 'idiot child' at the county lunatic asylum; here, perhaps, she found her vocation.

Although she must have been damaged by the experiences of her younger years (with her final period in the county lunatic asylum perhaps a long-term result) Harriet's defiance of the institutions that sought to control her and of social norms of the mid-19th century was remarkable and, in a way, magnificent. The statement attributed to her at her trial, whether it was, 'no man will conquer me', or that she would be, 'conquered by nobody', is resonant. And by April 1863, Harriet had, in a sense, won her battle with the Poor Law authorities. She was given 'outdoor relief' because the board of guardians were prepared to bend the rules to ensure that she did not disrupt the routines of Gressenhall workhouse.

After her marriage to William Head, Harriet spent most of the middle and later periods of her life in the mainly working-class community of Toftwood, the suburb on the south side of Dereham. Her life became less turbulent but not entirely stable. Harriet and her family moved house several times, probably as a result of changes in William Head's employment. Children arrived, and then grandchildren; and, with the latter, tragedy, as several died young—victims, no doubt, of the poor, insanitary and perhaps damp conditions in which they lived.

As a mature woman, Harriet still had a short temper and a capacity for violent rages. Perhaps reminded of her conflicts with the schoolmistresses at Gressenhall workhouse, she took exception to the actions of Emily Goodall, the schoolmistress at Toftwood board school, grasping her throat, pulling her hair, and pushing her across the room. Twelve years later, at the age of 50 or so, she threatened a later mistress, Ada Chapman, with extreme violence, to such an extent that Miss Chapman was afraid to walk to the school. In court afterwards, Harriet was defiant and seemed unconcerned about the prospect of prison or even hanging. A few years later, protective of the grandson for whom she took responsibility, she fell out with the district medical officer, Dr Belding, and with the school mistress Margaret Starling, abusing the latter and in all likelihood the former also. But it was not just with authority figures that Harriet had disputes; there were run-ins with neighbours too. Harriet could be a curmudgeon and, as she had done in the Bethlem hospital, there may have been occasions when she 'made herself obnoxious' to those around her by being quarrelsome and bearing grudges. Harriet's determination not to be defeated had an unattractive side: she pursued vendettas.

But there was a positive side too. What is perhaps most remarkable about Harriet's later life is that, having been on the receiving end of legal judgements in her youth, she learned to use the law for her own and her family's ends and to their advantage. Her claim in 1889, 'I know a good deal about law…it does me credit,' was fully justified. The manner in which she defeated a prosperous farmer and merchant in the county court, where the journalists covering the case acknowledged not only her passion but also her 'considerable skill', and the 'warm and pertinent answers' that she provided, are testimony to Harriet's intelligence and determination. She was still excitable and combative, but the anger was now more channelled and controlled. As seen in court in 1889, it was also accompanied by a measure of self-knowledge and self-deprecatory humour, as well as an ability to play to the gallery.

Harriet's relationship with William Head may have marked the first time when she had loved and been loved. William, who spent most of his working life with horses as an agricultural labourer and 'team-man', can be imagined, perhaps, as a very calm character. Harriet had four children with William, cared for and protected them with the tenacity of a tigress, and took her grandchildren under her wing as well, providing the orphaned Arthur with a home until he got married. Harriet's marriage to William Head may have had its tempestuous moments; it is striking that William and their son, Ernest, though they attended the petty sessions in 1889 where Harriet was charged with threatening Ada Chapman, were reluctant to stand surety for her, perhaps knowing too well from experience the potential for another outburst. Nevertheless, the family seems to have held together and Harriet's marriage lasted over 50 years. William outlived his wife but Harriet's longevity, in the light of all the issues relating to her health before her marriage, is remarkable. No one, surely, would have predicted in the 1850s that she would live to the age of 77 or 78 and see the first 16 years of the new century.

Harriet, above all, was a survivor.

Appendix: a selective timeline

1838 or 1839	Birth of Harriet Kettle.
7 April 1851	First appearance before the board of guardians of Mitford and Launditch Union, charged with a disciplinary offence.
13 September 1852	Ordered to appear before a magistrate; imprisoned in Walsingham house of correction for the first time, for 14 days.
10 January 1853	Ordered to appear before a magistrate: imprisoned in Walsingham house of correction for 42 days.
1853-1855	In Norwich; 'girl on the town'.
7 January 1856	Back in Gressenhall workhouse: reprimanded for refusing to perform a task of work having been refused clothes to leave.
21 January 1856	Ordered to appear before a magistrate; sentenced to 21 days in Walsingham house of correction for violent conduct. Afterwards, unable to give sureties for her good behaviour, sentenced for a further 12 months imprisonment.
16 July 1856	Removed from Walsingham house of correction to the county lunatic asylum, Thorpe.
31 March 1857	Discharged from the county lunatic asylum; possibly resumed sex work in Norwich.
1 November 1858	Back in Gressenhall workhouse: reprimanded for insubordinate conduct.
22 November 1858	Attempted to set fire to Gressenhall workhouse. Committed for trial and sent to Wymondham house of correction.
1 February 1859	Removed from Wymondham house of correction to the county lunatic asylum.
28 July 1859	Appeared at the summer assizes in Norwich but certified insane and returned to the county lunatic asylum.
28 March 1860	Trial at the Lent assizes in Norwich. Sentenced to 18

	months imprisonment and taken to Wymondham house of correction.
26 April 1860	Removed from Wymondham house of correction to the county lunatic asylum.
25 August 1860	Discharged from the county lunatic asylum and returned to Wymondham house of correction.
7 March 1861	Taken to the Bethlem hospital, St George's Fields, Southwark.
23 October 1861	Discharged from the Bethlem hospital. Returned to Norwich.
5 January 1863	Back in Gressenhall workhouse, pregnant.
End of March 1863	Left Gressenhall workhouse. Received outdoor relief in Dereham.
10 July 1863	Admitted to the county lunatic asylum following an overdose of laudanum.
26 April 1864	Discharged from the county lunatic asylum.
20 June 1865	Married William Head in Dereham.
24 November 1865	Baptism of Matilda, daughter of William and Harriet Head.
19 November 1867	Baptism of Ernest William, son of William and Harriet Head.
23 August 1871	Baptism of Alice, daughter of William and Harriet Head
26 November 1873	Birth of Laura, daughter of William and Harriet Head
1876-1877	Charged with assaulting Emily Eliza Goodall, mistress at Toftwood board school; bound over to keep the peace.
10 April 1880	Report on the final judgement in the county court case with Robert Potter.
2 March 1887	Birth of Leonard John Head, son of Matilda Head and first grandchild of William and Harriet Head. He died before reaching his first birthday.
27 May 1888	Marriage of Ernest William Head, son of William and Harriet Head, and Sarah Fulcher in Dereham.
1 February 1889	Charged with using threatening language to Ada Chapman, mistress at Toftwood board school; bound over to keep the peace.
20 November 1890	Birth of Horace Reginald Head, son of Laura Head and grandson of William and Harriet Head. He died before

	reaching his first birthday. Two other children born subsequently to Laura also died, one aged four and one as an infant.
21 January 1892	Birth of Arthur Fellows Head, son of Matilda Head and grandson of William and Harriet Head, followed (on 29 January 1892) by the death of Matilda Head.
4 July 1896	Birth of Alice Matilda Head, daughter of Ernest and Sarah Head, grand-daughter of William and Harriet Head.
31 January 1899	Birth of Herbert William Head, son of Ernest and Sarah Head, grandson of William and Harriet Head. He died before reaching his first birthday.
24 December 1899	Death of Ernest William Head, son of William and Harriet Head.
17 May 1900	Birth of Edith Sarah Head, daughter of Ernest and Sarah Head, grand-daughter of William and Harriet Head.
22 March 1903	Marriage of Alice Head, daughter of William and Harriet Head, and Frederick Guyton in Dereham.
26 July 1903	Birth of Blanche Maud Guyton, daughter of Frederick and Alice Guyton, grand-daughter of William and Harriet Head.
28 April 1906	Marriage of Laura Head and Leonard Ernest Frederick Martin in Ipswich.
8 May 1916	Death of Harriet Head nee Kettle.

Bibliography

Printed works consulted

David Adams, *The Revolt and Taming of the 'Ignorant': a Study of the Bircham Riots of 1835 and their Aftermath* (The Larks Press, Guist Bottom, 2013).

Joan Adams et al, *Early Nineteenth Century and Victorian Dereham* (WEA, East Dereham, 1989).

Patricia H Allderidge, *Criminal Insanity: Bethlem to Broadmoor*, in Proceedings of the Royal Society of Medicine, Vol 67, September 1974.

Lisa Appignanesi, *Mad, Bad and Sad: a History of Women and the Mind Doctors from 1800 to the Present* (Virago, London, 2008).

John E Archer, *'By a Flash and a Scare': Arson, Animal Maiming and Poaching in East Anglia 1815-1870* (Oxford University Press, Oxford, 1990).

Christopher Armstrong (ed), *Under the Parson's Nose* (The Larks Press, Guist Bottom, 2012).

Catharine Arnold, *Bedlam* (Simon and Schuster, London, 2008).

Christopher Barringer (ed), Norwich in the Nineteenth Century (Gliddon Books, Norwich, 1984).

Christopher Barringer, *Exploring the Norfolk Market Town* (Poppyland Publishing, Cromer, 2011).

Virgina Berridge and Griffith Edwards, *Opium and the People* (Yale University Press, New Haven, 1987).

Peter Carroll, *Lives and Loves of Letton Hall, Norfolk* (Jigsaw, Norwich, 2011).

Michael J Carter, *Peasants and Poachers* (The Boydell Press, Woodbridge, 1980).

Steven Cherry, *Mental Health Care in Modern England: The Norfolk Lunatic Asylum/St Andrew's Hospital, 1810-1998* (The Boydell Press, Woodbridge, 2003).

Kellow Chesney, *The Victorian Underworld* (Maurice Temple Smith, London, 1970).

Jerry Crowley and Andy Reid, *The Poor Law in Norfolk 1700-1850* (EARO,

Ely, 1983).

MA Crowther, *The Workhouse System 1834-1929* (University of Georgia Press, Athens, GA, 1981).

Anna Davin, *Growing Up Poor* (Rivers Oram Press, London, 1996).

Anne Digby, *Pauper Palaces* (Routledge and Kegan Paul, London, 1978).

Trevor Fisher, *Prostitution and the Victorians* (Sutton Publishing, Stroud, 2001).

CB Hawkins, *Norwich, a Social Study* (Warner, 1910).

Judy Hawkins, *The Wymondham Bridewell* (Wymondham Society, 1987).

E J Hobsbawm and G Rude, *Captain Swing* (Penguin, Harmondsworth, 1973).

Frances and Michael Holmes, *The Old Courts and Yards of Norwich* (Norwich Heritage Projects, 2015).

Alun Howkins, *Poor Labouring Men: Rural Radicalism in Norfolk 1870-1923* (Routledge and Kegan Paul, London, 1985).

Robert Hughes, *The Fatal Shore* (Collins Harvill, London, 1987).

NJ Jenson, *Wymondham Bridewell: the hidden past* (Wymondham Heritage Society, 2000).

Robert Lee, *Unquiet Country: Voices of the Rural Poor 1820-1880* (Windgather, Bollington, 2005).

Sean McConville, *English Local Prisons; Next only to Death* (Routledge, Abingdon, 1995).

Norval Morris and David J Rothman (eds), *The Oxford History of the Prison* (Oxford University Press, New York, 1995).

Rosemary O'Donoghue, *Norwich, an Expanding City, 1801-1900* (The Larks Press, Guist Bottom, 2014).

Stephen Pope, *Gressenhall Farm and Workhouse* (Poppyland Publishing, Cromer, 2006).

Philip Priestley, *Victorian Prison Lives* (Pimlico, London, 1999).

Andy Reid, *The Union Workhouse: A Study Guide for Teachers and Local Historians* (Phillimore, Chichester, 1994).

Vivienne Richmond, *Clothing the Poor in Nineteenth Century England* (Cambridge University Press, 2013).

Andrew Scull, *The Asylum as Utopia* (Routledge, London, 1991).

L Marion Springhall, *Labouring Life in Norfolk Villages* (London, 1936).

Susanna Wade Martins, *Historic Farm Buildings* (Batsford, London, 1991).

Susanna Wade Martins, *A Vicar in Victorian Norfolk* (The Boydell Press, Woodbridge, 2018).

Judith R Walkowitz, *Prostitution and Victorian Society: Women, Class and the State* (Cambridge University Press, 1980).

Bridget Yates, *Buns and Lemonade* (Harlequin Colour Print, East Dereham, 2020).

David Yaxley, *A Researcher's Glossary* (The Larks Press, Guist Bottom, 2003).

Websites used

ancestry.com: subscription website providing access to a wide range of records.

archive.org: access to digitised publications, notably, for this study, the Annual Reports of the Norfolk county lunatic asylum.

books.google.co.uk: access to published reports, for example the Annual Reports of the Poor Law Commission.

britishnewspaperarchive.co.uk: subscription website providing access to a huge but not comprehensive archive of British newpapers.

convictrecords.com.au: access to the records of convicts transported to Australia.

countyasylums.co.uk: access to data about county lunatic asylums, including those for Norfolk and Norwich.

digitalpanopticon.org: access to sources about prisoners and the justice system.

discovery.nationalarchives.gov.uk: access to catalogues and digitised material in The National Archives.

educationengland.org: access to key documents relating to the history of education.

findmypast.com: subscription website providing access to a wide range of records (including those of Bethlem Museum of the Mind).

freebmd.org,uk: access to records of civil registration of births, marriages and deaths, free of charge.

freereg.org.uk: access to the evidence in parish registers of baptisms, burials and marriages, free of charge.

fremantleprison.com.au: records of convicts transported to Western Australia.

geni.com: background on propertied families

historicengland.org.uk: background on historic sites around the country.

museumofthemind.org.uk: access to lists of the museum's archives.

nls.uk/collections/maps: access to early Ordnance Survey maps.

norfolk.gov.uk/.../picture-norfolk: access to visual sources on Norfolk.

norfolksources.norfolk.gov.uk: access to trade directories.

nrocat.norfolk.gov.uk: the Norfolk Record Office online catalogue.

poppyland.co.uk: access to lists of workhouse inmates and officers at Gressenhall.

prisonhistory.org: access to data about prisons, including those at Walsingham and Wymondham, and the convict hulks.

records.nsw.gov.au: for an index of convicts transported to new South Wales.

sql.qld.gov.au: the State Library of Queensland, Australia, for access to the convict transportation registers 1787-1867.

theclergydatabase.org,uk: background on Church of England clergy.

thepeerage.com: background on the families of peers.

ukcensusonline.com: subscription website providing access to census returns 1841-1911 inclusive, and also civil registration records.

walsinghamvillage.org: background on Walsingham house of correction.

wikipedia.org: background on more or less everything.

workhouses.org.uk: access to a large body of information about workhouses, including Gressenhall.

wymondhamheritagemuseum.co.uk: background on Wymondham house of correction, some of the buildings of which now house the Wymondham Heritage Museum.

Index

Printed in Great Britain
by Amazon